W9-CHM-148

Jane Austen

CLAUDIA L. JOHNSON

Jane Austen

WOMEN

POLITICS

AND THE

NOVEL

THE UNIVERSITY OF

CHICAGO PRESS

CHICAGO AND LONDON

The University of Chicago Press, Chicago 60637
The University of Chicago Press, Ltd., London

© 1988 by The University of Chicago
All rights reserved. Published 1988
Paperback edition 1990
Printed in the United States of America

03 02 01 00 99 98 97 96 95 94   3 4 5 6 7 8

Library of Congress Cataloging-in-Publication Data

Johnson, Claudia L.

  Jane Austen : women, politics, and the novel /
  Claudia L. Johnson
    p.   cm.
  Bibliography: p.
  Includes index.
  ISBN 0-226-40139-1

  1. Austen, Jane, 1775–1817—Political and social views.
2. Politics in literature.   3. Social problems in literature.
4. Women in literature.   I. Title.
PR4038.P6J64 1988
823'.7—dc19   87-27338
                                          CIP

This book is printed on acid-free paper.

FOR

Nicholas J. and E. Sandra Johnson

CONTENTS

ACKNOWLEDGMENTS

In one of her many enthusiastic moments, Marianne Dashwood declares, "I love to be reminded of the past . . . whether it be melancholy or gay, I love to recall it." I share Marianne's great love of remembrance, and so take particular pleasure now in thanking the many people and institutions whose assistance over the past few years has made this book and these happy recollections possible.

I am especially grateful to the Newberry Library, both for granting me a Monticello Fellowship during the years 1983–1984, when this book was first conceived, and also for continuing to support my research into its splendid holdings over the many months that have since brought this work to completion. Thanks are also due to Marquette University, to Oberlin College, and to the American Philosophical Society, all of whose generous support at various stages of my project enabled me to undertake research at the Huntington Library and at the Special Collections division of the University Research Library at UCLA.

I am much indebted to the many friends and colleagues who have been so kind as to read parts or all of this book from its beginnings to its completion. A. W. Litz, Margaret A. Doody, Dianne M. Dugaw, Jeffrey L. Spear, Edward Duffy, Christine Krueger, Thomas Jeffers, Wendy Wenner, and Albert J. Rivero have given me more than can ever be accounted for here in the way of proofreading, criticism, counsel, encouragement, and good argument. I reserve my deepest thanks for Catherine L. McClenahan, whose conversation at every stage has been a challenge, a delight, and a blessing; and most of all for Carol Kay, whose ability to bridge the learned and conversable worlds I shall always admire and strive to emulate.

Claudia L. Johnson

27 May 1987

ABBREVIATIONS

All references to Austen's writings are based on the standard editions by R. W. Chapman. Because these editions have since appeared in slightly revised and modified versions by Mary Lascelles and B. C. Southam, I mention here the dates of the issues I have used throughout this book, along with the abbreviations that will appear parenthetically in my text:

Minor Works (MW)—1980
Northanger Abbey (NA) and *Persuasion* (P)—1982
Sense and Sensibility (SS)—1982
Pride and Prejudice (PP)—1982
Mansfield Park (MP)—1980
Emma (E)—1982

Reference to Austen's letters are made parenthetically by date, and are based on the corrected, one- volume edition by Chapman printed in 1959.

THE FEMALE NOVELIST AND THE CRITICAL TRADITION

I am quite honoured by your thinking me capable of drawing such a clergyman as you gave the sketch of in your note of Nov. 16th. But I assure you I am not. *The comic part of the character I might be equal to, but not the good, the enthusiastic, the literary. Such a man's conversation must at times be on subjects of science and philosophy, of which I know nothing; or at least be occasionally abundant in quotations and allusions which a woman who like me, knows only her own mother tongue, and has read very little in that, would be totally without the power of giving. A classical education, or at any rate a very extensive acquaintance with English literature, ancient and modern, appears to me quite indispensable for the person who would do any justice to your clergyman; and I think I may boast myself to be, with all possible vanity, the most unlearned and uninformed female who ever dared to be an authoress.*

(*Letters*, 11 December 1815)

[Catherine] was heartily ashamed of her ignorance. A misplaced shame. Where people wish to attach, they should always be ignorant. To come with a well-informed mind, is to come with an inability of administering to the vanity of others, which a sensible person would always wish to avoid. A woman especially, if she have the misfortune of knowing any thing, should conceal it as well as she can.

(*Northanger Abbey*, 110–11)

Although Jane Austen's reputation has been secure since the mid-nineteenth century, she has remained one of the great anomalies of literary history. If few authors have occupied such an honored position in the ranks of great literature, just as few have inspired such divergent accounts of what exactly they are doing there in the first place. Accordingly, Austen has appeared to us in a number of contradictory guises—as a cameoist oblivious to her times, or a stern propagandist on behalf of a beleaguered ruling class; as a self-effacing good aunt, or a nasty old maid; as a subtly discriminating stylist, or a homely songbird, unconscious of her art.

Such variety points to more than the vicissitudes to which the reputations of all authors are subject. It bespeaks a basic and pervasive indecision about Austen's stature as an artist, an indecision due in large part to Austen's sex. The fact that Austen is a female novelist has made assessments of her artistic enterprise qualitatively different from those of her male counterparts. Because of it, she has been admitted into the canon on terms which cast doubt on her qualifications for entry and which ensure that her continued presence there be regarded as an act of gallantry. While the novel had proved especially attractive to eighteenth-century women writers precisely because it was not already the territory of men, starting from as early as around 1815, reviewers insist on a fairly rigid distinction between the "male" and the "female" novel. Austen's famous and, it seems, ironically self-deprecating letter to her talentless nephew, in which she contrasts his "manly, spirited Sketches, full of Variety and Glow," to her own "little bit (two Inches wide) of Ivory" (*Letters*, 16 December 1816), alludes to this emergent distinction, as does Scott's rather more earnestly self-deprecating reference to "The Big Bow-wow strain" in his own novels.[1] But the distinction between the "male" and "female" novel did not merely mark a difference, but also implied a hierarchy which reviewers sometimes made painfully explicit. One anonymous critic opens a series of articles in the *New Monthly Magazine* (1852) on "Female Novelists" by taking their inferiority as a starting point: "Perhaps, indeed— and some critics would substitute 'unquestionably' for 'perhaps'—none but a man, of first-rate power withal, can produce a first-rate novel; and if so, it may be alleged that a woman of corresponding genius (*quâ* woman) can only produce one of a second-rate order."[2]

The precondition of Austen's posthumous admittance into the canon was an apparent contentment to work artfully within carefully restricted boundaries which have been termed "feminine." But for those of Austen's female contemporaries who were eminent in the 1790s, this distinction was under construction. As important as gender difference was in itself, it did not confine women to a sphere in which formidable concerns could not be articulated. Review magazines of the 1790s treat female and male writers as menaces or allies of comparable magnitude. Among the monstrosities depicted in Gillray's "New Morality," which appeared in 1798 as the frontispiece to the first issue of the *Anti-Jacobin Review*, is a large Cornucopia of Ignorance. From this, novels by Mary Robinson, Charlotte Smith, and Mary Wollstonecraft have spilled into an ignominious heap, alongside works by Wakefield, Holcroft, Paine, Tooke, and the many other progressive male authors whose pages litter the scene. In the heat of controversies felt to shake the world, novels by women were acknowledged to express and mobilize political opinions every bit as effectively as Priestley's *Political Sermons* or Godwin's *Political Justice*. Offering little or nothing in the way of apology, women writers commonly took on urgent social, political, and theological questions, since assigned to the "masculine" sphere, and they have dropped out of later versions of literary history altogether as a result, leaving scarcely a trace. In 1814, a year after the publication of *Pride and Prejudice*, Fanny Burney published *The Wanderer, or, Female Difficulties*, a long and extremely ambitious novel composed largely before the turn of the century, in which she addresses many of the political and philosophical issues raised by the French Revolution, particularly as these related to the condition of women. As we shall see, there is nothing unique in Burney's having undertaken a novel of such massively political import. In fact, the only thing unusual about *The Wanderer* is that it was published so late, and that is what damned it. By 1814 the climate had changed for women writers, and the novel was stridently denounced by J. W. Croker in 1815 as the work of a shriveled hag. Novel and novelist alike have grown too old to delight discriminating male readers: "The vivacity, the bloom, the elegance, 'the purple light of love' are vanished; the eyes are there, but they are dim; the cheek, but it is furrowed; the lips, but they are withered." Just as Lord Merton had opined that women should not live after thirty, Croker implies that they should not write after thirty. Fiction by women must be fiction by young women—modest, delicate, wispy, delightful, everything he sees in *Evelina*—and as soon as a woman has anything significant to say, she is, as Croker puts it, "*épuisée*," past her career as a novelist and a woman. Accordingly, Croker ridicules Burney's effort to intensify her treatment of manners by linking them to political turmoil as the grotesque stratagem of "an old coquette . . . to compensate for the loss of the natural charms of freshness, novelty, and youth."[3]

Austen has been the beneficiary of these sorts of attitudes. In 1821 Archbishop Whately praises Austen for declining the didactic posture—which assumes the ambition as well as the authority to teach the public—and for opting instead to hint at matters of serious concern inobtrusively and unpretentiously.[4] Although Whately contends that Austen's indirection and subtlety are means of instruction rather than ends in themselves, he unwittingly began a tradition of praising Austen for what she does *not* do. Victorian readers from Lewes on, perhaps uncomfortable with their own admiration for an author deficient in high seriousness, dwell just as much on what Austen would not or could not do as on what she did. Richard Simpson insists repeatedly that Austen, "always the lady," had the good sense to avoid getting out of her depth: she "never deeply studied" the "organization of society," she had no "conception of society itself," no "idea" that clergymen and baronets speak and act in different ways.[5] Constructing a "myth of limitation," Victorian readers posit an Austen whose mind was without what Lewes called "literary or philosophic culture," so destitute of ideas that she had no choice but to ply the miniaturist's deft but inferior art for its own sake.[6] Thus the same modest acquiescence to work within feminine, commonplace limitations that wins Austen the indulgence of so many nineteenth-century reviewers and, in Lewes's words, a place "among great artists," also consigns her to a rank "not high among them."[7] Given Lewes's underhanded praise of Austen's achievement, it is no wonder that George Eliot and Charlotte Brontë should be so nonplussed to find Austen thrust at them as a model of artistry.

It may appear ungenerous to chide nineteenth-century critics and reviewers for patronizing Austen even as they grouped her with Shakespeare, but many of their misleading premises are still with us. Nowhere is this clearer than in R. W. Chapman's editions of Austen's novels, which have now influenced more than two generations of readers. The *Oxford Illustrated Jane Austen* is animated by an impulse markedly more antiquarian than scholarly. Though acclaimed, one suspects, almost as a matter of convention, the editions themselves are hardly models of rigorous textual scholarship, and to all appearances they do not intend to be. Chapman's annotations to Austen's literary and historical allusions are sketchy as a matter of editorial principle—his purpose having been, as Mary Lascelles informs us, only "to give to the text of an outstanding novelist care and attention *comparable to but not identical with* that hitherto reserved for classical authors and some English poets and dramatists"(P, 316, emphasis added). Chapman does not grant Austen "identical" attention because he evidently does not consider her to be a major author in the same sense that other authors are major authors. In the *Jane Austen Bibliography*, he dismisses Samuel Kliger's study of Austen's "neo-classicism" with telling annoyance: "the essay is polysyllabic, and open to the familiar objection that its subject would not have understood it."[8] Presumably because her sex made formal schooling impossible, Austen is held to be as removed from the sophisticated preoccupations of high culture as she is ignorant of the formidable rigors of big words—words which turn out to be as inoffensively elementary to eighteenth-century usage as "premeditated" and "antithesis."

Following Chapman, many an Austenian, amateur and professional alike, appealing to historical authority as well as decorum, has implied that her novels are off limits to the ponderous diction of literary scholarship. Since Austen herself would, as Chapman writes, "turn over in her grave" if she heard scholars describe her novels in tastelessly highfalutin terms, the apparatus of literary history and textual scholarship would misrepresent her enterprise. To Chapman, Austen is in the canon not because of her social vision or even because of her formidable artistry, but rather because she had the good fortune to be able and the good taste to be willing to record the elegant manners of her time.[9] And so, with an inexorable circularity, Chapman's edition of Austen creates the author it presumed, and the history it desired. Allusions to the riots in London, or the slave trade in Antigua, for example, are first passed over, and then believed not to exist at all. With their appendixes detailing Regency fashions in clothing, carriages, and modes of address, and their chronologies of events based on almanacs, Chapman's editions appear less to illuminate and to honor Austen's compositional process than to preserve the novels in a museumlike world situated somewhere between fiction and real life. As such, *The Oxford Illustrated Jane Austen* is a graceful monument to country life in Regency England, a time which twentieth-century readers have been prone to idealize into graciousness and tranquillity.

Normally, the publication of handsome, ostensibly "authoritative" editions is a signal that an author has been accepted as a serious contributor to the literary tradition, and is a call for scholars to elucidate his or her relationship to that tradition. But even though Austen studies have since become an industry of sorts, this process of legitimization could never be completed in her case. What Chapman pejoratively called the "philosophical approach" to Austen was in fact absurd, for the basic strategies of literary history—with its patrilineal models of influence and succession—are indeed inappropriate when applied to an author marginalized from the outset, an author agreed to be unconcerned with, probably even oblivious to, authors who make up the tradition. Scholars of course acknowledge that Austen avidly read the works of female novelists. But since these authors are likewise considered peripheral to the prestigious ranks of literary culture, they have not much counted. Thus while historical scholars since Chapman have attempted in a sense to justify the *Oxford Illustrated Jane Austen*, as Chapman himself did not, by affiliating Austen with important male authors or with pressing social and political issues, they deny her any direct access or pondered relation to them. Whether linking her to Shaftesbury, Rousseau, or Burke, for example, critics shuffle in fear of granting Austen too much, and taking away with one hand what they have given with the other, they couch their arguments about her intellectual antecedents and leanings in the vaguest possible terms of "affinity," "temperament," or "unconscious awareness."[10] Even Marilyn Butler—who has argued persuasively for Austen's relationship to the postrevolutionary "war of ideas"—contends at last not that her ideas were engaged and developed by that very war, but rather that "old-fashioned notions" were "given to her" by the "sermons" and "conduct books" that somehow "formed" her mind.[11] This account, however, actually denies Austen the dignity and the activity of being a warrior of ideas. Far from ever having wielded any herself, she purportedly imbibed the tendentious and intrinsically conservative propaganda she is imagined to have been indoctrinated with since childhood, without being able or inclined to consider the interests served by its representations. Having concluded that Austen's politics are unstintingly anti-Jacobin, and her morality so "preconceived and inflexible" as to preclude any interest in exploring or complicating the subjectivity of her characters, Butler is ready to subvert the premise which, in some ways, makes her own book possible, and to ask, with admirable, if perverse logic, whether Austen really does deserve her position in the canon: "[A]re we right to call her a great novelist at all?"[12]

The attempt of modern scholars to justify Austen's inherited place in the canon has been unsuccessful because we have not reconsidered how our assumptions about the education and attitudes available to Austen as a woman—assumptions which in turn depend on questionable versions of social and literary history—have stacked the deck against her from the start. If few go so far as Butler in seeing Austen as a propagandist for the reaction, most do agree that she is a "conservative." Yet when we scrutinize the bases on which this opinion rests, we find the question almost entirely begged. Assertions about her "Tory conservatism" are based not on statements by or about Austen in her novels or letters—no such statements exist—but rather on the belief that because she was a member of a certain class she reflexively accorded with all its values and interests. It is no accident, of course, that as modern readers find themselves more nostalgic for the stateliness and stability Austen's world is said to apotheosize, Austen's class gets higher and higher, and she herself is claimed to be more and more conservative. In her own time, this was hardly the case. Sir Walter Scott—who ought to know—contended that Austen's characters belong "chiefly to the middling classes of society," and Madame de Staël nailed Austen's work with devastating concision, "*vulgaire.*"[13] In our own century, however, Lord David Cecil has attempted to co-opt Austen, now the arbitress of good breeding, into the aristocracy. Even though Austen's father was propertyless, and even though she spent her most productive years as what Barbara Pym would call a "distressed gentlewoman," many readers contend that Austen was a socially confident member of the landed gentry and, with that, the "ruling class."[14] But whatever the station to which Austen is now assigned, she is not held to entertain an opinion independent of it. She is the "parson's daughter" or the "sailors' sister," and the mere identification of her kinship relations to the men in her family is judged enough to warrant the inference that her social opinions affirmed theirs as a matter of course.

Contrary to what one might expect, readers who by contrast consider Austen "subversive"—that is to say, at odds with the dominant values of her society—do not credit her with any corollary capacity for independence. Their conceptions of Austen's achievement are limited in identical ways by fixed and curiously unimaginative suppositions about what was possible, proper, and normal for women of her time. To them, Austen's social criticism is not the result of a reasonably considered outlook on society, or even of a simple ability to detect fools and knaves. Rather it is a symptom of emotional disability: she was a "nasty" old maid. Austen's most recent biographer is one of many to have considered his own absence to be the most remarkable and the most significant feature of Austen's life. The ironic conclusion of *Northanger Abbey*, by this account, reflects "Jane's" resentful realization that the happy ending of marriage would not bless her own life: Austen's peace "was surely on the brink of destruction, in her early twenties, as a result of loneliness, of sexual longing. *Northanger Abbey* shows her asking the old question: Where is the man for me?"[15] Statements such as these carry with them the implication that Austen's irony, her single most brilliant artistic achievement, was pathological, a problem any good husband could relieve, and that all social criticism written by women is borne of disappointment in love. Croker, it would appear, lives on.

Surveying more than a decade of Austenian criticism, one reviewer has suggested that the only genuinely "unanachronistic" Austen is the Tory conservative, and that modern approaches averring otherwise—feminist, Freudian, or Marxist discussions, for example—will finally appear ephemeral and wearisomely proliferative in the face of the sensibly corrective authority of "historical" scholarship.[16] But as we have seen, historical and biographical Austenian scholarship, sometimes merely methodologically naive and sometimes irrecoverably entrenched in logical fallacies, has always been preceded by very definite ideas about what it would find there. And in its decidedly modern nostalgia for an unalienated relationship to a calmer, more manageable world, it has not been fundamentally less skewed by modern projections than the readings historicists have deemed anachronistic.

The purpose of this study is not to eschew the historical approach to Austen, but rather to adopt it critically in order to reconceptualize the stylistic and thematic coherence of Austen's fiction by demonstrating how it emerges, draws, and departs from a largely feminine tradition of political novels, novels which are highly informed and often distinctively flexible, rather than ferociously partisan, in their sympathies. It is no longer possible, and no longer even necessary, to claim that I have constructed an ideologically objective or neutral methodology which transcends my own historicity as an investigator. The reader will observe that feminist theory and scholarship, as well as the new social and literary history, underpin my procedures.[17] But once my own historical perspective is acknowledged, it is not necessary to concede that it will be an impediment to inquiry. In fact, a consciousness of how the private is political, and a sensitivity to the problems women writers encounter living and writing in a male-dominated culture, can provide us with special grounds for a historical understanding of Austen's work. Few ostensibly "historical" truths are as stubbornly persistent and as entirely *a*historical as the belief that, with the exception of a few unseemly radicals, Austen and her ladylike contemporaries were not curious about or concerned with the moral implications of gender distinctions, and that as a sensible woman, Austen never mixed with the political debates of her time. Indeed, modern critics tend to view politics much as Catherine Morland viewed history—as a sphere "with men all so good for nothing, and hardly any women at all" (NA 108). But in the eighteenth- century novel this was not so. In general it never confined itself within the tidy disciplinary or sexual boundaries we have since drawn. *Robinson Crusoe, Rasselas,* and *Sir Charles Grandison,* for example, spill over into economics, philosophy, politics, religion, and conduct literature, and the novels written by Austen's female predecessors and contemporaries are no exception. Freely adapting works by Bolingbroke, Locke, Hume, not to mention Shakespeare, Burney's *The Wanderer* discourses at great length on suicide, the immortality of the soul, and the sentience of matter. Elizabeth Hamilton's *Memoirs of Modern Philosophers* (1800) extensively excerpts and footnotes Godwin's *Political Justice.* Maria Edgeworth's *Belinda* (1801), Amelia Opie's *Adeline Mowbray* (1804), Mary Hays's *Memoirs of Emma Courtney* (1796), Charlotte Smith's *The Young Philosopher* (1798), Sophia King's *Waldorf, Or, The Dangers of Philosophy* (1798), to name only a very few, assimilate or directly allude to Rousseau, Burke, Wollstonecraft, and Holcroft. In contrast to modern readers and writers, who draw the line between public and private at the threshold of an Englishman's home and then assign women to that apolitical space within its doors, late-eighteenth-century women read and wrote novels that undertook either to defend the nation from the contagion of "Jacobinism" or to improve the nation by pointing to the need for social reform. Dramatically exploring the philosophical rallying cries invoked on both sides of the debate—the catchwords about liberty, prejudice, reason, sensibility, authority, happiness—the feminine tradition of the novel was, pace Chapman, a "polysyllabic" one, and Austen, a compulsive reader of novels, was thoroughly acquainted with it.[18]

In reexamining the political ambience of Austen's fiction and that of her contemporaries, I depart from previous arguments in three related ways. First, avoiding the rhetorical traps set by the disputants themselves, I investigate a wide spectrum of responses to the social questions raised in England by the revolution in France. Political analysis cannot be left at the level of identifying an author's sympathies with this or that administration. Most of the novels written in the "war of ideas" are more complicated and less doctrinaire than modern commmentators have represented. It does not suffice to denominate writers as "conservative" or "radical" according to whether they were "for" or "against" the French Revolution. By the mid-1790s, with France and England at war and the Revolution and Terror faits accomplis, there were few English "Jacobins" around, and among professed "anti-Jacobins," there is far more disagreement than first meets the eye.[19] To be sure, West and More idealize and defend established power—power which, as we shall see, they do not hesitate to call by its proper name: "patriarchal." But Hamilton and Opie, for example, do not endorse the status quo without serious qualifications. They dutifully denounce reformist zeal, only to tuck away parallel plots which vindicate liberty, private conscience, and the defiance of authority, and thus discretely define broad areas where conservatives and progressives could agree, surely no part of the reactionary program. To group these authors together indiscriminately as "anti-Jacobin" is not only to blur crucial political distinctions, but it is also to overlook entirely the social and aesthetic problems authors face during times of reaction. Austen and her less-doctrinaire contemporaries do indeed participate in a polemical tradition, but to invoke a polemic is not necessarily to accept completely the loaded terms on which it is conducted or to endorse the foregone conclusions to which it invariably tends. Under the pressure of intense reaction, they developed stylistic techniques which enabled them to use politically charged material in an exploratory and interrogative, rather than hortatory and prescriptive, manner.

Secondly, though it is sometimes approached as if it rose out of a vacuum, I argue that the debate between "conservative" and "reformist" camps which informs the novels Austen read from the beginning through the end of her career must be placed in its prerevolutionary context of thought about rights, education, authority, happiness, and free agency if we are to appreciate what is distinctive about it. Before the French Revolution, Lockean ideas about happiness, education, judgment, autonomous choice, and the limited though necessary role of authority enjoyed general currency, and the English gentry, proud of its independence and suspicious of aristocratic prejudices, was wary of encroachments on its own authority. Later in the century, conservative observers opposed to reform were bewildered to find progressive rhetoric co-opting the positive valency of these very terms.[20] What had been an established tradition of political discourse wielded by guardians of the status quo could now be tapped by reformists' interests, and once the reaction was in full swing, ideas which before had been safe and acceptable enough now seemed to be pernicious doctrines: acknowledging pleasure and pain as moral prompters, as had Samuel Johnson, Austen's "favorite moralist" in prose, now could sound like proclaiming the primacy of license over duty; cherishing one's independence now could sound like the stubborn will to defy time-honored authorities and established forms.

Because the code words of conservative and reformist polemicists were not at first antithetical, but in fact often share a common tradition, representations of social and political debates in fiction are rarely as pat as modern commentators have considered them. As the matter is currently accepted, for example, "sensibility" is the cherished rallying cry of reformists, and it is lambasted by conservatives because it is said to promote dangerous moral relativism, to valorize unruly, generally sexual energies, and to foster radical individualism, instead of encouraging submission to social control. But "sensibility" is also the rallying cry of Burkean reactionaries who, anxious to discredit the presumptuous calculations of independent reason, cherish instead "feelings" and "affections" cultivated through the family. This overlay of politically sensitive terms surfaces in Austen's fiction, as in that of others, in illuminating and complicating ways. In *Sense and Sensibility*, for example, the "conservative" argument in behalf of sensibility is articulated by two of the novel's most abhorrent characters—Mr. and Mrs. John Dashwood, who use their tender solicitude for the future of their infant heir as an excuse to cheat their female relations out of their patrimony. Conversely, when Marianne Dashwood challenges the justice of social conventions which require her to conceal honorable affections, she bases her argument on an appeal to *reason*, not on an appeal to the sanctity of individuals' feelings. Thus the fact that *Sense and Sensibility* shatters Marianne's vehement feelings is surely no proof that Austen is a conservative. Even though Godwin's *Memoirs of the Author of a Vindication of the Rights of Woman* (1798) presented her as a Rousseauvian heroine of sensibility, Mary Wollstonecraft herself is more suspicious of sensibility than Austen is, and in *Memoirs of Modern Philosophers*, a novel deemed "anti-Jacobin," Hamilton praises Wollstonecraft generously for refuting Rousseau's recommendation of sensibility. The rhetoric of "sensibility" is, then, fully as volatile as that of "true liberty." Because Austen and many of her contemporaries are fully aware that the codes employed by the two opposing camps are not always so discrete and mutually exclusive, they are more able to take a measured view of social and political problems, and are more willing to give quarter to opposing platforms than their more partisan counterparts.

Finally, unlike many previous commentators, I consider Austen's sex to be a crucially significant factor, not only in the formation of her social opinions, but also in the development of aesthetic strategies for writing about them. This is only fitting, since the idea that great literature is genderless was entirely alien to Austen's generation, particularly traumatized as it was by social upheaval. Years ago, Lionel Trilling observed that Emma Woodhouse was remarkable for having "a moral life as a man has a moral life."[21] Unable, like so many of his forebears, to credit Austen with a bright idea, Trilling quickly reassures us that Austen surely had no ax to grind in presenting Emma as a "new woman." But in fact, the extent to which women have or ought to have moral lives in the same way men have moral lives was very hotly and accessibly debated in Austen's time, as were other issues pertaining to female sexuality in particular and sexual difference in general. In endowing attractive female characters like Emma Woodhouse and Elizabeth Bennet with rich and unapologetic senses of self-consequence, Austen defies every dictum about female propriety and deference propounded in the sermons and conduct books which have been thought to shape her opinions on all important matters. Although many novels written from the beginning until the end of Austen's career referred positively or negatively to *The Rights of Woman*, no allusions were necessary to remind audiences that female characterization, such as Emma's or Fanny's, was already a politicized issue in and of itself, and Austen's handling of this problem is perhaps the most independent of all her contemporaries.

But for a woman novelist writing at the end of the eighteenth century, the issue of gender affected more than choices of characterization, and indeed it eventually called into question the act of authorship itself. No woman novelist, even among the most progressive, wished to be discredited by association with Mary Wollstonecraft, particularly after Godwin's widely attacked *Memoirs* disclosed details about her sexual improprieties and suicide attempts. Moreover, as the reaction intensified, the fear of being branded a treasonous Jacobin obliged moderately progressive novelists to appear more conservative than they really were. Their horror at the Revolution and Terror notwithstanding, Burney, Edgeworth, Hamilton, and Opie—conservatives all by most reckonings—feel in varying degrees too marginal as women in their society to idealize established power, too compromised by the customary social structures which conservative discourse upholds. As a consequence, they smuggle in their social criticism, as well as the mildest of reformist projects, through various means of indirection—irony, antithetical pairing, double plotting, the testing or subverting of overt, typically doctrinaire statement with contrasting dramatic incident. In addition to adopting and perfecting such techniques, Austen shares with these, as well as with unequivocally radical novelists, such as Wollstonecraft and Hays, the device of centering her novels in the consciousness of unempowered characters—that is, women. This technique, instead of vindicating the status quo (the professed objective of "anti-Jacobin" controversialists, after all) enables Austen to expose and explore those aspects of traditional institutions—marriage, primogeniture, patriarchy—which patently do not serve her heroines well.

In a famous passage of *Northanger Abbey*, Henry Tilney undertakes to tutor Catherine Morland on the intricacies of the picturesque. Catherine proves such an eager and receptive "scholar" that Henry soon fears straining her powers of absorption, and closes his lecture by turning it adroitly from landscape to politics to silence:

> . . . by an easy transition from a piece of rocky fragment and the withered oak which he had placed near its summit, to oaks in general, to forests, the inclosure of them, waste lands, crown lands and government, he shortly found himself arrived at politics; and from politics, it was an easy step to silence. (NA 111)

If Catherine is brought to silence, we should not be surprised: at the outset of the novel, Austen lays it down as axiomatic that Catherine is intimidated by and deferent to self-assured men. But we should not assume that just because Catherine is awed by Henry Tilney, Austen is as well. The speech which reposes Catherine in silence, far from proving that women must steer clear from matters as arcane as politics, shows on the contrary that all subjects lead to it, that the very landscape—with its withered oaks and enclosed lands—calls it perforce to mind. And part of the larger structural irony of the novel is that Catherine talks about politics every time she opens her mouth, whenever she considers the harshness of General Tilney's paternal authority, for example, or questions Henry's judgment. Despite Austen's having mockingly boasted "with all possible vanity" that she, much like Catherine, was "the most unlearned and uninformed female who ever dared to be an authoress," the "authoresses" she habitually read were hardly uninformed, and exactly how and why Austen saw fit to suggest that they and she were otherwise is the subject of this book. When we compare Austen's novels to those of her more conspicuously political sister-novelists—conservative and progressive alike—we discover that she routinely employs a lexicon of politically sensitive terms, themes, and narrative patterns that she inherited from their fiction, and that she, like Catherine again, often discusses politics all the time without making announcements about it beforehand. By opting in this manner to retain the same preoccupations as her more conspicuously political contemporaries, without, however, alluding as they did to the topical considerations which had originally animated them, Austen was able not to depoliticize her work—for the political implications of her work is implicit in the subject matter itself—but rather to depolemicize it.

"Seldom, very seldom," as Austen wrote in *Emma*, "does complete truth belong to any human disclosure; seldom can it happen that something is not a little disguised, or a little mistaken" (E 431). Austen was well aware that the political novels written in her own generation were "human disclosures" in which much had been disguised and mistaken. As we shall see, her only apparent "silence" on matters political is a creditable choice of strength rather than a decorous concession to "feminine" weakness or ignorance. Austen's silence is an enabling rather than inhibiting strategy. Such "silence" permitted her to rewrite the lexicon of conservative discourse, showing, for example, how Sir Thomas's word "advise" means the "advice" of "absolute power," and thereby to dismantle myths propounded by anti-Jacobin novelists without seeming necessarily to imply a Jacobin wish to see society radically reconstituted. Paradoxically perhaps, only by appearing to move from politics to silence was it possible for Austen to find a voice which had in a sense already been spoken for by the reaction, and in the process to disclose more while disguising less.

CHAPTER ONE

THE NOVEL OF CRISIS

"Profligate *as I knew you to be, I was not prepared for such a sight.
. . . And this is the reward for all the cares I have taken in your Education; for all my troubles & Anxieties; and Heaven knows how many
they have been! All I wished for, was to breed you up virtuously; I
never wanted you to play upon the Harpsichord, or draw better than
any one else; but I had hoped to see you respectable and good; to see
you able & willing to give an example of Modesty and Virtue to the
Young people here abouts. I bought you Blair's Sermons, and Coelebs
in Search of a Wife, I gave you the key to my own Library, and borrowed
a great many good books of my Neighbours for you, all to this purpose.
But I might have spared myself the trouble—Oh! Catherine, you are
an abandoned Creature, and I do not know what will become of you.
I am glad however, she continued softening into some degree of Mildness, to see that you have some shame for what you have done, and if
you are really sorry for it, and your future life is a life of penitence
and reformation perhaps you may be forgiven. But I plainly see that
every thing is going to sixes & sevens and all order will soon be at an
end throughout the Kingdom."*

"*Not however Ma'am the sooner, I hope, from any conduct of mine,
said Catherine in a tone of great humility, for upon my honour I have
done nothing this evening that can contribute to overthrow the establishment of the kingdom."*

"*You are Mistaken Child, replied she; the welfare of every Nation
depends upon the virtue of it's [sic] individuals, and any one who offends
in so gross a manner against decorum and propriety is certainly hastening it's [sic] ruin."*

(Jane Austen, "Catharine, or The Bower"
[1792–1809]) (MW 232–33)

*When posterity shall know that these principles characterize the
close of the eighteenth century, it will cease to wonder at the calamities*

*which history will then have recorded. . . . Should it therefore be told
to future ages, that the capricious dissolubility (if not the absolute
nullity) of the nuptual tie and the annihilation of parental authority
are among the blasphemies uttered by the* moral *instructors of these
times: should they hear, that law was branded as a vain and even unjust
attempt to bring individual actions under the restrictions of general
rule; that chastity was defined to mean only individuality of affection;
that religion was degraded into a sentimental effusion; and that these
doctrines do not proceed from the pen of* avowed *profligates, but from
persons* apparently *actuated by the desire of improving the happiness
of the world: should, I say, generations yet unborn hear this, they will
not ascribe the annihilation of thrones and altars to the successful arms
of France, but to those principles which, by dissolving domestic confidence and undermining private worth, paved the way for universal
confusion.*

(Jane West, *Tale of the Times* [1799])[1]

The reactionary ideology which evolved in England during the 1790s left
a rich and paradoxical legacy: even as it required women to be amiably
weak, retiring, and docile so to assure the authority, the chivalry, even
the identity of men, it not only stimulated but also empowered women's
commentary on political affairs. To be sure, women novelists had never
been wanting for subjects before the Revolution in France. But after it,
those largely domestic subjects, concerning which they had been acknowledged to have some wisdom, were brought to the forefront of national life and were infused with dignity as well as urgency. In the preface
to her early radical novel, *Desmond* (1792), Charlotte Smith claims to
derive her authority to speak about France and England solely from her
relation to men: "But women it is said have no business with politics—
Why not?—Have they no interest in the scenes that are acting around
them, in which they have fathers, brothers, husbands, sons, or friends
engaged?"[2] However, like virtually every political novel of the period, of
no matter what persuasion, *Desmond* goes on to show that women's
"business with politics" is not indirect, undertaken simply out of concern
for closely related male agents in the public arena. On the contrary it
shows that every major aspect of women's lives already serves a political
agenda. Whereas it had before been implicit, it was now unavoidably plain
that women's education, their manners, their modesty, their reading, their
opinions about personal happiness, their power of choice in matrimony,

and their expectations from married life were all matters of increasingly anxious public concern.

It is this touted momentousness of female conduct or, more precisely, the ways such momentousness is appealed to in order to intimidate women themselves, that Austen unmasks in her early fragment "Catharine, or the Bower." Drafted in 1792, just prior to the first wave of reaction, "Catharine" continued to interest Austen as late as 1809, after the reaction had become a full-blown tradition, and after Austen understood its implications more clearly. Emended literary allusions sharpen the focus of the earlier effort. Archbishop Secker's often reprinted *Lectures on the Catechism of the Church of England* (1769) is replaced with the more timely, politically repressive *Coelebs in Search of a Wife* by Hannah More, which had just been published. In the sketch, Catharine has done nothing but be the astonished and unwilling object of a silly fellow's impulsive gallantries. But to her censorious aunt, Mrs. Percival, Catharine plays a major role in a national drama. Because, in Mrs. Percival's view, "the whole race of Mankind were degenerating," because "all order was destroyed over the face of the World" and "the whole Nation [will] speedily be ruined" (MW 200, 212), Catharine's alleged "Impudence" is a grievous offense: the stability of the kingdom depends on the unbesmirched chastity and prudent matches of eligible girls. However unlikely a candidate for treason, Catharine is, momentarily at least, convicted as a "*Profligate*" lost to "Modesty and Virtue," and as such she shoulders responsibility for the ruin of the kingdom.

The significance Mrs. Percival ascribes to female modesty may appear caricatured beyond credible proportions. And indeed, in Austen's hands, portentous moralizing on female virtue would remain not simply a laughable, but also a very mean undertaking that reflects back unfavorably onto the speaker: consider, for example, Mary Bennet's series of glib "moral extractions" collected from conduct books on the subject of the loss of reputation in a woman; or Mr. Price's brutal remark about the adulterous Maria Rushworth, "If she belonged to me, I'd give her the rope's end as long as I could stand over her" (MP 440). But for professedly conservative novelists, Mrs. Percival's association of female "profligacy" with political calamity would appear prophetic and not in the least exaggerated, and if we look closely at their productions, Austen's differences with conservative apologetics will stand out in bold relief. Like Mrs. Percival, the real-life Jane West was obsessed with the depravity of "the times." In fact, it became the motive for her long and very successful career as a novelist: "Tho' I by no means think them [novels] the best vehicles for 'the words of sound doctrine,'" she writes in the introduction to *The Infidel Father*

(1802), "yet, while the enemies of our church and state continue to pour their poison into unwary ears through this channel, it behooves the friends of our establishments to convey an antidote by the same course."[3] As the excerpt above clearly shows, the world to West appeared to be teetering on brink of "universal confusion," and destruction would be wrought, not by violent revolution or military invasion, but rather by laxity in the morals of private individuals; for her too, as for Austen's Mrs. Percival, the pivotal figure in either the continuance or the annihilation of political order is a woman. In *Tale of the Times*, however, the woman in question is not, like Catharine, a clever and ingenuous young girl harassed by a coxcomb, but rather a mature and judicious married lady. Lady Geraldine Monteith's downfall occurs because she permits herself to feel unhappy with her whoring and gaming husband: to disapprove of his irresponsibility as a landowner and a father, to wish her lot in life were better, and finally to repose confidence in another man. West underscores the political nature of Lady Geraldine's offenses by making that other man be a smooth-talking Jacobin spy who has diabolically contrived these plots of conjugal infelicity from the very start, with no other end in view than to gain Lady Geraldine's trust and, by abducting and raping her, to ruin forever the stock of one of the country's oldest and finest families.

West's conviction that "private worth" and "domestic confidence" alone can secure the nation's survival against the forces of anarchy derives from Burke's arguments in *Reflections on the Revolution in France* (1790) and its sequel, *Letter to a Member of the National Assembly* (1791). These works provided conservative novelists with their paradigms, character types, and catchwords, and progressive novelists with their targets and counterplots. As scholars have long observed, the *Reflections* is striking for the degree to which it presents a vast and multifaceted series of events in France as a unitary family drama. In this drama the state is figured as a persecuted, "almost naked" queen fleeing a gleeful band of would-be rapists in order to seek the protection of her husband, the king, whose once awesome person is no longer able to command the respect necessary to hold the disruptively libidinous energies of his subjects in check:

> History will record, that on the morning of the 6th of October 1789, the king and queen of France, after a day of confusion, alarm, dismay and slaughter, lay down, under the pledged security of public faith, to indulge nature in a few hours of respite, and troubled melancholy repose. From this sleep the queen was first startled by the voice of the centinel at her door, who cried out to her, to save herself by flight—that this was the last proof of fidelity he could give—that they were upon him, and he was dead. Instantly he was cut down. A band of cruel ruffians and assassins, reeking with blood, rushed into the chamber of the queen, and pierced with an

hundred strokes of bayonets and poniards the bed, from whence this persecuted woman had but just time to fly almost naked, and through ways
unknown to the murderers had escaped to seek refuge at the feet of a king
and husband, not secure of his own life for a moment.[4]

In presenting the political act as a sexual act, the violation of the queen
as an assault on the king's authority, Burke does more than articulate
anxious oedipal fantasies. He describes what happens when a political system and the dominant figures within it no longer command the sentimental life—the aspirations, inhibitions, and loyalties—of its subjects. In
self-proclaimed contrast to crazed French ideologues who would break with
time-honored traditions in order to create a new society based on rational
principles, Burke apotheosizes the patriarchal ideal and the social and sentimental structures which enforce it: the retired life of the country gentleman, the orderly transmission of property, the stabilizing principle of
generational continuity, the grateful deference of youth to venerable age,
and of course the chastity of wives and daughters which alone can guarantee the social identity of men and heirs.[5] As the course of the novel
would subsequently attest, Burke's writings about the French Revolution
were, among other things, embryonic political novels in and of themselves, and not simply discursive political commentary. This is clear not
only in the famous "gothic-pathetic" passages dealing with Marie Antoinette, for the prurience of which he was ridiculed at the time, but also
in sections which come closer to the workaday world of domestic comedy
than to the phantasmagoric world of gothic horror with which he is usually associated.[6] In exposing the revolutionaries' agenda, Burke describes
a "plot"—lifted from Rousseau's La nouvelle Héloise—which would be
rewritten, elaborated, confirmed, or refuted in countless novels to come:

> The rulers of the National Assembly are in good hopes that the females of
> the first families in France may become an easy prey to the dancing masters,
> fiddlers, pattern-drawers, friseurs, and valets de chambres, and other active
> citizens of that description, who having the entry into your houses . . . may
> be blended with you by regular and irregular relations. . . . The great ob-
> ject of your tyrants is to destroy the gentlemen of France. . . . [These ty-
> rants] propagate principles by which every servant may think it, if not his
> duty, at least his privilege to betray his master. By these principles, every
> considerable father of a family loses the sanctuary of his house.[7]

Dwelling fretfully on the vulnerability of patriarchal authority through
seduction, Burke props up the fathers of "considerable families" by justifying the institution over which they preside. To Burke, the family and
its immediate environs in the neighborhood—described with pathos calculated to endear as "our little platoon"—is not simply a metaphor for

or microcosm of the state, but a basic political unit in its own right. Because it establishes a network of mutual interests and nurtures such civilizing and affiliating "affections" as fond solicitude and trusting dependency, unselfish benevolence and grateful submission, Burke regards the love of family as "the first principle (the germ as it were) of public affections. It is the first link in the series by which we proceed towards a love to our country and to mankind."[8] Having defined the patriarchal family not simply as the linchpin of generational continuity but also as the locus of socialization and hence the object of revolutionary schemes of subversion, Burke then generates a fearsome novel of manners in which moral survival and decency are at stake. Following the outlines of Burkean "plots," the novels written in his shadow take the rights of parents over daughters, of husbands over wives, and the superiority of "prejudices" favoring established modes of behavior to "rational principles" dictating innovative social conduct as their basic starting points; feminine desire and illicit sex constitute their basic crises.

Because, among conservative novelists of Austen's generation, Jane West was the most distinguished to dramatize Burkean fictions with little adulteration, it is fitting that an outline of the conservative novel begin with her. Although in her early career she published plays and poems (including an elegy on Burke), prose appears to have been West's favored medium for supporting Tory politics and the high church. Even as an already well-established and well-reviewed novelist, West posed no threat which Austen did not feel equal to meet. After predicting in one of her letters that she would like Scott's *Waverley* almost in spite of herself, Austen continues, "I am quite determined however not to be pleased with Mrs. West's *Alicia de Lacy*, should I ever meet with it, which I hope I may not.—I think I *can* be stout against any thing written by Mrs. West" (*Letters*, 28 September 1814). At least one reason why Mrs. West failed to awe her younger and as yet obscure rival is that by idealizing the patriarchal family with unremitting earnestness and insistence, she went where Austen had no wish to follow. West's early *Advantages of Education* (1793)—a thinly fictionalized conduct book for mothers as well as daughters—clearly exposes the problems poorer women face living outside institutionalized pales of power and protection. But her later work—written in the wake of the treason trial of 1794 and the repressive legislation of 1795—would never again expose established institutions to criticism, but boldly announces its commitment to vindicating the status quo, and to proving, as she writes at the outset of *Tale of the Times*, that "filial and conjugal ties are no remnants of feudal barbarisms, but happy institutions, calculated to promote domestic peace."[9]

The very defensiveness of this program shows West's familiarity with the radical challenges reformers were leveling at the traditional family structure, and a survey of anti-Jacobin novelists shows them to be very well informed. A shrewd propagandist, West, however, never writes the radical opposition into her novel long enough to let it speak for itself. But the nefarious Jacobin in Elizabeth Hamilton's extremely popular conservative novel *Memoirs of Modern Philosophers* (1800) has studied Godwin on the subject of the family, and Hamilton even supplies the footnotes. As he explains them, the tenets West and other conservatives cherish—such as "*filial duty*, and *family affection*, *gratitude to benefactors*, and *regard to promises*"—are really no more than mere "prejudices" which "aristocratical pride and selfishness have interwoven into the constitution of society" in order to legitimize and perpetuate its supremacy.[10] For her part West did not so much endeavor to refute such assertions as she did to neutralize the opprobrium attached to them. The moral center of *Tale of the Times* is, appropriately enough, the heroine's father, Sir Anthony Powerscourt, who rules over his household like a "prudent monarch", always responsible with his "prerogative" and always infallible in his moral judgments. Resigning himself to make the best of the birth of a daughter, Sir Anthony tactfully encourages the suit of a modest and distantly related young man who, among his many unimpeachable qualifications, bears the family name. Sir Anthony's subscribes to West's intrusively expressed views that a country gentleman of such ancient stature does best to bestow his heiress "on her father's nearest male relation," a man who lives in the neighborhood and who will "continue to diffuse the same noble benevolence and patriarchal hospitality" to tenants, villagers, and visitors that his forebears have for generations before him. Sir Anthony's aim is clearly to promote social coherence by stirring in the breasts of dependents a warm and mutually binding sense of gratitude for his paternal solicitude that it has been the work of ages to form.[11] From his point of view, therefore, it is not base vainglory, but an unselfish sense of responsibility to his family and community, past and future, that prompts him to insert clauses about the continuance of his name and the care of his tenants into the nuptual agreements when his daughter, to her infinite misfortune, ignores his good advice and marries a rich but irresponsible lord for the will-o'-the-wisp of romantic love.

As the outlines of West's characteristic plot make clear, unequivocally anti-Jacobin novelists—West, More, King, Mary Anne Hanway, and men such as Issac Disraeli, Charles Lucas, Robert Bisset, and George Walker—

depart markedly from earlier fiction. Not in their works will we find the stock-in-trade elements of social criticism which abound in novels by Fielding and Richardson, for example: gluttonous and sycophantic clergymen, tyrannical fathers, wastrel eldest sons, or comic plots favoring the romantic energies of the young over the inflexibility and greed of the old.[12] In an atmosphere of reaction, such material was politically sensitive, particularly after the Treasonable Practices and Seditious Meetings Acts of 1795 extended the definition of treason to include any criticism of the government. Social criticism was the inheritance of reformers bent on exposing the corruption of established power by taking the part of the dispossessed. Mary Wollstonecraft's *The Wrongs of Woman, or Maria* (1798) would show that the society sentimentalized by Burke authorizes brutish and mercenary husbands to run through their wives' fortunes and to immure them without legal interference; Elizabeth Inchbald's *Nature and Art* (1796) would show that the same magistrates who condemn ruined women to death also seduce and abandon village beauties in order to advance their careers and protect the blood of their families; Charlotte Smith's *Desmond* would show an insouciant lord praising his dog above his mother and sisters, and a plantation owner insisting that black slaves do not object to being flogged.

But having pointedly committed themselves to an anti-Jacobin position, conservative novelists have little choice but to idealize authority per se—the authority of laws, of conventions, of customs, and of course, of standard figures embodying them: fathers, husbands, clergymen. To do any less would be to surrender their first position and grant that the reformers they tried to discredit as maniacal and treasonous had legitimate grievances after all. Accordingly, in West's work, the yoke of patriarchal authority is light, and its power wise and benign. West opens *A Gossip's Story* (1796), for example, by exploding the silly "romantic" notion that behind every deceased wife is a tyrannical husband. When it is rumored that one Sir William has seduced and abandoned women, an unwary or reflexively progressive reader might conclude that West is granting that women are at a disadvantage. But as it turns out, the female "victims" had plied their wily arts, and thus had only gotten what they deserved. Though highborn lords or squires in West's works are often lax and sometimes even themselves misled by progressive theories, modest country gentlemen are generally models of rectitude. In *Tale of the Times* the clergyman is a figure of sound moral vision, and if the venerable patriarch Sir Anthony has any fault, it is only that he is too kind to prohibit his daughter's marriage of choice. Described as a man of feeling, Sir Anthony would never abuse his power, and no sensible person would ever oppose it. Holding fast to principles of "religion and morality," Sir William does not recognize "the claims of female supremacy," and thus he rightly assumes that it is rather his wife's duty to oblige him than his to submit to her ill-tempered petticoat government. We are to understand that the constraints he as a husband is empowered, indeed obligated, to place upon his silly wife are for her own good. She is not allowed to ridicule the clergy, to indulge in witty repartee, to wear hats piled high with fruit, or to attend masquerades: "What woman of spirit," West writes with ponderous irony, "could brook such restrictions?"[13]

Not all conservative novelists cared to idealize the status quo so confidently. Elizabeth Hamilton's novels are unmistakably conservative in their defense of established forms, but they are also remarkable in their refusal to be inflexibly doctrinaire and in their readiness to recognize and give way to at least some progressive social criticism. In the very process of refuting "Jacobin" doctrine, Hamilton's *Memoirs of Modern Philosophers*, as suggested above, cites and reproduces it at great length. And the voice it is allowed to possess here, as in novels by Amelia Opie and Fanny Burney, is listened to and heeded, even if only in part. Hamilton acknowledges that aristocrats have reprehensible "prejudices." One of the reliable moral guides in this novel's subplot is haughtily dismissed as ungrateful and fanatical by a worldly lord for declining a proffered living of six hundred pounds a year which depended solely on subscribing to the Test Act oath. To legitimize independence, defiance, and private conscience even when it controverts the church establishment, as Hamilton does throughout *Modern Philosophers*, is to share the platform of reform with progressive novelists. In *The Cottagers of Glenburnie* (1808), Hamilton even presumes to tell lords that they should teach their sons to apologize to their servants. But Hamilton is careful to keep her social criticism well this side of radicalism. While discussing masculine abuses of domestic power, Dr. Orwell, the normative center of *Memoirs of Modern Philosophers*, emphatically claims, "It is impossible that a real Christian should ever be a tyrant. To gratify the passion for dominion, or to exercise the pride of power, can never be the object with him who has imbibed the spirit which pervades the philosophy of JESUS."[14] In this manner, abuses which reformers would argue are intrinsic to existing power structures themselves are dismissed as adventitious, as genuine but purely personal failures on the part of individuals. Although far less doctrinaire than West, Elizabeth Hamilton shares her unwillingness to examine, as Austen does in *Mansfield Park*, for example, when authority itself can be morally problematic.

Concerning the question of a father's or husband's authority, Hamilton is every bit as strict as West. In Austen's novels, parental neglect is often just as apt to be benign as anything else. But conservative novelists preach submission without repining, and fault fathers only for being too indulgent: in *The Cottagers of Glenburnie*, Mr. Stewart timidly refuses to exercise his "right to dictate" to his daughter, whining "I cannot bear to see my child unhappy. I have not courage to encounter sour looks, and all the murmurings of discontent."[15] Similarly, in *Memoirs of Modern Philosophers* Captain Delmond is so fond of his daughter and so convinced of her intellectual superiority that he lets her read anything she wants and thus leaves her vulnerable to the seductive appeal of Jacobin doctrines. Here the villainous Vallaton runs through a sequence of professions that come straight from the pages of Burke's *Reflections* and *Letter:* beginning as an orphan, a thankless valet, a hairdresser, a writer, and finally as a patriot, he travels to England in order to make mischief in good families. This he accomplishes by convincing Julia Delmond that she has no moral obligations to her doting father, that filial gratitude ought not interfere with a child's free choices, and that promises are not binding once they no longer meet the approbation of our judgment. Once assenting to these maxims, the weak-headed Julia betrays her good father and the unexceptionable young man he has chosen for her, and elopes with Vallaton, only to be debauched, abandoned, and left to die repentant in an insane asylum. For this unhappy fate, Julia's freethinking and foolishly indulgent father claims some responsibility, having by paternal example as well as precept "encouraged her to throw off the prejudices of religion . . . to consult the dictates of her mind, instead of the dictates of the gospel."[16]

Clearly the fictions conservative writers contrive do not invite us to inquire when the authority of fathers over children is ever morally compromising, because the debate in which they are engaged requires them to demonstrate that the family itself is preeminently moral and moralizing. The good girl in *Modern Philosophers* underlines the sad moral to Julia Delmond's tale in this transparently Burkean way:

> "What shall we say to this sort of philosophy . . . which cuts the ties of gratitude, and pretends to extend our benevolence by annihilating the sweet bonds of domestic attachment? Should this system prevail,—'Relations dear, and all the charities of father, son, and brother,' would soon be no longer known."[17]

Considered from within the compelling rhetorical structures conservative novelists build, to suggest, as Austen, among many others, frequently does, that fathers, sons, and brothers themselves may be selfish, bullying and unscrupulous, and that the "bonds of domestic attachment" are not always sweet, is to attack the institutions which make morality possible and so to contribute to the dissolution of the government. In her *Letters Addressed to a Young Man* (1801), West instructs future husbands in the political importance of family government and the political subversiveness of attacks upon it. Exploding the "new theory of morals" which holds that "subjection is servility, and authority tyranny" and that "liberty and independence are such indefeasible rights, that even between parent and child, no such sentiments as authority and obedience should subsist," West follows counterrevolutionaries who, equating motive with results, insist that enlightenment writers have conspired to bring about the Revolution, to abolish "Christianity, regular governments and all social institutions" and wickedly to "*eradicate* from the human breast the *fundamental* principles of piety and virtue."[18]

In either championing or challenging the patriarchal family, the novelists of the 1790s employ a lexicon of sensitive terms which signal their partisanship and prefigure the outcomes of their plots. In part because of its association with philosophes such as Voltaire and Diderot, the word "philosophy," for example, acquires particularly volatile implications that sometimes ring like challenges in the very titles of novels. The reform-minded Charlotte Smith would entitle her book *The Young Philosopher* (1798) because it features a noble young man who dares to think for himself, to form his own judgments on the basis of reason and good sense, and thus to dissent from the self-serving amoral "prejudices" of his ossified aristocratic family. Employed within the matrix of counterrevolutionary ideolology, however, "philosophy" is a bad word, denoting that system of outrageous and ostensibly newfangled theories privileging private judgment and justifying the chimerical and hedonistic pursuit of personal happiness. Accordingly, Sophia King entitles her novel *Waldorf, or, the Dangers of Philosophy* (1798) because it features a hapless anti-hero who gets entangled in specious principles about morality and atheistical philosophy that ruin the lives of all around him and leave a trail of suicides and death in his unwitting wake.[19]

After, though not exclusively because of, Burke, "philosophy" is associated with arrogant sophisms which, following from the oft-caricatured premise "whatever is is wrong," attack beliefs and customs that have been tried by time. As Hamilton put it in her satiric novel *Translation of the Letters of a Hindoo Rajah* (1796), English philosophers are not men "deep in knowledge, either moral or natural," but people who without knowledge "entertain a high idea of their own superiority, from having the temerity to reject whatever has the sanction of experience, and common sense."[20] Although Hamilton—confounding the conservative lexicon—tried to rescue the term "philosophy" from infamy by linking it with the teachings of Christ, in conservative fiction as a whole "philosophy" is what bad men appeal to in order to justify theft in terms of the greater good, and what loose women blather about when they desert fathers, husbands, and children. Philosophy is in its nature specious, a rationalization of either fatuous or calculated selfishness. In *Modern Philosophers*, the ugly and slovenly feminist—a caricature of Mary Hays—rationalizes a silly romance with the following jumble of radical jargon:

> "By what moral tie am I bound to consult the inclinations of my mother? The only just morals are those which tend to increase the bulk of enjoyment. . . . [I]s not happiness and pleasure the only true end of our being? When we attain these, do we not promote general utility? These are the sublime principles of philosophy!"[21]

Happiness is not the end of our being, and weak-minded young men and women should be preserved from thinking so. As Issac Disraeli complains in *Vaurien* (1797), politically dangerous ideas are too accessible. The "speculations of philosophy" were formerly "told only in whispers, or published with a solicitous ambiguity." But now, unfortunately, any one who can read at all can find "philosophic scepticism" and "political inquiry" anywhere, and as a result they are "of greater importance in society, than in any preceding period."[22] To the degree that "philosophy" convinces people of their own entitlement to happiness, it destabilizes the hierarchical network of social and familial interdependencies that conservative novelists cherish.

But not all the villains or anti-heroes in conservative fiction are gross charlatans happy to employ "reason" in order to justify their mean actions. Some are earnest seekers after truth, and it is precisely their penchant for reflection that gets them into trouble. Woe to the indulgent parents who let their daughters read without the strict supervision Austen mocks in Mrs. Percival's tirade. Otherwise, the philosophy daughters are likely to come across in their reading will convince them that their opinions about questions relative to themselves matter, and it will urge them to subject received ideas to their own consideration, to choose what is best and preferable for themselves. Generally regarded as a grimly and patly conservative novelist, Amelia Opie was personally acquainted with progressives and radicals such as Godwin, Holcroft, and Inchbald, and although from 1801 on, her novels surely do ride on the waves of reaction, they are decidedly unenthusiastic about the forms they appear to advocate. In *Adeline Mowbray* (1804)—a novel which features a variation on the Godwin-Wollstonecraft relationship—a nineteen-year-old woman of unquestioned moral superiority reads extensively and then forms and lives out her unconventional view that the matrimonial relationship is consecrated only by the "honor" of its equal partners, not by a legal ceremony which "sanctions and perpetuates the dearest of all monopolies, and erects a sacred barrier to guard his [i.e., the husband's] rights."[23] After listening to the hapless Adeline explain her "opinions," Dr. Norberry, the novel's moral guide, explodes with indignation, "In your opinion!—Pray, child, how old are you?" an incident reconfigured in *Pride and Prejudice*, where Lady Catherine likewise attempts to discredit the forthright Elizabeth Bennet by asking her age.[24] Whatever Lady Catherine's point, Dr. Norberry's is that individuals in general—let alone inexperienced young girls—are not better judges about what is good for society in general or themselves in particular than is the accumulated wisdom of the ages, and that our own opinions, however sincere or even sensible, must accordingly bear less weight than the dictates of convention in determining our manners.

If conservative fiction opposes the autonomous efforts of reason unfavorably to the traditional practices enjoined by prejudice, they by necessity tended to discredit reflection itself. In *Adeline Mowbray*, the heroine's mother, when yet a birdbrained child spoiled by her parents as a "genius," reads Locke's *The Conduct of the Understanding*. Commended throughout the eighteenth century, Locke's little volume is a conduct book for the mind which, among other things, exhorts us to avoid such pitfalls to sound reflection as prejudice, haste, indistinctness, narrowness, and carelessness of language. When only a young girl, Mrs. Mowbray is so impressed with Locke's book that she presumes to recommend it to her parents so that she can teach them how "to think."[25] Opie invites us to consider the preposterousness of this act virtually self-evident, implying as it does that those simple and too fond parents, who have always done their duty, somehow have never really thought before and need to learn how now. Similarly King's *Waldorf, or the Dangers of Philosophy*, opposes the good wise man, "Zenna, the Magician," to the meretricious wise man, "Hardi Lok, The Philosopher." In so doing King endeavors to taint Locke by associating him with the English radical Thomas Hardy, who was tried and acquitted in the treason trials of 1794. Once dubbed "the sagacious," extensively quoted by no less than Samuel Richardson precisely for his didactic value, Locke now appears to be a subversive rationalist.

Try as Burke did to differentiate the Revolution of 1688 from the French Revolution, to which sympathizers such as Price had compared it, a native tradition of political notions was being appropriated by reformers. In *Desmond* for example, Charlotte Smith opposes Burke's "fine sounding periods" to the more solid reasonings of Locke's *Treatises of Government*, giving particular emphasis to his refutation of Filmer's *Patriarcha*, his critique of custom, and his censure of the practice of attempting to bind posterity to present obligations.[26] Political conservatives were thus in the uncomfortable position of having to rewrite English history and the lexicon of political rhetoric that served it. As a result, once-acceptable words such as "reason," "judgment," "liberty," "impartiality," "happiness," and "independence" had to be redefined and stripped of any good moral or political raison d'être. Conservative novelists, then, minimize the necessity for reflection. The good girl in *Memoirs of Modern Philosophers*, contemplating the philosophical manias that have wrought such havoc in her village, declares "May we . . . never suffer ourselves to be seduced from the plain path of piety and peace."[27] For her, there is not much to reflect or opine about: the path of duty is always clear, and obedience to parents, fathers, and husbands is always proper. Far from requiring the endorsement of our reason, the established forms of state and family save us where reason fails. Thus the plots of conservative fiction do not so much clarify or simplify moral problems as they deny that any exist.

For women in particular, debates about reason, prejudice, happiness, authority, and independence were not academic. To a public progressively more anxious about the respect for authority and the inviolability of marriage as an institution that orders, sanctifies, and perpetuates the interests of society, it is particularly important that young ladies be prevented from entertaining idiosyncratic opinions or intensely personal expectations about marriage and family. With the countryside full of Jacobin riffraff out to ruin English families by seducing women away from fond fathers and rightful husbands, female modesty—that is to say, the extent to which women do not feel, express, and pursue their own desires—is no less than a matter of national security. Mimicking and thus exposing the self-serving logic of this anxiety, Mary Robinson's progressive *The False Friend: A Domestic Story* (1797) assigns the following speech to a conniving Lord Arcot threatened by new ideas about women: "If a wife breaks the fetters of matrimonial restraint, though we all know that women were born to be slaves, why, forsooth, she is only called a lover of liberty."[28] Of course the objective of late-eighteenth-century feminists was not to apologize for adultery—although it certainly seemed that way to astonished conservative readers—but rather to plea for female autonomy, and thus to give women a broader scope for "liberty" than what they currently had.

Writers such as Wollstonecraft and Hays exposed and deplored the double standard in a liberal moral philosophy which is founded on rights to liberty and happiness all share prior to social contracts solely by virtue of being human, but which, in prohibiting women from making choices about their own lives, dictates fundamentally different codes of morality for men and women, unfits women for moral as well as for domestic duties, and entraps them in infantine dependency. In the early 1790s, the assertion that morality has no gender was not alarming or distinctively radical, though some male readers apparently felt that the recognition of women's rights necessarily entailed a diminution of their own. No Burkean man of feeling he, the boorish Lord B. in Gilbert Imlay's *The Immigrants* (1793) complains that it is "now looked upon as quite *brutish*, for a man to go to bed to his wife in a state of *intoxication*," and furiously resenting not only the complaints of women, but also the encroaching feminization of men's manners, he predicts that if a male "tyranny" does not reassert its rights, "a female *empire would destroy every thing that was beautiful, and which the talents of ages had accumulated.*"[29] Although it was her second refutation of Burke's *Reflections*, most reviewers considered Wollstonecraft's *Vindication of the Rights of Woman* in 1792 as yet another, largely commendable attack on the kind of female education which promoted superficial accomplishments and imbecilic helplessness to the exclusion of rationality, reflection, and usefulness.[30] Even as late as 1796, Bage referred favorably to Wollstonecraft's *Vindication* throughout *Hermsprong* without any apparent anxiety about how his approval might be construed. As the reaction wore on, however, and as Wollstonecraft's unconventional sexual conduct became public knowledge, conservative audiences were shocked to realize that if women were indeed educated and permitted to act like "rational creatures," they might consider themselves entitled, as free agents, to frame their own desires and pursue happiness on their own terms, rather than be content as dutiful daughters or submissive wives.

This threatening prospect loomed in Mary Hays's *Memoirs of Emma Courtney* (1796). An autobiographical critique of obsessive romantic love and the conventions that can render it tragic, this novel features a woman who proposes repeatedly to a man in letters detailing her qualifications to make him happy. Greeted as a recommendation of self-pity and shamelessly persistent female indelicacy, *Emma Courtney* instantly became the bugbear of anti-Jacobin novelists who hastened to reaffirm male supremacy and to redraw the lines of sexual difference. To male authors of reactionary fiction especially, supporting the rights of woman became synonymous with advocating the unleashing of rapacious female sexuality. What other motive, after all, could a woman have for wishing to eschew the modesty that customarily restrains her desires? Thus the malicious Jacobin Marauder in Charles Lucas's *The Infernal Quixote* (1801) begins his project of debauching Miss Emily by mixing "the most pernicious doctrines with the most grateful flattery," both of which are calculated to make her more susceptible to his designs upon her chastity: "Why should there be any inferiority in the one sex than the other? In what are we superior to you? . . . were your education not so confined, I doubt not you would equally rival us in the most learned studies."[31] Robert Bisset's thinly fictionalized *Modern Literature: A Novel* (1804) strikes Wollstonecraft and Rousseau with the same blow. Wollstonecraft, appearing under the name "Jemima," tries to win sisters over to her cause by describing the ease of promiscuity and the convenience of having foundling hospitals for unwanted offspring.[32] While early readers considered Wollstonecraft dour and asexual, in the index to the *Anti-Jacobin Review* of 1798, Wollstonecraft is listed under the word "Prostitution"; with gleefully puerile salaciousness Richard Polwhele treats her suggestion that children overcome false modesty by studying the reproductive capacities of plants as tantamount to advocating priapism. Similarly, in Edgeworth's *Belinda* (1801), the feminist Harriot Freke barks her championship of the "rights of woman" and to that end dresses like a man, shakes hands with everyone, speaks loudly, arranges a duel between two women, and encourages adultery and female-initiated proposals.[33]

The novels and conduct books by Hannah More and Jane West advance the strictest programs for female subordination and the most repressive standards of female propriety to counteract the influence of progressive ideas about women. Writing with avowedly counterrevolutionary intentions, West promotes a model of female excellence that is defined exclusively from the male point of view: as she writes in *The Gossip's Story*, "the attentive, submissive daughter will make a tender obliging wife; the retired, amiable maid, will form the prudent domestick matron."[34] Presenting marriage as a social duty and not as a source of personal felicity, West frowns on marriages of affection. Had the otherwise dutiful Lady Geraldine not credited her own (needless to say fallible) preferences in choosing a husband, and had she consented instead to accept the sensible man her sensible father picked out for her, the convoluted tragedy in *Tale of the Times* could not have occurred. "[M]utual attachment," West decides conclusively, "is unnecessary in a union between two worthy people."[35] Although West admits that marriage places a larger burden on women than on men, she insists without compromise that husbands, no matter how reprehensible, must always be able to depend absolutely on the continuance of their wives' devotion. Thus, though Geraldine's husband, Lord Monteith, is painted unflinchingly as a selfish brat who virtually pushes his wife into the arms of another man, he is never assailed for his wrongdoing. The subordination of women is absolutely maintained. This system, as West explains in *The Infidel Father*, may be "inconvenient," but women can learn to work it to their advantage. Rather than put "the lordly creature" on his guard with demands or assertions of rights, women can "appear to *retire* . . . as if you feared that he was going to commence hostilities" and thus by acknowledging his power, ameliorate it. In *Tale of the Times*, however, even this ploy does not work, for docility only stings the guilt-ridden husband with more bitterness. In any case, fundamental questioning of "our governors" will only lead to a reactionary backlash of "stricter coercion" in domestic authority, and West does not say it would be ill-deserved.[36]

If West showed women their duty, she did not insist that they like it. A stoic cheer would suffice. The task of teaching women actually to cherish standards of female excellence which serve the patriarchy fell to Hannah More, who is today known mostly for the evangelical teaching and reactionary propaganda she addressed to lower and middle classes, the audience for her immensely popular *Cheap Repository Tracts*. But as Austen's revisions to "Catharine, or The Bower" testify, *Coelebs in Search of a Wife* reached more affluent audiences as well, and Austen herself took note. *Coelebs* dramatizes the paradoxes of female subordination in their most ludicrous form, though it must be acknowledged that most readers did not think so, since it went into some thirteen editions in its first year. Having much earlier disdained to read Wollstonecraft's *Vindication* because its very title seemed absurd and indecent, More sets out in *Coelebs* to elaborate a construction of sexual difference which confirms male superiority, and to recommend the strictest and most excruciatingly proper model of female delicacy. In order to do so, More adopts the masculine point of view. Her protagonist, Coelebs, is a supremely eligible and fastidious bachelor who travels the nation around in search of a good wife, a commodity very hard to find: learned ones cannot cook, stupid ones cannot think about religion, and other poor creatures can do neither. Whereas advocates of women's rights had argued that the moral duties of men and women are identical, More maintains the "absolute *morality*," the *"positive duty of being agreeable at home"* as the only desideratum of feminine virtue. Indeed, deviations from truth, religion, modesty, and decorum alike are conceived not as failures of morality per se, as Wollstonecraft, for one, would hold, but rather as failures of "agreeableness" that will make a woman undesirable as a daughter or wife.[37] The anti-heroine Amelia Rattle, for example, is frowned upon because she is intrepid; because, far from deferring to men in conversation, she does not hesitate to express her opinions forcibly; because she is strong enough to spring onto a carriage without masculine assistance and exuberant enough to cry out "drive on" without inhibition—these last two infractions earning her the epithet "little hoyden" from the incredulous Coelebs. Clearly, vitality, confidence and self-sufficiency are not marriageable qualities, and Amelia's most glaring defect is her utter indifference to the judgment of him whose approval is the litmus test of feminine, that is, wifely, worth. The fair Lucilla Stanley, however, is another story. She does not speak until spoken to, and even then only in the presence of her immediate family; she is the best cook, menu planner and household manager in the county; she is a blessing to her parents and a godsend to the village poor; she is devoutly though unostentatiously religious; she is educated enough to appreciate men's cleverness in conversation but feminine enough never to wish to engage in or rival it herself; she believes that female accomplishment should be cultivated only insofar as it "improves herself, it embellishes her family society, it entertains her husband, it informs her children."[38] In short, Lucilla Stanley is the perfect wife.

By recommending a diffidence so complete as almost to amount to contented self-erasure, More encounters aesthetic as well as logical problems. The invariably dutiful and retiring Lucilla is only talked about. The perfectly proper lady can not be represented at all, for a woman so delicately receded will not permit herself to be seen or heard or otherwise differentiated from a nonentity. How then can More as a novelist praise, and by praising make attractive to women readers, a modest and feminine ambition precisely to have none, to go unnoticed? Coelebs tries—"How modestly flattering her manner. . . . How intelligent her silence! How well-bred her attention!"—but silence so unbroken cannot be distinguished from insipidness or imbecility.[39] Even worse, by adopting the masculine persona, More unwittingly encourages young ladies to indulge the pathetic fantasy of the powerless: to believe that rich and sensible men spend all their time examining the minutiae of female manners and dreaming of a woman whose perfect modesty and domestic economy render her not only commendable but utterly irresistible. Although More—with Wollstonecraft—denounces "Mahometan education" which only makes "woman an object of attraction," she herself does essentially the same, for her novel suggests that catching a husband is the only motive for female virtue.[40]

Concerning the question of sexual difference, as well as every other aspect of anti-Jacobin ideology, many women novelists found it impossible to toe the party line. Partly because the subject of sexual difference itself has only recently been seen to carry political significance, much of the social criticism of women novelists considered unequivocally conservative has been overlooked. Indeed, strain shows even in the postures of such unequivocally counterrevolutionary writers as West and More. Authorial self-styling is a sticky business for a woman publicly committed to championing female subordination.[41] West tries to palliate the forward, unfeminine act of publicity sometimes by employing the pseudonym "Prudentia Homespun"; sometimes, in an effort that points forward to Elizabeth Gaskell, by adopting the disingenuously self-deprecating persona of the village "old maid," a well-meaning "gossip" with nothing better to do; and sometimes by denying her sex altogether and aggrandizing her interest in the moral welfare of young Englishmen with the adjective "paternal." Hannah More also chafes from time to time. Her preface to *Strictures on the Modern System of Female Education* (1799) placates would-be critics with the assurance that she is not so presumptuous as to claim herself free from the faults she censures in her sex. Adopting the viewpoint of a male protagonist in *Coelebs in Search of a Wife*, whatever its awkwardness in some respects, was certainly an enabling device in others, for with it More-Coelebs can disapprove of women displaying their learning, on the one hand, and parade her own unfeminine knowledge of ancient languages on the other.

But for women writers who, like Austen, were sceptical about reactionary ideology, more was at stake than the embarrassment of finding it impossible to practice what they preached. Indeed, because many women novelists felt their marginality to patriarchal culture far more acutely than West or More, they had no wish to advocate comparable codes of female propriety and sexual difference which, if taken seriously, would compromise the act of authorship itself. However, because reactionary apologists arrogated all moral authority to themselves, effectual dissent on the subject of sexual difference and the host of topics constellated around it was difficult, not to say downright dangerous. Accordingly, taking part in the "war of ideas" during a time of intense reaction posed severe aesthetic problems. How could authors use the urgently important subjects postrevolutionary polemics opened up to them without getting entangled in the inexorable binary oppositions that very polemic set into motion? How could they arraign the patriarchal family without seeming thereby to embrace amoral and treasonous doctrines? How could they question the wisdom of convention without seeming to prefer the principle of total singularity? How could they advance progressive ideas about the situation of women without seeming to recommend Wollstonecraft's sexual irregularities and her suicide attempts? To write novels of social criticism, authors had to develop strategies of subversion and indirection which would enable them to use the polemical tradition without being used completely by it.

Such strategies are more conspicuous with respect to the advocacy of sexual difference than to any other facet of reactionary ideology. Sceptical women novelists try to engage in incisive social criticism and at the same time to assure touchy readers that *they* are not uppity and insubordinate women, by creating a new and short-lived character-type: the freakish feminist, or "female philosopher," as she was then called. A sop thrown to gullible readers, this figure espouses the feminist principles of the 1790s in a ridiculously caricatured form, and is duly mocked throughout the novel and contrasted unfavorably to modest and sensible young ladies. In

Memoirs of Modern Philosophers, for example, Bridgetina Botherim bears the brunt of Hamilton's antifeminist satire: fat, ugly, crippled, slovenly, and short—Bridgetina is taller sitting down than standing up—she decries the retiring modesty and household duties that cramp female genius. Bridgetina is thus the opposite of Austen's Charlotte Lutterell in *Lesley Castle*, who, by living and breathing syllabubs, cheeses, and "devouring" plans, satirizes female domesticity in the very process of epitomizing it with a vengeance so assertive that it has long since ceased to serve patriarchal purposes. Bridgetina, by contrast, is stung by suggestion that she might know how to cook pudding: " 'A pudding,' repeated Bridgetina, reddening with anger, 'I do assure you, sir, you are very much mistaken, if you think that I employ my time in such a manner.' " Indeed, Bridgetina spends her time reading deep in novels and metaphysics and is, as her benighted mother remarks, "far too learned to trouble herself about doing any thing useful."[42] As embodied by Bridgetina, at least, feminist tenets are ludicrous rather than pernicious.

But Bridgetina Botherim, like many another female philosopher in turn-of-the-century fiction, is not the author's last word on the rights of woman. If anything, appearing as she does to be proof perfect that her creator is innocent of any radical intent, the freakish feminist actually frees the author to advance reformist positions about women through the back door.[43] Once having discredited Bridgetina, Hamilton is secure enough to praise Mary Wollstonecraft's criticisms of Rousseau and to present her as a "very sensible authoress" who does not deserve the abuse with which "superficial readers" treat her. Vilifying Bridgetina, then, makes it possible for Hamilton to argue with Wollstonecraft that Christ's "morality was addressed to the judgment without distinction of sex."[44] In *Translation of the Letters of a Hindoo Rajah*, Hamilton doubles up overtly and covertly feminist characters to the same effect: the silly Miss Ardent is mocked for her disdain of domestic duties and her entirely unfounded pride in her "*masculine understanding*," but the lovely Lady Grey, without aspiring to feminism, is praised for her powerful and informed mind and for the quiet but firm strength she shows when her husband's illness makes it necessary for her to run the whole estate by herself.[45] Maria Edgeworth similarly distances herself from feminist controversy, only to sneak moderately feminist suggestions into her novels and stories. In *Belinda* (1801), Harriot Freke proclaims her championship of the rights of woman, and her name alone discredits her. But having burlesqued Harriot Freke in one chapter of *Belinda*, Edgeworth can expose what genuinely *is* irrational about the code of female delicacy in many another. Similarly, in "The Modern Griselda" (1805), Edgeworth indicts Griselda's perverse drive for marital dominion only to establish the domestic equality of a contrasting couple as ideal. Fanny Burney goes the furthest in *The Wanderer, or, Female Difficulties*, where the anti-heroine's feminist ravings, though duly dismissed by "sensible" characters, provide accurate running commentary on the humiliation and injustice suffered throughout the novel by the heroine, Ellis. More than merely a reassuring diversionary ploy, Burney's female philosopher, however vulnerable to criticism herself, is an indispenable element of the novel.

To be sure, the mere presence of risible women touting female genius and liberty is a symptom of the pressure under which women novelists labored and of the political sensitivity of even mildly profeminist platforms. At the same time, however, the freakish feminist represents an ingenious way of undermining the polemical logic of anti-Jacobin apologists. The use of this historically specific figure, who virtually disappears after 1815, testifies to the determination of many women novelists to advance rather than forestall social criticism, for it enabled women to argue a position similar to Wollstonecraft's in *Vindication of the Rights of Woman* at a time when her life and works were in disgrace: promoting the moral equality and rational cultivation of women actually serves to stabilize society by making women into more useful helpmates and engaging companions than the submissive and retiring creatures anti-Jacobin propagandists idealized in their novels and conduct books. As a rhetorical device, the freakish feminist exemplifies the effort of sceptical novelists to subvert the anti-Jacobin novel from within, as it were, to use its own conventions against itself, to establish an alternative tradition by working within an existing one in a different way and to a different end.

This procedure of using apparently conservative material in order to question rather than confirm it illuminates the artistic choices of authors who, like Austen, make no explicit announcement about engaging in social criticism in the first place. At first glance, Laura Montreville in Brunton's *Self-Control* (1811) appears to be the very model of repressive female modesty. But Brunton tacitly avers otherwise by playing her off against tropes about feminine manners established in previous novels. True, Laura may delicately swoon from time to time, but when anyone attempts to wrest her *self*-control from her hands, she can seize the reins, spring on and off curricles, and shout with a "powerful voice," all of which physically assertive activities Coelebs censures in the feminist "hoyden" Amelia Rattle.[46] Like Brunton, Austen too must render her dues unto conventions about female modesty, and though she analyzes these conventions methodically in *Mansfield Park*, the constraints they posed surface in all her novels. Austen's notorious refusal to depict her heroines in the act of saying "yes" to proposals of marriage, for example, is often chalked up to personal inadequacy, to a peculiar inability on her part to confront emo-

tion. "What did she say?" the narrator teasingly asks concerning the proposal scene in *Emma*, "Just what she ought, of course. A lady always
does" (E 431). But exactly what a "lady" *can* say, and just as important,
how it can be depicted in fiction are riddles *Emma* cannot answer. If those
gaps in Austen's novels indicate any authorial inability, it is only an inability to crack the ironclad logic of female delicacy, according to which a
proper woman openly and ardently avowing intense personal desire can
scarcely be imagined, much less represented. Accordingly, although Austen, like Brunton, is, happily, rather unusual among her contemporaries
in declining to create a ridiculous female philosopher, she too dissents
from conduct-book moralizing about women by subversively using motifs that already have a political resonance to them. For example, when
Elizabeth Bennet muddies her petticoats by running through the countryside to visit her sick sister, Austen is alluding to an incident in *Memoirs
of Modern Philosophers* where Bridgetina Botherim does the same while
taking a vigorous walk. The issue in both cases, of course, is not clean-
liness, but rather the unseemliness of female "energy." In Hamilton's
novel, Bridgetina's "energies" are laughed off as yet another Godwinian
absurdity. But in *Pride and Prejudice*, Elizabeth's exercise brings a flush
of vitality to her face which the gentlemen find sexually attractive, and
if Darcy concedes that he would never allow his sister to traipse around
like that, Bingley allows that Elizabeth's run bespeaks an amiable concern
for her sister's health. By quietly reassembling what had previously been
unambiguous and politically sensitive material about female conduct,
Austen and Brunton, like the more conspicuously politicized sister-novelists from whom they draw, are challenging repressive anti-Jacobin dicta
about women without fuss or fanfare.

   If, as we have seen, women novelists were able to appropriate a reactionary type in order to advance modest but distinctly reformist positions
about female manners, they developed other narrative strategies to examine Burkean premises about marriage and patriarchy while eluding the
accusation that they favored a radical reconstitution of society. Both the
subtlest and the most radical of these is the use of ironic parallels or multiple plots which belie, rather than underscore, didactic contrasts between
good girls and bad girls, good families and bad families, good attitudes
and bad attitudes, and which, by thus decentering the prescriptive thrust
of the plot, call our attention to moral problems Burkean conservatives
minimize. Opie's *Adeline Mowbray* is positively dizzying in the degree
to which it invalidates all answers, conservative and radical. Typically read
as "the usual cautionary tale of the anti-Jacobins," this novel does indeed
feature an emancipated woman who lives to regret it.[47] Falling prey to
the seductive radical critique of marriage, she lives with her spouse "in

honor" outside of marriage, only to suffer social opprobrium and isolation so acute as to convince her to renounce her arrogant eccentricity. Adeline finally concludes that marriage is "beneficial to society" because it protects children, enforces constancy, and "has a tendency to call forth and exercise the affections, and control the passions."[48]

This entirely Burkean conclusion would be unassailable if any marriage in the novel actually were presented in a benign light. But on the contrary, without making an issue of it the novel shows that marriage does no such thing. One of the defenders of religion and marriage in the novel, Sir Patrick O'Carrol, is himself a fraud, a would-be rapist, a bigamist, and a misogynist. Yet another husband, a glutton, begrudges his wife her food and virtually starves her to death—"being no advocate for the equality of the sexes, he thought it only a matter of course that he should fare better than his wife." To make matters worse, he is conspicuously oblivious to the softening influence of paternity: he loathes his newborn son and, lest we missed Opie's first reference to bigamy, deserts him and his mother to take up house with another woman in Jamaica.[49] Living outside marriage may not be good for women, but in *Adeline Mowbray* living within it is certainly not much of an improvement. If the heroine finally affirms the social and moral efficacy of marriage, nothing else in the novel does. Rather than compare a radical social position unfavorably to a Burkean one, Opie plays both ends off against the middle, in much the same way as Austen inconclusively plays the improper Mary Crawford off against the proper Fanny Price in *Mansfield Park*. Both novelists proffer an abundance of orthodox pronouncements, not as definitive and incontestable truths around which to structure their novels, but as propositions that their novels test and turn inside out.

Even when weaving less polemically charged plots, novelists such as Opie, Inchbald, Burney, Edgeworth—and Austen—collapse the antithetical structures that conservative apologists employ in order to validate their ideas. Their novels complicate the simpler world of Burkean fiction, where fathers are judicious and clergymen are pious; where the duties of daughters are clear, and where wives are either grave and good or petulant and power hungry; where villains and heroes occupy entirely different moral universes, and where right and wrong are mutually exclusive categories. West's *A Gossip's Story*, for example, tirelessly reiterates the moral difference between two daughters, one good, decorous, obedient, and contentedly married to a modest country gentleman her father appoints, and the other bad, romantic, self-willed, and doomed to a connubial infelicity of her own choosing. But Inchbald's *A Simple Story* (1791)—like *Sense and Sensibility*—sets up tropic antithetical contrasts and simplicities only the more systematically to dismantle them throughout the course of the narrative by suggesting that the differences are more apparent than real. The two symmetical parts of *A Simple Story* are often taken to reinforce the moral differences between the frivolous and flighty woman of the first half and her sober, disciplined, and obedient daughter in the second. But the two plots suggest just as unmistakably how impossible it is for either woman, try as she may, to survive the cold and withering grip of Dorriforth's authority. In much the same way, *Sense and Sensibility* apportions its titular qualities to each of the sisters, and they, furthermore, are deluded in identical ways about their equally shadowy, weak, and unworthy suitors.

The novels of women authors not specifically reformist, but nevertheless sceptical of conservative ideology, deal with the same types and situations as Burkean fiction, but refuse to play them out in precisely the same ways. The several favorable allusions to Burke in Edgeworth's *Belinda*, for example, may prompt an inattentive reader to conclude that the novel is unequivocally partisan. But even though Edgeworth—like West, More, and Hamilton—brings to her fiction the same didactic habits that typify her work on manners and education, she defies her own tendencies to be exemplary in *Belinda*, and scrambles the Burkean codes she sets up. One expects an uppity wife with a penchant for "government" to presage an honorable, if abused, old patriarch of a husband, but in fact Lord Delacour is every bit as boorish, selfish, and pathetic as his wife; the sight of female duelists may raise our eyebrows, but the bigotry and coarseness of the mob that gives them chase is more unnerving still; Harriot Freke leaves us cold when urging female forwardness, but when good girls like Miss Portman are treated like chattel, and others, like Virginia, are admired for their vacuity and docility, Freke's fury with female delicacy does not sound unreasonable after all. Reformist writers employ Burkean oppositions only to question their distinctness and in the process to undo them, thus permitting a degree of moral complication, even disorientation, which counterrevolutionary novelists deplore. It is no accident, after all, that *Northanger Abbey*, a novel which bows gracefully to *Belinda*, closes with a not inconsequential question for the fiction of her time: "I leave it to be settled by whomsoever it may concern, whether the tendency of this work be altogether to recommend parental tyranny, or reward filial disobedience" (NA 252). Instead of laboring towards ringing didactic conclusions, the novelists with whom Austen affiliates herself in *Northanger Abbey* employ the same interrogative, rather than declarative, narrative methods Austen devoted her career to refining, methods which serve moderately progressive rather than reactionary political outlooks.[50]

But Jane Austen singles out another author for honorable mention as a model in *Northanger Abbey*, Fanny Burney. With her broad canvasses, her penchant for feminizing the picaresque, and her fascination with the mad and bizarre, Burney seems little akin to Austen. Her fiction, however, bears on Austen and the tradition of the political novel in especially crucial ways. Unlike Burkean conservatives, Burney adopts the narrative vantage point of marginal figures, and the way patriarchy looks from that angle is none too comforting. The political ramifications of this simple reversal of perspective must not be underestimated, for it gives a voice to characters whose opinions about patriarchy Burke, for one, did not solicit. Well before the revolution and reaction, Burney's novels had problematized patriarchal figures by representing the discrepancy between how they really are and how they seem in the eyes of ingenues who idealize them, clearly the formula Austen follows in *Northanger Abbey* and in *Mansfield Park*. *Evelina* (1778) depicts female experience as a continual process of fending off assaults, where preceptors are incompetent or unavailing, and where protectors cannot readily be distinguished from predators. With greater claims to ambition and more discernible traces of frustration and ambivalence, *Cecilia* (1782) dramatizes how patriarchy itself subsists on the actual eradication of female selfhood. Buckling beneath the pressure of her uncle's posthumous will that she maintain his surname and her prospective husband's insistence that she adopt his, the heroine loses not only her inheritance but also quite literally her identity, undergoing repeated fits of madness and amnesia that leave her exhausted, eroded, and numb with indifference by the time her story ends. Burney's later experiences at Court as a Keeper of the Queen's Robes and her horror at the Terror did not abate her tendency to question how well women are served by the institutions that purport to protect them. At least part of her enterprise in *Camilla* (1796) is to show once again how women are compromised, not by prowling strangers, but by the very preceptor figures on whose selfish, overbearing, poor, or merely limited judgment they are obliged to rely, and how the modesty that is urged upon them as the crowning excellency of their sex is an intolerably oppressive double bind. By the time Burney turned to her final novel, she went a logical step further and reworked Wollstonecraft's *The Wrongs of Woman, or Maria* from the point of view of a single character. *The Wanderer* exposes the injustices and prejudices women endure when, obliged to live without male protection, they slip down the social ladder into the same kind of indigence that menaces Jane Fairfax.[51]

To be sure, Burney never openly challenges the principle of paternal or of paternalistic authority; nor does she systematically question conventional pieties about female docility. Sometimes the paternal figure is so formidable that Burney, in marked contrast with Wollstonecraft, *displaces* conflict either onto a powerful female figure, Mrs. Delvile, for example, or onto distanced or defused surrogates. And when a patriarch is brought to his feet—as Sir John Belmont is in *Evelina*—it is only amidst protests from the young girl he has injured. These acts of displacement or denial in themselves are strategies of social criticism that surface conspicuously in Austen's fiction—Lady Catherine, for example, being less awesome and therefore more assailable than any male counterpart, and fathers such as Mr. Woodhouse or Sir Walter Elliot being depotentiated altogether. Nevertheless, if Burney and Austen draw back with ambivalence where Wollstonecraft and Hays step forward with confidence, their worries about the moral unreliablity of patriarchal figures and their dubiousness about the social conventions which privilege the prerogatives of men at the cost of confining the choice of women are not any the less perceptible. By writing from the viewpoint of dispossessed characters who themselves do not question the legitimacy of Burkean loci of moral and social stability, Burney and Austen alike are able to show, beneath the nominally conventional surfaces of their novels, truths about the absence or arbitrariness of fathers, the self-importance of brothers, and the bad faith of mentors which, if not as daring or sweeping, are still as disturbing as any of the indictments made by radical novelists.

The Revolution in France gave rise to the novel of crisis in England, a novel in which the structures of daily life are called into doubt and in which the unthinkable just keeps happening. In one novel a wife, spouting off about the immoral tendency of matrimony, leaves her husband and children; in another, a husband, cramped for money, uses his authority to sell his wife to a rich friend. In one novel, the "philosophy" of a radical prompts him to look forward to that glorious age when female chastity shall "be considered as a weakness and the virtue of a woman estimated according as she has had the energy to break its mean restraints"; and in another, the "prejudice" of a reactionary landowner teaches that women are "a race of subordinate beings, formed for the service and amusement of men; and that if, like horses, they were well lodged, fed, and kept clean, they had no right to complain."[52] In some novels, benighted or ungrateful daughters desert their good fathers only to expose themselves to shame and drive those reverend gentlemen to extremities of grief; in others, greedy fathers brutally force their daughters into disastrous marriages in order to consolidate their estates. Finding themselves at the heart of unsettling moral and political debates, Austen's only slightly older contemporaries image forth visions of domestic horror which vary according to their political sympathies. For some, the unthinkable is living outside sacred and time-honored structures; for others, on the contrary, it is living inside of them. For both, however, the moral as well as aesthetic center has ceased to hold, and despair, confusion, weariness, and apocalyptic dread or yearning strain the fabric of their narratives and push their characters to violence, madness, and suicide.[53]

The novels of Jane Austen focus on the discourse rather than the representation of politics. Alluding only rarely to actual events outside her famously placid villages, Austen does not, it is true, explicitly invoke the French Revolution; but from the 1790s—the formative years of her career—until the end of her career, she is constantly evoking the tradition of fiction in England to which it gave rise: from Mrs. Percival's admonitions about female virtue and national security in "Catharine, or The Bower," to the staging in *Mansfield Park* of Inchbald's version of *Lover's Vows*, featuring a woman's proposal of marriage, and finally to Mrs. Croft's untroubled insistence in *Persuasion* that women are "rational creatures" who can and indeed who must seize the reins lest the carriage overturn. Austen may slacken the desperate tempos employed by her more strenuously politicized counterparts, but she shares their artistic strategies and their commitment to uncovering the ideological underpinnings of cultural myths.

CHAPTER TWO

THE JUVENILIA AND *NORTHANGER ABBEY:*
THE AUTHORITY OF MEN AND BOOKS

Jane Austen's earliest literary productions are the fruit of unparalleled self-assurance. With very little ado, Austen proclaims the dignity of her genre as well as the authority of her own command over it—both at a time when such gestures were rare. Unlike her predecessors, Austen pointedly refuses to apologize for novels. By contrast, Fielding's efforts to elevate his own fiction by affiliating it with the classical tradition bespeak his nagging doubts about its status, not to mention his own status in dealing in it; Richardson's prefaces and editorial pronouncements reflect uneasiness about the moral tendency of his work; and women novelists irked Austen no end by marginalizing their work and having their own heroines deny reading anything so frivolous as novels at all: " 'Do not imagine that *I* often read novels,' " Austen mimicks, " '—It is really very well for a novel.'—Such is the common cant.—'And what are you reading Miss ———?' 'Oh! it is only a novel!' replies the young lady" (NA 38). Regarding herself and her colleagues as "an injured body" plagued not simply by reviewers' cant, but even worse, by their own self-defeating habits of internalizing and reproducing it, Austen counters for the first and final time in her career, that novels are works "in which the most thorough knowledge of human nature, the happiest delineation of its varieties, the liveliest effusions of wit and humour are conveyed to the world in the best chosen language" (NA 38). Never again would similar gestures of self-justification appear necessary. Austen's readiness to assume her qualifications to vindicate fiction is more than an outpouring of youthful enthusiasm. It bespeaks a profound confidence which no previous novelist of either sex possessed. Because the acuity and independence of Austen's mature social criticism emerge from her authorial confidence and self-consciousness, it is worth considering closely the first stirrings of both.

From the earliest writings on, Austen's confidence took a remarkably assertive form. Virginia Woolf was one of the first to observe that Austen's early work, generally viewed as precocious diversions for the family circle, was *not* amateurish and contentedly unaspiring, undertaken solely to entertain adored parents, cousins, and siblings. Honoring the "rhythm and shapeliness and severity" that mark even the earliest of Austen's sentences, Woolf finds that "Love and Freindship," for example, was "meant to outlast the Christmas holidays." To Woolf, Austen was from the very start a committed artist "writing for everybody, for nobody, for our age, for her own," and the most salient quality of her artistry is the unnerving effrontery of its laughter: "The girl of fifteen is laughing, in her corner, at the world."[1]

To sit in amused judgment upon the world requires a degree of audacity we do not generally associate with girls of fifteen looking on from their corners.[2] But Austen did not confine the keen presumption of her laughter to the snobs, hypocrites, and bumblers who constitute "the world." Like most eighteenth-century novelists and poets, Austen initiated her career by parody. Austen's parodic juvenile writings are exercises in authority which announce both a superiority of judgment which entitles her to authorship and a determination to level that judgment against predominating literary conventions—conventions which would soon be conspicuously freighted with political urgency. Throughout the juvenilia Austen derives her vitality from systematically exploring and dismantling the conventions that governed the literary form available to her. Her fiction of the late 1780s—and later the 1790s—was, in other words, more than a playpen where a precocious girl poked fun at silly fads and people. It was also a workshop, where the would-be artist first set hand to the tools of her trade, identifying operative structures and motifs, and then turning them inside out in order to explore their artificiality and bring to light their hidden implications. "Jack and Alice", for example, shocks us into the recognition of how little innocent our acts of reading are, for virtually every sentence of this tour de force turns uproariously on itself to disrupt expectations we had no idea we were nursing to begin with. The temporal displacement of the opening sentence irreverently mocks what George Eliot more soberly called "the make believe of a beginning":

> Mr. Johnson was once upon a time about 53; in a twelvemonth afterwards he was 54, which so much delighted him that he was determined to celebrate his next Birthday by giving a Masquerade to his Children & Freinds (MW 12).

Like all parody, Austen's sentence here is hyperconventional and anti-conventional at one and the same time, unfolding a series of codes which first appears unitary, only then to diverge into confounding incongruity. Austen thus begins with the predictable "once upon a time," the ostensible purpose of which is to situate us in the narrative present. But much to our bewilderment, by mid-sentence we are transported with no discernible purpose not one but two years before—or is it after?—the "beginning." Only after a few double takes will we be able to orient ourselves. And even then the process of reexamination will turn up doubts generated by the word "about" which we did not notice when reading the passage through for the first time, and which threaten the import of the entire sentence. By concluding with an allusion to masquerade, among the most hackneyed motifs in eighteenth-century fiction, Austen placidly resumes the conventionality that began with "once upon a time," only now that conventionality has been undermined. Austen's sentence thus prohibits us from reading naively, as Catherine Morland does at first, for her style continually makes itself subject to doubt. Here it has rendered us wary of the formulas which introduce fiction, but in *Mansfield Park* similar kinds of techniques will be deployed more ambitiously to make us wary of Burkean discourse itself.

But throughout the juvenilia, Austen does more than debunk novelistic formulas and have done. As a rule her treatment of them obliges us instead to slow down and to consider more carefully the realities they conceal. In "Jack and Alice," Austen, following Swift and Johnson, intrudes upon the rarefied pastoral atmosphere of sentimental fiction a variety of embarrassing objects that pastoral generally contrives to exclude: "A few days after their reconciliation Lady Williams called on Miss Johnson to propose a walk in a Citron Grove which led from her Ladyship's pigstye to Charles Adams's Horsepond" (MW 18). When Austen, by such techniques as reduction, reversal, literalization, or hyperbole, seems most to "make strange" the conventional elements of fiction, she often only alerts us to how strange they were before they were tampered with. The understatement in Laura's description of the parameters of her experience in "Love and Freindship," for example, turns out to be all too slight:

> Our neighbourhood was small, for it consisted only of your mother. . . .
> Isabel had seen the World. She had passed 2 Years at one of the first Board-
> ing schools in London; had spent a fortnight in Bath & had supped one
> night in Southampton (MW 78).

Here stock phrases are transformed by reduction into nonsense: a neighborhood becomes virtually one person; the "World" is diminished to a provincial girl's boarding school. And yet in a manner that looks forward to the mature Austen's polyvalent irony, the laughter here turns back on itself. Once we have had our laugh, it becomes clear that Austen has not so much reduced stock phrases such as "the world" as she has taken them at their face value in certain situations. Emma Woodhouse's "neighbourhood" is quite as small, hardly affording her a single friend, and far from having seen the "world," she has never even seen the sea. Thus if first we are struck by the difference between a young lady's world and the real world, next it is likely that their sameness will appear equally unsettling. Such syntactical child's play may not appear to merit sustained attention, but Austen in fact refined patterns and rhythms very similar to these throughout her career, as the following excerpt from *Persuasion* attests:

> Be it known then, that Sir Walter, like a good father, (having met with one or two private disappointments in very unreasonable applications) prided himself on remaining single for his dear daughter's sake. For one daughter, his eldest, he would really have given up any thing, which he had not been very much tempted to do (P 5).

Austen's irony typically functions like a Mobius strip, first setting up two clear and discrete planes, and later showing them on the contrary to be coextensive. As in the juvenilia, the reader here hurries along only at her or his own risk, for the second half of Austen's statement will not really make "known" what the first half says it will—that is, how Sir Walter is a "good father"—but will rather double back to belie a professed design. Sir Walter's self-sacrifice in remaining single is subverted by parenthetical information relating his attempts to remarry, while the claim that he would "really" give up anything for a daughter is shaken by the assurance that he has never been so disposed. Rather than appearing as a "good father," then, Sir Walter appears to be a poor father indeed.[3]

It is important that we see Austen's early work as exercises in stylistic and generic self-consciousness and not principally as expressions of personal belief, if we are to appreciate what is distinctive about her mature productions. "Love and Freindship", for example, is typically read as a fledgling *Sense and Sensibility*, a scathing satire on the unseemliness of excessive feeling. But Austen's parody, here as elsewhere, is never so essentially prescriptive nor so unitary. "Love and Freindship" parodies the destinies inscribed by sentimental fiction, not the perniciousness of sentiment, and to overlook this layer of detachment in the sketch is to miss many of its most hilarious jokes. Here characters themselves are sometimes bewildered to discover that their very status as sentimental characters dictates otherwise gratuitous courses of action. Edward Lindsay, for example, is roused to manly opposition even when his father plights him to a woman he adores: "No never exclaimed I. Lady Dorothea is lovely and Engaging; I prefer no woman to her; but know Sir, that I scorn to marry her in compliance with your wishes. No! Never shall it be said that I obliged my Father" (MW 81). Edward has no reason to defy his father, just as Laura has no reason to conceal his name "under that of Talbot"

(MW 80), except for the fact that both characters live in a fictive world which requires that they do.

In the juvenilia, as in the mature works, we will look in vain for unqualified and securely embedded norms that enable and oblige us to conclude that Austen is simply "against" impetuous feeling, for example, and "for" the authority of parents. As George Steiner has observed, Austen's "radically linguistic" style makes such "assured reading" difficult because it is always encoding reality in a "distinctive idiom," an idiom which, I would emphasize, we are always given specifically to understand is only an idiom.[4] Austen does not target feelings because the characters in "Love and Freindship" are selfish any more than she targets landowners because in "Henry and Eliza: A Novel" they behave like slavedrivers: "As Sir George and Lady Harcourt were superintending the Labours of their Haymakers, rewarding the industry of some by smiles of approbation, & punishing the idleness of others, by a cudgel, they perceived . . . a beautifull little Girl not more than 3 months old" (MW 33). And surely she is not against either of these any more than she is against morality itself when she exposes the unfeeling pomposity and self-interest of homiletic discourse: "We all know that many are unfortunate in their progress through the world, but we do not know all that are so. To seek them out to study their wants, & to leave them unsupplied is the duty, and ought to be the Business of Man" (MW 71). In each of these instances, Austen's enterprise is not to scold her characters as, say, West or More would, but rather to expose the perspectivity of various discourses and to demonstrate how stock figures, expressions, and paradigms are not faithful or innocuous representations of reality, but rather themselves are constructions, which promote certain agendas and exclude others. From the age of fifteen on, Austen, sceptical and unawed, refuses to be lulled by her medium and is determined to illuminate the interests served by its broadest structural outlines down to the subtlest details of its words, rhythms, and cadences. As we shall see, the achievement of the juvenilia would serve Austen particularly well once the stakes became higher—when the discourse she would challenge claimed to represent political truth, and when authorial audacity was more of a risk.

When Austen began to compose her full-scale parody *Northanger Abbey* sometime in the mid-1790s, the gothic novel had already been thoroughly imbued with political implications.[5] As Ronald Paulson has put it, "By the time *The Mysteries of Udolpho* appeared (1794), the castle, prison, tyrant, and sensitive young girl could no longer be presented naively; they had all been familiarized and sophisticated by the events in France."[6] Paulson's short catalogue of gothic images would seem implicitly to serve the progressive agenda to protect the powerless and the feminine from the abuses of a decaying but still powerful patriarchy, and some progressive novelists, such as Eliza Fenwick in *Secresy, or, The Ruin on the Rock* (1795) or Wollstonecraft in *The Wrongs of Woman, or Maria,* did employ the form or much of its imagery for precisely such purposes. Charlotte Smith, of course, combined politics and gothicism most regularly, as in *The Old Manor House* (1793) and *Marchmont* (1796). In the overtly polemical *Desmond,* in fact, her own heroine calls attention to how gothic "excesses" figure forth realities which young girls ought to know about. Coming to gothic fiction only after her unhappy marriage, she reports how she now devoured

> the mawkish pages that told of damsels, most exquisitely beautiful, confined by a cruel father, and escaping to a heroic lover, while a wicked Lord laid in wait to tear her from him, and carried her off to some remote castle—Those delighted me most that ended miserably. . . . Had the imagination of a young person been liable to be much affected by these sorts of histories, mine would, probably, have taken a romantic turn, and at eighteen, when I was married, I should have hestitated whether I should obey my friends [sic] directions, or have waited till the hero appeared. . . . But, far from doing so, I was, you see, "obedient—very obedient . . ."[7]

Would that Geraldine *had* had the benefit of gothic fiction to show her how to be disobedient and teach her what to suspect from her protectors. The distresses she reads about, alas, are now her own: her family commanded her unsuitable marriage for money, her husband is plotting to sell her to a rich duke, her treacherous family, entrapping her with words like "duty" and "obedience," is now confining her because they suspect that her "hero"—the progressive Desmond—will rescue her. To Smith, as to other reform-minded novelists, the gothic was not a grotesque, but in some ways a fairly unmediated representation of world "as it is," if not as "it ought to be."

But in Radcliffean gothic, the focus of Austen's parody, the political valence of gothicism is not so clear, and this despite the conservatism of Radcliffe herself. True, *The Mysteries of Udolpho* affirms a Burkean strain of paternalism by reiterating negative object lessons in the need for regulating violently subversive passional energies, lessons which apply equally to Emily, Valencourt, and Montoni.[8] But when one shows how fathersurrogates like Montoni wield legal and religious authority over women in order to force marriages and thereby consolidate their own wealth, one is describing what patriarchal society daily permits as a matter of course, not what is an aberration from its softening and humanizing influences. The cozy La Vallée, presided over by the benevolent father St. Aubert, and the isolated Udolpho, ruled by the brooding and avaricious Montoni, can be seen not as polar opposites, then, but as mirror images, for considered from the outside, protectors of order and agents of tyranny can look alarmingly alike. Struck by the same double message in turn-of-the-century architecture, Mark Girouard relates the Gothic revival in English country houses specifically to the "spectre of the French Revolution" and subsequent reassertion of authority: "Country houses could project a disconcerting double image—relaxed and delightful to those who had the entrée, arrogant and forbidding to those who did not."[9]

Radcliffe's novels present the double image Girouard elucidates, for they provide a Burkean rationale for repression, as well as describe the grounds for rebelling against it. In *The Italian* (1797) especially, stock characters, images, and situations veer almost entirely out of control, and a conservative agenda is maintained only by pacing the action of the novel so rapidly as to hinder reflection on politically sensitive issues intrinsic to the material—such as the extent of familial authority, the tension between private affections and public obligations, and the moral authority of the church and its representatives. The movement of the novel as a whole is to cover up. We needn't be alarmed at the ease with which fathers *could* murder daughters, because Schedoni turns out not to be Ellena's father after all; we needn't worry about the lengths to which aristocratic families go to prevent their sons from marrying beneath them, because Ellena turns out to be nobly born; we needn't protest the corruption of religious institutions, for the officers of the Inquisition, after a few perfunctorily gruesome threats of torture, finally acquit themselves as responsible ministers of truth and justice. As if unwilling herself to follow through with the potentially radical implications of her material, Radcliffe opens creaking doors to dark and dreadful passages only to slam them shut in our faces.

It has seemed to many readers that Austen's parody in *Northanger Abbey* debunks gothic conventions out of an allegiance to the commonsense world of the ordinary, where life is sane and dependable, if not always pleasant.[10] But by showing that the gothic is in fact the inside out of the ordinary, that the abbey does indeed present a disconcerting double image, particularly forbidding and arrogant to one who, like Catherine Morland, does not have an entrée, *Northanger Abbey* does not refute, but rather clarifies and reclaims, gothic conventions in distinctly political ways. Austen's parody here, as in the juvenilia, "makes strange" a fictional style in order better to determine what it really accomplishes, and in the process it does not ridicule gothic novels nearly as much as their readers. Clearly the danger for a reader like Henry Tilney, too often mistaken for an authorial surrogate, is to dismiss gothic novels as a "good read"—as a set of stock situations and responses to them which need not trouble us with a moment's serious reflection after we have put the book down. He is, in fact, a perfect reader for Radcliffe's particularly evasive brand of escapist thrills about the horrors that occur in safely remote Catholic countries. By contrast, the danger for a reader like Catherine is to mistake gothic exaggerations for unmediated representation, to fail to recognize their conventional trappings. Thus while Henry categorically denies the gothic any legitimately mimetic provenance, Catherine imagines that no more or less than the literal imprisonment and murder of an unhappy wife is the only crime a bad man can be charged with. By making the distrust of patriarchy which gothic fiction fosters itself the subject for outright discussion, Austen obliges us first to see the import of conventions which we, like Henry perhaps, dismiss as merely formal, and then to acknowledge, as Henry never does, that the "alarms of romance" are a canvas onto which the "anxieties of common life" (NA 201) can be projected in illuminating, rather than distorting, ways. Austen may dismiss "alarms" concerning stock gothic *machinery*—storms, cabinets, curtains, manuscripts—with blithe amusement, but alarms concerning the central gothic *figure*, the tyrannical father, she concludes, are commensurate to the threat they actually pose.

In turning her powers of parody to a saliently politicized form, Austen raised the stakes on her work. Imperious aristocrats, frowning castles, dark dungeons, and torture chambers were safe enough before 1790, and sometimes in the juvenile sketches, such as "Henry and Eliza" and "Evelyn," they surface in uproariously telescoped fashion. But once social stability was virtually equated with paternal authority, gothic material was potent stuff, and in *Northanger Abbey* Austen does not shy away from it. If anything, she emphasizes the political subtext of gothic conventions: her villain, General Tilney, is not only a repressive father, but also a self-professed defender of national security. To Catherine, the General seems most like Montoni—that is, "dead to every sense of humanity"—when he, "with downcast eyes and contracted brow," paces the drawing room gloomily, pondering political "pamphlets" and the "affairs of the nation" (NA 187). By depicting the villain as an officious English gentleman, publically respected on the local as well as national level, and "accustomed on every ordinary occasion to give the law in his family" (NA 247), *Northanger Abbey*, to use Johnsonian terms, "approximates the remote and familiarizes the wonderful" in gothic fiction, and in the process brings it into complete conjunction with the novel of manners. This conjunction is reinforced by the two-part format of the novel. The world which Catherine is entering for the first time comprises Bath and

Northanger Abbey, both of which are menacing and "strange"—Catherine's recurrent expression—to one whose "real power," as Eleanor Tilney says of herself, "is nothing" (NA 225).

Just as conspicuously as *Mansfield Park, Northanger Abbey* concerns itself explicitly with the prerogatives of those who have what Eleanor calls "real power" and the constraints of those who do not. Henry Tilney is far from believing that women in general, much less Catherine or his own sister, have no "real power." To him, women's power—in marriage, in country dances, in daily life generally—is limited, but very real: "[M]an has the advantage of choice, woman only the power of refusal" (NA 77). Henry's aphorism describes the conditions of female propriety as they had been traditionally conceived, and as they were reasserted throughout the 1790s by conservative advocates of female modesty. Women, by such accounts, are not initiators of their own choices, but rather are receivers of men's. If the "power of refusal" seems detrimental or frustrating in its negativity, it is still better than nothing, for it does not leave women without any control of their destinies: women may not be permitted to pursue what they want, but they may resist what they do not want. But in Austen's novels, as in so much eighteenth-century fiction about women, women's power of refusal is severely compromised. Many Austenian men—from Collins to Crawford to Wentworth—cannot take "no" for an answer.

In *Northanger Abbey,* bullying of various sorts is rampant, and Tilney's confidence in the feminine power of refusal is put to the test. Indeed Catherine's own friends have no scruples about lying in order to force her to comply with them rather than keep her own engagement with the Tilneys, and when caught in his lie, John Thorpe, with the apparent concurrence of Catherine's brother, "only laughed, smacked his whip . . . and drove on," overbearing her refusal: "angry and vexed as she was, having no power of getting away, [Catherine] was obliged to give up the point and submit" (NA 87). When mere lying and abduction are not apropos, James and the Thorpes join forces to compel Catherine to surrender her power of refusal. Together, they "demand" her agreement; they refuse her "refusal;" they "attack" her with reproach and supplication; and they resort to emotional manipulation ("I shall think you quite unkind, if you still refuse"), fraternal bullying ("Catherine, you must go"), and eventually even to physical compulsion ("Isabella . . . caught hold of one hand; Thorpe of the other" [NA 98–100]). So little is Catherine's brother inclined to respect woman's "only" power, refusal, that he defines, if not feminine, then at least sisterly virtue as a sweet-tempered yielding of her will altogether to his: "I did not think you had been so obstinate . . . you were not used to be so hard to persuade; you once were the kindest, best-tempered of my sisters" (NA 99–100). The moral and physical coercion of powerless females which figures so predominantly in gothic fiction is here transposed to the daytime world of drawing room manners, where it can be shown for the everyday occurrence it is, but no less "strange" for all that.

Against the selfishness of James Morland and the bluster of John Thorpe, Henry Tilney stands out, not in opposition, but if anything in clearer relief, for his unquestioning confidence in his focality and in the breadth of his understanding prompts him to preempt not only the female's power of refusal but indeed even her power of speech in analogous ways, without doubting the propriety of his doing so. Brothers are treated with great respect in Austenian criticism, certainly with much more than they deserve if *Northanger Abbey* and *The Watsons* are considered with due weight. Because it is assumed that Austen's feelings for her brothers— about which we actually know rather little—were fond and grateful to the point of adoration, the sceptical treatment brother figures receive in her fiction has been little examined. Between Thorpe's remark that his younger sisters "both looked very ugly" (NA 49) and Tilney's reference to Eleanor as "my stupid sister" (NA 113), there is little difference, for in each case, the cool possession of privilege entitles them to disparaging banter, not the less corrosive for being entirely in the normal course of things. On most occasions, however, Tilney's bullying is more polished. A self-proclaimed expert on matters feminine, from epistolary style to muslin, Tilney simply believes that he knows women's minds better than they do, and he dismisses any "no" to the contrary as unreal. On the first day he meets Catherine, for example, he tells her exactly what she ought to write in her journal the next morning—the entry he proposes, needless to say, is devoted entirely to the praise of himself. Female speech is never entirely repressed in Austen's fiction, but instead is dictated so as to mirror or otherwise reassure masculine desire. But when Catherine protests, "But, perhaps, I keep no journal," Henry, flippantly but no less decisively does not take her "no" for an answer: "Perhaps you are not sitting in this room, and I am not sitting by you. These are points in which a doubt is equally possible" (NA 27). That, it would appear, is that, if for no other reason than that Henry himself has said so. But—for all we know to the contrary—Catherine does *not* keep a journal, and this will not be the first time that Henry, believing, as he says here, that reality itself is sooner doubted than the infallibility of his own inscriptions, will with magisterial complacence lay down the law. The effect for a woman like Catherine, "fearful of hazarding an opinion" of her own "in opposition to that of a self-assured man" (NA 48), is silencing, even when she knows she is right. Catherine would no more dream of opposing Henry here than she would the General himself when he announces that even his heir must have a profession, for as Austen makes clear, silence is exactly what he wishes: "The imposing effect of this last argument was equal to his wishes. The silence of the lady [Catherine] proved it to be unanswerable" (NA 176).

Henry too, then, takes away the feminine power of refusal, simply by turning a deaf ear to it. In this respect, he is more graceful, but he is not essentially different from the General, who asks Eleanor questions only to answer them himself, or from John Thorpe, who declares that his horses are unruly when they are manifestly tame. The characteristic masculine activity in *Northanger Abbey* is measurement, a fiatlike fixing of boundaries—of mileage, of time, of money, and in Henry's case, of words. Although these boundaries turn out to be no less the projection of hopes and fears than are the overtly fanciful stuff of gothic novels, they are decreed as unanswerable facts, and the self-assurance of their promulgators enforces credence and silences dissent. Because Henry dictates the parameters of words, the kind of control he exercises extends to thought itself, the capacity for which he describes in explicitly sexual terms. Appearing to consider his respect for "the understanding of women" a somewhat unwarranted concession, Henry quips, "nature has given them so much [understanding], that they never find it necessary to use more than half" (NA 114). A great stickler for words, he bristles at any loosening of strict definition—such as relaxing the terms "nice" and "amazement"—and he is in the habit of "overpowering" offenders with "Johnson and Blair" (NA 108) when their usage transgresses prescribed boundaries. But when Catherine and Eleanor get entangled in their famous *malentendu* concerning "something very shocking indeed, [that] will soon come out in London" (NA 112), linguistic looseness has served them where Henry's correctness could not. To Catherine, of course, what is shocking, horrible, dreadful, and murderous can only be a new gothic novel; to Eleanor it can only be a mob uprising of three thousand. Henry regards the interchangeability of this vocabulary as proof of a feminine carelessness of thought and language which is regrettable, laughable, and endearing at the same time, and he enlightens them by vaunting his manliness and his lucidity: "I will prove myself a man, no less by the generosity of my soul than the clearness of my head" (NA 112).

Henry may be bantering again, but politically speaking the linguistic and intellectual superiority he boasts is no joke. During the 1790s in particular, privileged classes felt their hegemony on language, and with that power, seriously challenged by radical social critics—some of them women, and many of the men self-educated—from below, and as one scholar has recently demonstrated, conservatives met this challenge by asserting that the superiority of their language rendered them alone fit for participation in public life. Tilney's esteemed Dr. Johnson played a posthumous role in this process, for those "aspects of Johnson's style that embodied hegemonic assessments of language" were "developed and imitated" as proper models.[11] With the authority of Johnson and Blair behind him, then, Henry is empowered to consider feminine discourse—conversation or gothic novels—as either mistaken or absurd, and in any case requiring his arbitration. The course of the novel attests, however, that the misunderstanding between Catherine and Eleanor is plausible and even insightful: political unrest and gothic fiction are well served by a common vocabulary of "horror" because they are both unruly responses to repression. Such, however, is not how Henry reads gothic novels, nor how he, in effect, teaches Catherine to read them. Indeed, the reason Catherine assents to ludicrously dark surmises about the cabinet is not that her imagination is inflamed with *Radcliffean* excesses, but rather that she trusts *Henry's* authority as a sensible man, and does not suspect that he, like John Thorpe but with much more charm, would impose on her credulity in order to amuse himself. "How could she have so imposed on herself," Catherine wonders. But soon she places the blame where it belongs: "And it was in a great measure his own doing, for had not the cabinet appeared so exactly to agree with his description of her adventures, she should never have felt the smallest curiosity about it" (NA 173). This exercise of power by "the knowing over the ignorant" is, as Judith Wilt has argued, "pure Gothic," and it is structured into the system of female education and manners.[12] In "justice to men," the narrator slyly avers that sensible men prefer female "ignorance" to female "imbecility"—let alone to the "misfortune" of knowledge—precisely because it administers to their "vanity" of superior knowledge (NA 110–11). Catherine's tendency to equate the verbs "to torment" and "to instruct" seems less confused given the humiliating upshot of her lesson in the gothic at Henry's hands.

But Henry, as we have seen, does not know everything. And what he does not know about gothic fiction in particular is explicitly related to his political outlook. Even though Austen spares us Tilney's "short disquisition on the state of the nation" (NA 111)—delivered in part to bring Catherine to "silence"—she does not hesitate to caricature his conservative tendency to be pollyannaish about the status quo. Catherine is a "hopeful scholar" not only in landscape theory but also in gothic novels, and her sensitivity to the lessons they afford far surpasses the capacity of her tutor, because her position of powerlessness and dependency give her a different perspective on the status quo. Gothic novels teach the deferent and self-deprecating Catherine to do what no one and nothing else does: to distrust paternal figures and to feel that her power of refusal is continuously under siege. While still in Bath, Catherine does not feel com-

pletely secure with the attentiveness of Mr. Allen's protection; she feels
impelled "to resist such high authority" (NA 67) as her brother's on the
subject of John Thorpe's powers of pleasing ladies; and though she finds
it almost impossible to doubt General Tilney's perfect gentility, she cannot ignore the pall he casts on his household. Further, gothic novels teach
Catherine about distrust and concealment, about cruel secrets hidden beneath formidable and imposing surfaces. Before she goes to Northanger,
she expects to find "some awful memorials of an injured and ill-fated nun"
(NA 141), and what she eventually turns up there about the injured and
ill-fated Mrs. Tilney is not that wide of the mark. If these were to be the
"lessons" inculcated to flighty young girls, it is small wonder conservatives should feel that they should be expunged. Writing as late as 1813,
the high Tory Eaton Stannard Barrett considered gothic fiction still dangerous enough to warrant savage burlesquing in his own novel *The Heroine*. His anti-heroine's first and most heinous offense is to take gothic
novels seriously enough to doubt her good father's paternity, and with
that to resist his authority. From such delusions, it is only a short step to
the three volumes of utter dementia that finally land her in a lunatic asylum. As the sensible Mr. Stuart patiently explains to her at the end, novels
like *Coelebs* and *The Vicar of Wakefield* "may be read without injury,"
but gothic novels "present us with incidents and characters which we can
never meet in the world," and are thus "intoxicating stimulants."[13]

   Such of course is precisely the lesson Henry would impress upon Catherine, and it is a lesson he himself believes. When Henry Tilney learns
that Catherine has suspected his father of murder, he is stupefied by a
"horror" which he has "hardly words to ———" (NA 197). Evidently,
Johnson and Blair do not supply Henry with words adequate to what gothic
novels describe all the time, and the reason the manly and "clear-headed"
Henry never read gothic fiction sensitively enough to realize this is that
it insists on a doubleness which he finds semantically, as well as politically,
imponderable. Because he considers England as a uniquely civilized nation, where church, education, laws, neighborhoods, roads, and news-
papers make heartless husbands and their crimes rare, improbable, almost
unknown, the gothic "horror" Catherine intuits is as preposterous and
even as subversive as the earlier malentendu about the "shocking" news
from London. But gothic fiction represents a world which is far more
menacing and ambiguous, where figureheads of political and domestic order silence dissent, where a father can be a British subject, a Christian, a
respectable citizen, *and* a ruthless and mean-spirited tyrant at the same
time, one who, moreover, in some legitimate sense of the term can "kill"
his wife slowly by quelling her voice and vitality. When General Tilney
sacrifices decency to avarice and banishes the now reluctant gothic heroine

into the night, he proves that "human nature, at least in the midland countries of England" *can* in fact be looked for in "Mrs. Radcliffe's works" and those of "all her imitators" (NA 200). We are never informed of Henry Tilney's reflections on this occasion, and have no reason to suppose him cognizant of the need to revise his lecture to Catherine and to acknowledge the accuracy of her suspicions. But by the end of the novel, Catherine at least is capable of reaching this conclusion on her own: "in suspecting General Tilney of either murdering or shutting up his wife, she had scarcely sinned against his character, or magnified his cruelty" (NA 247).

Given the political ambience of British fiction during the 1790s, it is not surprising that of all Austen's novels, *Northanger Abbey*, arguably her earliest, should be the most densely packed with topical details of a political character—enclosure, riots, hothouses, pamphlets, and even anti-treason laws authorizing the activities of "voluntary spies" (NA 198).[14] The political contemporaneity of *Northanger Abbey* does not stop with these allusions and with its critical treatment of paternal authority, but indeed extends to another, related theme: the status of promises. The obligation to abide by promises is an important moral rule in the history of political thought, especially since it underlies the contract theory of Locke as well as older natural law theories. At the end of the century, however, the very idea of promises had been radically criticized by Godwin as one of many possible kinds of socially mediating agencies of human decision and practice which cramp the judgment of the individual subject. Debates about the value and violability of promises figure prominently in turn-of-the-century fiction. In anti-Jacobin novels, pernicious or merely benighted characters philosophize as they break their words and betray their trusts left and right. In *The Modern Philosophers*, for example, Hamilton presents the attack on promise keeping as one of the centerpieces of "new philosophy": Vallaton reasons that the "nobler" intervening purpose of spending money with which he has been entrusted absolves him from the prior obligation to deliver it to someone else, as he had promised; Mr. Glib releases himself from marriage—"the mistake he has so happily detected"—quoting Godwin and decrying matrimony as "an odious and unjust instititution"; and the ugly Bridgetina urges a man to break his engagement to another women by ranting "Who can promise forever? . . . Are not the opinions of a perfectible being ever changing? You do not at present see my preferableness, but you may not be always blind to a truth so obvious."[15]

Since social stability depends in large part on keeping one's word, it is not surprising that Godwin's critique of promises and trusts proved upsetting to conservative readers. But for reform-minded novelists, keeping promises is more likely to promote cynical and sterile legalism than social cohesiveness. Stopping well this side of Godwin's radical critique of promises, they expose how the sanctity of promises is something for underlings always to observe and for perfidious overlords to omit whenever it suits their interests. Without trumpeting its political relevance, Inchbald shows in *A Simple Story* that breaches of promise are countenanced by the powerful all the time. When Dorriforth's wife breaks her marital vows, she is justly banished into shameful oblivion. Yet Dorriforth, formerly a Catholic priest, had reneged on his vow of celibacy with the full approval of his confessor and the community because doing so enabled him to inherit an immense fortune and thus to enhance the worldly power of the Church. When expedience dictates, powerful characters routinely break their promises—of celibacy, fidelity, secrecy—with complete impunity, and in fact without as much as acknowledging such acts as breaches, while sustaining other promises, particularly punitive ones against subordinates, with inhumane strenuousness. In *Northanger Abbey* Austen, like Inchbald, dramatizes the implications of promise breaking and keeping as a function of the power of the characters concerned.

Breaking engagements and words of honor of all sorts is the predominant activity in *Northanger Abbey*. Instances may vary in intensity, but they all amount to the same thing: Isabella's "engagement" to marry James Morland; Catherine's "engagement" to walk with the Tilneys; Henry's "promise" to wait and read *The Mysteries of Udolpho* with his sister; General Tilney's pompously worded assurance "to make Northanger Abbey not wholly disagreeable" (NA 140) to Catherine, to name only a few. The issue of promise breaking, of course, predates the social criticism of the 1790s, and can thus illustrate the polarization that took place as the reaction wore on. Richardson's Grandison can criticize fashionable lying on generally accepted grounds, but in the 1790s, the topic is marked as radical. An eighteenth-century reader would have recognized as a breach of trust General Tilney's order to deny Catherine at the door when he and his daughter were really at home. Much to the annoyance of the conservative Issac Disraeli, social reformers in their typical way made far too much of this, the domestic prerogative of every gentleman, and thus in *Vaurien*, he has the Jacobin windbag, Mr. Subtile, denounce the practice of "denying yourself when at home. I would not commit such a crime if a bailiff demanded admittance. It is a national system of lying and impudence."[16] Catherine could have read in her mother's copy of Richardson's novel that Grandison scorns the practice, and with his example in mind, Lady Williams in "Jack and Alice" pronounces it "little less than downright Bigamy" (MW 15), a simile which highlights the promissory character of civility and monogamy. It is no accident that manners in Bath seem as "strange" to Catherine as the behavior in gothic fiction, for in both nothing is predictable and no one can be depended upon, least of all the figures one has been taught to trust. When the deceived Catherine meditates on "broken promises and broken arches; phaetons and false hangings, Tilneys and trap-doors"(NA 87), her associations betray a seepage of the gothic into the quotidian that begins to localize her anxieties. Henry, as we have seen, discredits gothic novels because he believes that English "law" itself, as well as the pressure of "social and literary intercourse" (NA 197), enforces decency. But in depicting a strange world of broken promises and betrayed trusts, Catherine's gothic novels and *Northanger Abbey* alike denude familiar institutions and figures of their amiable facades in order to depict the menacing aspect they can show to the marginalized.

Henry Tilney explicitly raises the issue of promises, and his famous conceit jocularly likening marriage to a country dance is striking for the anxiety it persistently evinces about infidelity:

> "We have entered into a contract of mutual agreeableness for the space of an evening, and all our agreeableness belongs solely to each other for that time. Nobody can fasten themselves on the notice of one, without injuring the rights of the other. I consider a country-dance as an emblem of marriage. Fidelity and complaisance are the principal duties of both; and those men who do not chuse to dance or marry themselves, have no business with the partners or wives of their neighbours. . . . You will allow, that in both, man has the advantage of choice, woman only the power of refusal; that in both, it is an engagement between man and woman, formed for the advantage of each; and that when once entered into, they belong exclusively to each other till the moment of its dissolution; that it is their duty, each to endeavour to give the other no cause for wishing that he or she had bestowed themselves elsewhere, and their best interest to keep their own imaginations from wandering towards the perfections of their neighbours, or fancying that they should have been better off with any one else." (NA 76–77)

Frederick Tilney's subsequent interference with the dancing, as well as marital plans, of Isabella Thorpe and James Morland engages the serious subjects Tilney flippantly raises here. Given the centrality of illicit sexuality to the fiction of the time, Henry's disquisition rings with special significance, especially since it is always attempting to forestall the threat of faithlessness. In comparison to that of her contemporaries, Austen's fiction is exceedingly discreet. Though she never excludes the illicit entirely, she displaces it onto the periphery of her plots. But from there it exercises considerable influence. Henry's speech is the closest Austen gets to commentary on the subject of fidelity until *Mansfield Park*, and even there the topic is integrated into the dramatic fabric of the plot, rather than isolated and discussed as an abstract issue, as it is here. To Catherine, of course, Henry's comparison is absurd, since an engagement to dance merely binds people "for half an hour," while "[p]eople that marry can never part" (NA 77). Catherine feels this difference acutely, and her failure to appreciate Henry's humor is another instance of the wisdom she unwittingly articulates throughout the novel. After all, the deceased Mrs. Tilney and her gothic avatar, the "injured and ill-fated nun" (NA 141) whose memorials Catherine expects to find at Northanger, both epitomize the lot of females immured in remote abbeys who would not have the power to leave even if they were not bound by indissoluble vows. To be sure, Austen is emphatically not recommending the passage of divorce laws, as had novelists such as Imlay, Godwin and Holcroft. But neither does she here or anywhere else in her fiction overlook the desolation experienced by those who have more than enough "cause for wishing that [they] had bestowed themselves elsewhere" (NA 77).

Few characters in *Northanger Abbey* have kept promises as faithfully as Mrs. Tilney, not even Henry who, as we have seen, is not above imposing on Catherine's credulity for the sake of a joke. Henry finds the formulation "faithful promise" ludicrous. The self-appointed monitor of Catherine's language, he rather atypically sputters at some length about its redundancy: "Promised so faithfully!—A faithful promise!—That puzzles me.—I have heard of a faithful performance. But a faithful promise—the fidelity of promising!" (NA 196). Henry naturally disapproves of the phrase because in one very important matter at least he is so eminently faithful: at the end of the novel, Henry feels himself so "bound as much in honour as in affection to Miss Morland," that nothing the angry General does can "shake his [Henry's] fidelity," and nothing can justify the General's "unworthy retraction of a tacit consent" (NA 247). A faithful subject in a civilized land, Henry, despite what the ingenuous Catherine considers his satirical turn, is too sanguine to acknowledge the aptness of the phrase in a world where almost all promises are not faithful. Isabella Thorpe, of course, is the most conspicuous promise breaker in the novel: "Isabella had promised and promised again" (NA 201) to write, Catherine exclaims, as yet unaware that Isabella's promises—of friendship or love—routinely give way to interest. But Isabella's faithlessness is so foregrounded that it is possible to overlook how it functions to implicate promise breakers like the General and others who, because they possess power, breach trust with impunity. Conservative novels, such as *A Gossip's Story*, counterbalance the moral instability of selfish and flighty females with the sobriety and responsibility of firm father figures, and thus provide a benign rationale for paternal repression. But in *Northanger Abbey* these two tropic figures are mutually illuminating, for in every respect except the position of authority, General Tilney and Isabella Thorpe are similar characters who cause disorder because they never mean what they say.

Already thinking about dropping James Morland in favor of Frederick Tilney, Isabella remarks, "What one means one day, you know, one may not mean the next. Circumstances change, opinions alter" (NA 146). The mutability Isabella describes does release people from some engagements. After Catherine is apprised of Isabella's duplicity, she admits, "I cannot still love her" (NA 207), without appearing to realize how her behavior here exemplifies the pertinence of Isabella's earlier observation on the justness of dissolving certain promises. But Isabella's faithlessness, like the General's, results, not from a change of heart, but from a choice of policy favoring wealth. Just as Isabella chooses Frederick Tilney solely because he, as the General states, "will perhaps inherit as considerable a landed property as any private man in the county" (NA 176), General Tilney courts Catherine solely because he believes her to be heiress to Mr. Allen's large estate. Thus the two figures who most belittle the advantages of wealth also, to Catherine's bewilderment, pursue it the most greedily and unscrupulously. In Isabella's case, of course, this means, as Eleanor Tilney puts it, "violating an engagement voluntarily entered into with another man" (NA 205–6). In the General's case, this means, in effect, stealing Catherine from another man who had at the time "pretty well resolved upon marrying Catherine himself" (NA 244).

The self-interest which prompts Isabella to deploy her charms in order to secure Captain Tilney is surely no more dishonorable than that which prompts the General "to spare no pains in weakening [Thorpe's] boasted interest and ruining his dearest hopes" (NA 245). In very important respects it is less so, for the General's superior position obligates him to consider the care of dependents, let alone invited guests, more conscientiously. Unlike Captain Tilney, Catherine is an unsuspecting party to brute self-interest, and as a woman is wholly dependent upon the good will and guidance of superiors. As it turns out, however, Catherine's trust that the General "could not propose any thing improper for her" (NA 156) is sorely misplaced. Having strong-armed Catherine into Northanger Abbey, "courting [her] from the protection of real friends" (NA 225) and encouraging her sense of "false security" (NA 228), he just as authoritatively thrusts her out, without any qualms about violated trust, and without "allowing her even the appearance of choice" (NA 226). While the pledges made to dependents ought to be observed with, if anything, greater attention, General Tilney appears to believe that they do not matter and can therefore be flouted without inviting the embarrassments of social reproach which Henry believes, in Burkean fashion, restrain the insolent from abusiveness. Indifferent to the "patriarchal hospitality" which a conservative novelist like West associated with men of his position, the General banishes Catherine from his house precisely *because* he considers her beneath the imperatives of common civility: "to turn her from the house seemed the best, though to his feelings an inadequate proof of his resentment towards herself, and his contempt of her family" (NA 244). To depict the respectable country gentleman not as one who binds himself benevolently and responsibly to inferiors, but who on the contrary behaves as though his social superiority absolved him from responsibility to inferiors, is to cross over into the territory of radical novelists, whose fictions expose petty tyrants of General Tilney's ilk. Not until *Persuasion* would Austen again arraign a figure of his stature so decisively.

For Isabella, the matter stands quite differently. Merely mercenary herself, she is outmatched by Frederick Tilney. A permutation of the gothic villain, he appears on the scene with no other purpose than to gratify his vanity of dominion by breaking a preexisting engagement. Backing away from the depiction of the violation of vows within marriage, Austen nevertheless imputes to a representative of the ruling class—an oldest son, heir, and guardian of national security—an activity which conservative novelists impute to the minions of Robespierre. If Henry's earlier speech on marriage and country dances is a reliable guide, then Isabella does not bear sole responsibility for the jilting of James Morland. At that time Henry, annoyed by Thorpe's ostensible civilities to Catherine, argues, "He has no business to withdraw the attention of my partner from me . . . our agreeableness belongs solely to each other, and nobody can fasten themselves on the notice of one, without injuring the rights of the other" (NA 76). Remembering this, Catherine questions Henry closely about his brother's brazen interference and until the end of the novel finds it impossible to believe that Captain Tilney would connive at breaking others' promises and knowingly injure "the rights" of her brother. Whatever her own inattention, Isabella believes that Frederick Tilney is attached to her: "he would take no denial" (NA 134), and in this novel refusing the denials of women is a very common activity, no matter how pleasing Isabella may have found it in the present case. Because Captain Tilney not only "fastens" himself on her attention, but pledges an intention to marry where none exists—in Catherine's words he "only made believe to do so for mischief's sake" (NA 219)—Isabella's breach of promise to Morland looks less self-willed. If she has acted only to secure her own interest, she in turn has been acted upon by Frederick only to destroy

James's. Ever the defender of the status quo, Henry does not consider Frederick's trespasses to bespeak any remarkable fault. But when he imputes the whole affair to Isabella's heartlessness, the unconvinced Catherine replies with a scepticism that marks the beginning of her detachment from Tilney's judgment and her awareness of its partiality: "It is very right that you should stand by your brother" (NA 219).

As garrulous and high-spirited as it is, *Northanger Abbey* is an alarming novel to the extent that it, in its own unassuming and matter-of-fact way, domesticates the gothic and brings its apparent excesses into the drawing rooms of "the midland countries of England" (NA 200). With the exception of Isabella, who is herself betrayed, the agents of betrayal are figures from whom Catherine has every right to expect just the opposite. James Morland, hardly a sage or exemplary figure, is not only an eldest son, but is also destined for the Church, as Austen repeats; and yet he considers promises of so little importance that he countenances and even participates in abusive attempts to compel his sister to break her engagements. More formidable personnages—General Tilney and his son—with insolent abandon flout agreements basic to civility. Depicting guardians of national, domestic, and even religious authority as socially destabilizing figures, *Northanger Abbey* has indeed appropriated the gothic, in a distinctively progressive way. Catherine, unencumbered by the elaborate proprieties that tie the hands of gothic heroines, is free to make blunt declarations and to ask embarrassing questions that expose the duplicity and the deficiency of those on whom innocence such as her own ought to rely. Whether she is thanking her brother for coming to Bath to visit her, asking Henry what Captain Tilney could mean by flirting with an engaged woman, or trying to reconcile the General's claims of liberality with his anticipated objections to Isabella's poverty, she is discovering—unwittingly perhaps, but with stunning accuracy—the betrayals of paternal figures and the discourse they wield. It is no accident, then, that Austen can back gracefully out of the impasse to which she brings Catherine at the end only by resorting to an authorially underscored *surplus* of the conventions she parodies. Alluding to the "tell-tale compression of the pages before them" which can only signal that "we are all hastening together to perfect felicity" (NA 250), and declining to describe Eleanor's newfound husband because "the most charming young man in the world is instantly before the imagination of us all" (NA 251), Austen turns Radcliffean conclusions, which labor to undo disturbing and subversive implications, back on themselves: the General's "cruelty," we are assured, was actually "rather conducive" (NA 252) to the felicity of Henry and

Catherine, since it provided them with the occasion to get to know each other. But carrying over the practice of her juvenilia into her mature work, Austen draws attention to the artificiality, rather than the *vraisemblance*, of her conclusion, and implies in the process that the damage wrought by the likes of General Tilney is in fact not resolvable into the "perfect felicity" of fiction, and that the convention of the happy ending conceals our all-too-legitimate cause for alarm.

A fitting sequel to the juvenilia, *Northanger Abbey* considers the authority of men and books, women's books in particular, and suggests how the latter can illuminate and even resist the former. Having been "ashamed of liking Udolpho" (NA 107) herself, Catherine regards novels as a preeminently feminine genre which men are right to pooh-pooh as they do: "gentlemen," she explains, "read better books" (NA 106). Henry pounces with a characteristically conclusory retort: "The person, be it gentleman or lady, who has not pleasure in a good novel, must be intolerably stupid" (NA 106). Here, as elsewhere, Henry's position is more glib than acute, because Austen herself claims a value for fiction that goes well beyond the pleasure of suspense which Henry appears to think is the only thing gothic novels have to offer: "when I had once begun [*The Mysteries of Udolpho*], I could not lay down again" (NA 106). But *Northanger Abbey* is a dauntlessly self-affirming novel, which Austen undertakes to place alongside *Cecilia*, *Camilla*, and *Belinda* as likewise displaying "the greatest powers of the mind" and "the most thorough knowledge of human nature" (NA 38).

Of course *Northanger Abbey* stands beside *The Italian* and *The Mysteries of Udolpho* as well, since parodies are acknowledgments of respect, as well as acts of criticism. Austen's display of human nature in *Northanger Abbey* is necessarily coupled with Radcliffe's, and is executed by showing the justification for gothic conventions, not by dismissing them. Continuously sensitizing us to the mediating properties of gothic conventions, Austen provides the readers of her own as well as Radcliffe's novels with the distance necessary to see the dark and despotic side of the familiar and to experience it as "strange" rather than as proper and inevitable. *Northanger Abbey* accomplishes its social criticism, then, not only by what it says, but also by how it says it, for Austen creates an audience not only able but also inclined to read their novels and their societies with critical detachment.

CHAPTER THREE

SENSE AND SENSIBILITY: OPINIONS TOO
COMMON AND TOO DANGEROUS

Well before the establishment of "the subversive school" in Austenian criticism, Austen's more acute admirers perceived what Margaret Oliphant called her "fine vein of feminine cynicism" about the worldliness around her, and Reginald Farrer considered such cynicism so radical that he called Austen "the most merciless, though calmest, of iconoclasts."[1] Charges of cynicism and iconoclasm particularly befit *Sense and Sensibility*, for this dark and disenchanted novel exposes how those sacred and supposedly benevolizing institutions of order—property, marriage, and family—actually enforce avarice, shiftlessness, and oppressive mediocrity. In *Sense and Sensibility* there are no dependable normative centers—no sane Gardiners or hale Crofts who serve as havens from the fatuity and vitiation rampant elsewhere. Edward Ferrars certainly cannot serve in this capacity, for his own derelictions are part of the problem. And the other eligible figure, Colonel Brandon, refuses the voice of moral censor. Anticipating his concurrence, Elinor laments that Marianne's "systems" set "propriety at nought" (SS 56). But Brandon, unlike Elinor herself, has had that "better acquaintance with the world" (SS 56) which Elinor would prescribe to Marianne. Knowledge of the world has only made him value the "romantic refinements of a young mind" such as Marianne's all the more, and regret that those "opinions" that pass as proper in the world are "too common, and too dangerous" (SS 57). Well might Brandon cherish Marianne's defiance of worldly commonplaces, since the world of *Sense and Sensibility* harbors such moral nullities as John Dashwood, who is "well-respected" precisely because "he conducted himself with propriety" (SS 5), and Lady Middleton, that exemplar of decorum, who instinctively hates the superiority of the Dashwood sisters: "because they were fond of reading, she fancied them satirical: perhaps without exactly knowing what it was to be satirical; but *that* did not signify. It was censure in common use, and easily given" (SS 246).

Of all Austen's novels, *Sense and Sensibility* is the most attuned to progressive social criticism. Like their counterparts in the political fiction of the 1790s, when "Elinor and Marianne" was drafted, the characters here are exceptionally conscious of how ideology, that only apparently natural system of priorities, practices, and attitudes, delimits all our social behavior, and the novel as a whole assails the dominant ideology of its time for privileging the greedy, mean-spirited, and pedestrian.[2] *Sense and Sensibility* is not, as it is often assumed to be, a dramatized conduct book patly favoring female prudence over female impetuosity, as if those qualities could be discussed apart from the larger world of politics. Indeed, it is only because that larger world around them is so menacing in the first place that the manners of young ladies are of such consequence. Provided she appear proper and play the sycophant to wealth and power, a cold-hearted heroine like Lucy Steele finds a place in the world. But for romantic heroines like Elinor and Marianne, who in their own ways challenge the commonplace, the scenario reads quite differently. Whereas conduct books teach young women the social codes they must adopt if they are to live acceptably as wives and daughters, fully integrated into their communities, *Sense and Sensibility* makes those codes and the communities that dictate them the subject of its interrogation, and what is at stake finally is not propriety, but survival. While it has seemed to virtually all readers that Marianne's very independence from the dominant mores of her society subjects her to Austen's satire, in many ways the case is just the opposite. In this novel, the destiny assigned to romantic heroines is betrayal—and this at the hands of "respectable" country gentlemen. If Marianne has resisted the codes which not only require but reward calculation and coldheartedness, she has submitted without resistance to those which dictate desolation and very nearly death as the price of feeling.

As we have seen, conservative ideologues met the threat posed by the revolution in France and the voices of reform in England by reasserting the political momentousness of the family, and this usually meant maintaining its power to inculcate moral affections and to channel self-interest in socially constructive and cohesive ways. In *Translation of the Letters of a Hindoo Rajah*, Elizabeth Hamilton tries to stem the tide of social criticism by burlesquing those who oppose the traditional family. The facile atheist Mr. Vapour damns himself with every word, as he looks forward to the dawning of a new age when the mores which entrench the ruling class will give way to the happiness of all:

> "Benevolence will not then be heard of; gratitude will be considered as a crime. . . . Filial affection would, no doubt, be treated as a crime of a still deeper dye, but that, to prevent the possibility of such a breach of virtue, no man, in the age of reason, shall be able to guess who his father is, nor any woman to say to her husband, behold your son. Chastity, shall then be considered as a weakness and the virtue of a female estimated according

as she has had sufficient energy to break its mean restraints. . . . By destroying the domestic affections, what an addition will be made to human happiness! And when man is no longer corrupted by the tender and endearing ties of brother, sister, wife, and child, how greatly will his dispositions be meliorated."[3]

The radical critique of the family per se that is ridiculed here called attention to the possible narrowing or otherwise negative aspects of this institution, and novelists of manners could draw on problems this critique disclosed without necessarily being thoroughgoing radicals themselves. To be sure, *Sense and Sensibility* nowhere expresses Mr. Vapour's Godwinian impatience for the dissolution of society as we know it and for the coming of the age of reason. Still, his rhapsody helps disclose the progressive provenance of Austen's novel. Virtually all the social evils Mr. Vapour decries relative to domestic life are decried in *Sense and Sensibility* as well, not with his doctrinaire positiveness or his unworried anarchism, of course, but with Austen's distinctive dubiety. What is dismissed in an anti-Jacobin novel is taken quite seriously in Austen's. In an unsigned notice in the *British Critic*, one of Austen's first reviewers notes the "perplexity in the genealogy of the first chapter" where "the reader is somewhat bewildered among half-sisters, cousins, and so forth."[4] This mild complaint is also a shrewd observation: the knot of relatives vying for property calls our attention to the *dis*orderliness of family life, in marked contrast to the stabilizing clarity and tender esprit de corps conservative apologists associate with "our little platoon." Unlike the openings to the other novels, the first sentences here begin a generation before the Dashwoods come to Norland Park and seize immediately on the archetypical: "the old Gentleman" who heads the Dashwood family is never individuated enough to have a Christian name. In fact, he is not so much a person as he is an institution—a modest gentry Everyman: not extraordinary, but respectable; not ancient, but "long settled in Sussex" (SS 3).

Austen ushers the story in a generation early and describes her venerable patriarch with such unwontedly obtrusive abstraction in order to highlight what would otherwise be unremarkable: the succession of property through sons. No sooner does Austen introduce all the Dashwood relatives and their respective incomes than she abruptly reports, "The old Gentleman died," bequeathing his estate first to his nephew, Mr. Henry Dashwood, and then "to his son, and his son's son" (SS 4), specifically depriving Henry Dashwood of power to settle even a portion of his inheritance upon his wife and daughters. We are repeatedly reminded that the patrilineal succession of Norland is at once utterly commonplace and painfully arbitrary. Given the wealth and property already in his posses-

sion, the Norland estate, we are informed, is "not so really important"
to John Dashwood "as to his sisters" (SS 3). And in his dotage, "the old
Gentleman" secures his property to the male infant because, having once
or twice chanced to tickle the old man's fancy, the tot "outweigh[s] all the
value of all the attention which, for years, he had received from his niece
and her daughters" (SS 4). Clearly, to anyone acting within the framework of patriarchal ideology—take John Dashwood for example—"the
old Gentleman's" choice, far from being eccentric, appears perfectly natural. But Austen enables, indeed invites, us to stand far enough outside
that ideology for a moment to see it as capricious rather than steady, and
her later description of Mrs. Ferrars's habit of owning, disowning, and
reowning sons corroborates this perception: "Her family had of late been
exceedingly fluctuating. For many years of her life she had had two sons;
but the crime and annihilation of Edward a few weeks ago, had robbed
her of one; the similar annihilation of Robert had left her for a fortnight
without any; and now, by the resuscitation of Edward, she had one again"
(SS 373). The renewal of Edward's filial existence, however, is only partial, for he never recovers his supposedly immutable status as the eldest
son. "Can any thing be more galling to the spirit of a man," remarks John
Dashwood, "than to see his younger brother in possession of an estate
which might have been his own?" (SS 269). How galling, we wonder,
would John Dashwood have found the sight of *half sisters* in possession
of an estate that might have been his own? Though the "old Gentleman's"
partiality for little Harry has proved singularly profitable to John Dashwood, we have seen that it depends more on the caprices of momentary
self-will than on steady and time-honored principles.

If the continuities and affiliations of the patriarchal family seem less
than settled and settling, its pretensions to cultivating moral affections
appear even less convincing. *Sense and Sensibility* methodically examines
the lot of women who have become marginalized due to the death or simple absence of male protectors. In a father's absence, of course, the brother
should serve, and here the conscientious father, gasping on his deathbed,
obliges his son solemnly to promise to provide for his widow and three
daughters. John Dashwood is momentarily touched. Though generally
"cold hearted, and rather selfish" (SS 5), a "recommendation of such a
nature at such a time" is affecting. The prospect of his own enlarged wealth
and the power of benevolence it promises "warmed his heart and made
him feel capable of generosity.—Yes, he would give them three thousand
pounds: it would be liberal and handsome! It would be enough to make
them completely easy. Three thousand pounds! he could spare so considerable a sum with little inconvenience.' " (SS 5). Sceptical as we may
be of this delicious self-congratulation, John Dashwood is feeling in ac-

cordance with the sentimental theories conservative ideologues applaud. Generosity and self-interest unite in his benevolence: the power to supply assistance is gratifying, and the prospect of publicity—"it would be liberal and handsome!"—demonstrates at once a fitting sensitivity to the opinion of his neighbors which every gentleman should possess and a proper desire for dignity to which a respectable man like John Dashwood ought to aspire.

In *Sense and Sensibility* at least, sentiments do not function as blamelessly as apologists for patriarchy would have us believe, because the family, far from being the mainspring for all moral and social affections, is the mainspring instead for the love of money, the principal vice in *Sense and Sensibility*, and in so much progressive fiction. Soon forgetting the sweet sensations of self-approving generosity, John Dashwood robs Elinor, Marianne, and Margaret of their inheritance, in defiance of his "solemn promise" (SS 14), precisely on the grounds, as he and his wife manage to convince themselves, that they are not really his sisters. Considering them sisters might deprive his son, the only proper object of his affections, of his birthright:

> What possible claim could the Miss Dashwoods, who were related to him only by half blood, which she considered as no relationship at all, have on his generosity to so large an amount. It was very well known that no affection was ever supposed to exist between the children of any man by different marriages; and why was he to ruin himself, and their poor little Harry, by giving away all his money to his half sisters? (SS 8)

If his half sisters are really "no relation at all," then it is "absolutely unnecessary, if not highly indecorous" to assist them with anything more than small, purely "neighbourly acts" (SS 13). To the principal spokesman for the ideology of the patriarchal family, then, the family very severely restricts, rather than enables and broadens, acts of generosity, and all considerations—even promises to dying patriarchs—can be dropped by appealing to the future needs of the toddling male heir: "Harry will regret that so large a sum was parted with. If he should have a numerous family, for instance, it would be a very convenient addition" (SS 9). Scarcely able to feel kindness "towards any body beyond himself, his wife, and their child"(SS 8), John Dashwood cannot believe that all sensible men do not delimit their moral universes as narrowly. His mind staggers at the disinterestedness of Colonel Brandon's motives for giving Edward Ferrars a modest living: "Really!—Well, this is very astonishing!—no relationship!—no connection between them!" (SS 294).

In comparison to the exclusive character of family affections as formulated and enacted by John Dashwood, Sir John Middleton's unstinting generosity to kinswomen he has never even met comes as a surprise as well as a blessing. But in endowing her boisterous squire with a surplus of sociable affections and the "real satisfaction of a good heart" (SS 33), Austen is not so much mollifying her critique of the gentry family as she is extending it further in a different direction. The family circle is just not as sufficient for Sir John and his Lady as it is for the John Dashwoods. Domestic society is irksome to them: "Sir John was a sportsman, Lady Middleton a mother. He hunted and shot, and she humoured her children: and these were their only resources" (SS 32). Such resources afford no durable satisfaction. Sir John's "independent employments were in existence only half the time" (SS 32)—that is, during hunting season—and Lady Middleton's one enjoyment is essentially insatiable. Refusing to endorse the emerging tendency to sentimentalize maternity, Austen defines "a fond mother" as "the most rapacious of human beings" (SS 120). Under such circumstances, expanding outwards beyond the family is a matter of survival. A constant supply of visitors "was necessary to the happiness of both; for . . . they strongly resembled each other in that total want of talent and taste which confined their employments, unconnected with such as society produced, within a very narrow compass" (SS 32). The hospitality they practice, then, is not a tribute to patriarchal munificence, but rather an antidote to domestic boredom. As fortunate as Sir John's good nature turns out to be for them, Elinor and Marianne have more than one occasion to find being drawn into Barton almost as oppressive as having been shut out of Norland.

Mrs. Palmer and her "droll" husband complete Austen's survey of married life. Mrs. Jenning's silences her son-in-law's periodic eruptions of insolence by reminding him of what polite people usually do not say about unhappy marriages:

> "Aye, you may abuse me as you please," said the good-natured old lady, "you have taken Charlotte off my hands, and cannot give her back again. So there I have the whip hand of you."
> Charlotte laughed heartily to think that her husband could not get rid of her; and exultingly said, she did not care how cross he was to her, as they must live together. (SS 112)

To remind Mr. Palmer of the irreversibility of his conjugal misery is indeed to have "the whip hand" of him, for inasmuch as Mrs. Jennings's aim was solely to get her daughter off her hands, his abuse now hardly matters, especially since Charlotte, to his perpetual annoyance, is too vacuous to feel its sting. While the country gentlemen of conservative fiction lead peaceful yet purposeful lives managing their estates and overseeing the affairs of their neighborhoods with a benevolent eye, the sour Mr.

Palmer, running for Parliament, is understandably fatigued by the efforts "to make every body like him" (SS 113). Life at the manor, while it restrains his rudeness, worsens rather than rectifies all of his deficiencies: "nice in his eating, uncertain in his hours; [and] fond of his child," he "idle[s] away the mornings at billiards" instead of managing the business of his estate (SS 304–5). What with her inane cheerfulness and "his Epicurism, his selfishness, and his conceit" (SS 305), the Palmers live without affection, talent, or moral culture, and they complement Austen's relentlessly harsh satire on contemporary marriage.

If conservative novelists held that the patriarchal family regulated and improved the passions, in *Sense and Sensibility* the family tends to be the locus of venal and idle habits. When we read the novel exclusively as a discussion of female propriety, a quasi-allegorical representation of "sense" and "sensibility," we overlook just how much material it devotes to the manners of men of family. In fact, *Sense and Sensibility* methodically examines the sexual relations gentlemen pursue, either to strengthen patriarchal interests or to relieve the tedium of their existences, which are doomed to dependency and ennui until the death of a near relation will supply the money and liberty they crave. The stories of the two Elizas dramatize each of these possibilities.

The depiction of illicit sexual behavior was a possibility always open to Austen. The refusal to center her fiction on problematic sexual passion distinguishes Austen from her contemporaries, conservative and progressive alike. Seduced and abandoned women are the stuff of many a prerevolutionary English novel, preeminently *Clarissa*, but they positively crowd the pages of the political novel, in conservative fiction attesting to the vulnerability of the nation's decent families to rootless marauders, and in progressive fiction attesting to the abuses of established power. For Austen, however, to have foregrounded the tales of the Elizas would have entailed earmarking a progressive stance, which she evidently did not want to do. Their stories, while stopping decidedly short of pardoning failures of female chastity, nevertheless divulge the callousness of the ruling class, and they would not be out place beside such unequivocally radical novels as Hays's *Victim of Prejudice* (1799) and Inchbald's Rousseauvian *Nature and Art* (1796). As if to defuse the sensitivity of the subject matter, Austen distances herself from the story of the two Elizas by tucking it safely within the center of *Sense and Sensibility* and delegating its narration to the safe Colonel Brandon. But if this inset tale is never permitted to become central, it nevertheless is linked to the larger story in *Sense and Sensibility* through the use of common thematic and descriptive details. In fact, the part-to-whole relationship here functions in much the same way gothic fiction does in *Northanger Abbey*. In both cases, worst-case scenarios with highly conventionalized contours are invoked in order to illuminate what is "too common and too dangerous" about the "ordinary" experiences of her heroines.

In *Sense and Sensibility*, the age of seventeen is the turning point for unprotected females. It is at this age that the first Eliza, a rich orphan, is forced by her uncle, Brandon's father, to marry his eldest son specifically in order to fill the family coffers: "Her fortune was large, and our family estate much encumbered" (SS 205). No pains are spared to heighten Eliza's persecution. Her longstanding and mutual love for Brandon is brutally prohibited, and after an attempted elopement, she is locked up until she submits to her uncle's demand: "She was allowed no liberty, no society, no amusement, till my father's point was gained" (SS 206). Miseries of an evidently unspeakable sort follow her in her married life. Brandon is too gentlemanly to detail a brother's depravities to a young lady like Elinor, but he intimates them with tantalizing indirection: "His pleasures were not what they ought to have been, and from the first he treated her unkindly" (SS 206). Brandon does everything possible to exonerate Eliza, short of pardoning her adultery outright: "Can we wonder that with such a husband to provoke inconstancy, and without a friend to advise or restrain her . . . she should fall?" (SS 206). Cheated out of her own patrimony, Eliza is not given a "legal allowance . . . adequate to her fortune, nor sufficient for her comfortable maintenance" (SS 207), and is thus left after her divorce "to sink deeper in a life of sin" (SS 207), melancholia, and mortal illness. Eliza's fate testifies to the failures of conservative ideology. As an orphan and an heiress, Eliza is a creature so vulnerable that she ought to melt the honorable breast of a Burkean man of feeling. But Eliza's uncle is not in the least susceptible to the melting sensations of solicitude and protectiveness. Rather than feel for the helplessness of his dependent, he looks only to keep up his country estate, while her dissolute husband no sooner possesses a wife's fortune than he abuses the wife herself. Far from being a cautionary tale about the duty of fidelity, Eliza's story, like so much of the central matter in *Sense and Sensibility*, indicts the license to coercion, corruption, and avarice available to grasping patriarchs and their eldest sons.

When the second Eliza is seventeen, she too, in the absence of responsible paternal protection, falls victim to unscrupulous male designs. Unlike Wickham, a propertyless upstart, and unlike the roving seducers in anti-Jacobin fiction, Willoughby is a landed gentleman, in straitened circumstances, but respectable nonetheless. His faults are explicitly related to the corrupt social practices of which he is himself in some senses the victim. While he awaits "the death of [his] old cousin . . . to set [him] free" (SS 320), Willoughby has nothing better to do than accumulate debts and prey on women. The only women available for his dark purposes are the unsheltered and unprotected—like Eliza Williams, and later Marianne Dashwood. Indeed, if Willoughby sports with Marianne only to gratify his vanity, "careless of her happiness, thinking only of [his] own amusement" (SS 320), his intentions for Eliza were always even less honorable. Willoughby is strikingly unrepentant about debauching Eliza and abandoning her and his child by her, and he even appears to consider the fact that he "did not recollect" (SS 322) to give her his address an adequate defense for his negligence. Willoughby's failure as a gentleman and a father are attributed to a deficiency of sensibility. As Colonel Brandon puts it, "[Willoughby] had already done that, which no man who *can* feel for another, would do" (SS 209). Not unlike Brandon's father and brother, Willoughby is governed by the need for money to support the habits of his class: "it had been for some time my intention to re-establish my circumstances by marrying a woman of fortune" (SS 320). Thus while Eliza's seduction is born of anomie, her abandonment is born of avarice, for when Willoughby's aunt vows to disinherit him unless he marries the girl, Willoughby simply states, "That could not be" (SS 323). The "dread of poverty" (SS 323) precludes this even more surely than it does a marriage to Marianne.

The most striking thing about the tales of the two Elizas is their insistent redundancy. One Eliza would have sufficed as far as the immediate narrative purpose is concerned, which is to discredit Willoughby with a prior attachment. But the presence of two unfortunate heroines points to crimes beyond Willoughby's doing, and their common name opens the sinister possibility that plights such as theirs proliferate throughout the kingdom. This redundancy has a generalizing effect, for it invites us to consider how much male behavior in *Sense and Sensibility* redoubles with what is depicted in their tales. The parallels between the Eliza stories and Marianne's experiences are overt. The bearing of the Eliza stories on Edward's treatment of Elinor and Lucy Steele, on the other hand, is, though submerged, more disturbing, because Edward is often regarded as the positive foil to Willoughby: modest, retiring, indifferent to dead leaves. But Edward too forms an early attachment out of the idleness endemic to landed gentlemen as presented in *Sense and Sensibility*. Although Edward, unlike Willoughby, is still under a parent's thumb, he too is holding out for an inheritance that will give him the money and the independence he needs to sustain, not an extravagant, but still a rather aimless life as a private gentleman. In the meantime, he expresses no interest in the energetic management of a country estate and discloses no enthusiasm or talent for a profession, not even the Church. Edward himself describes his relationship with Lucy Steele as a "fancied attachment" (SS 362), and as such it is not different from Willoughby's early feelings about Eliza, whose tenderness towards him "for a very short time, had the power of creating [a] return" (SS 322). But gentlemen in *Sense and Sensibility* are uncommitted sorts. They move on, more or less encumbered by human wreckage from the past. No sooner does Edward, like Willoughby, bind himself to one woman than he proceeds to engage the heart of another. Elinor moralizes upon Willoughby's faults. But not so quick to "scold the imprudence which compliments" herself (SS 368), she is not inclined to worry about Edward's similar, though less glaring, defects. When Elinor chides him for being inconstant to Lucy, Edward tepidly replies:

> "I was simple enough to think, that because my *faith* was plighted to another, there could be no danger in my being with you; and that the consciousness of my engagement was to keep my heart as safe and sacred as my honour. I felt that I admired you, but I told myself it was only friendship . . . [that] I am doing no injury to anybody but myself." (SS 368)

Elinor chalks up all of Willoughby's "behaviour . . . from the beginning to the end" to "selfishness" (SS 351), but she appears not to notice that Edward's self-defense is animated solely by self-concern. While Willoughby at least admits to having amused himself with Marianne "without any design of returning her affection" (SS 320), Edward never hints at any consciousness that he may carelessly have created an attachment in Elinor that he had no intention of reciprocating. As different as Edward and Willoughby are individually, as English gentlemen many of their failures are identical. In marked contrast to the Darcys and Knightleys of this world, they are weak, duplicitous, and selfish, entirely lacking in that rectitude and forthrightness with which Austen is capable of endowing exemplary gentlemen when she wishes. In *Sense and Sensibility*, as in *Persuasion*, these faults are described as the effects of established and accepted social practices for men of family, not as aberrations from them. It is their commonplace lapses towards women that render female manners so desperately important and so impossibly problematic.

All of Austen's novels in varying degrees address the question of female modesty. As early as *Northanger Abbey*, Austen reminds us how wrong, by conventional standards, Catherine is to dwell on Henry after so short an acquaintance: "if it be true, as a celebrated writer [Samuel Richardson] has maintained, that no young lady can be justified in falling in love before the gentleman's love is declared, it must be very improper that a young lady should dream of a gentleman before the gentleman is first known to have dreamt of her" (NA 29–30). Of course, as Richardson himself was writing *Rambler* 97, his own Harriet Byron was not only falling in love first, but openly discussing the fact. Austen's heroines are often equally heterodox. Blissfully ignorant of the exigencies of female propriety, Catherine both dreams and loves first without harming and certainly without disgracing herself. Austen's other novels, however, burden their heroines with acquired notions about propriety that restrain the spontaneous or unequivocal expression of feelings. Jane Bennet, for example, almost loses Bingley altogether precisely because she modestly forebore to show affection enough to convince him of her love before a declaration on his part, and throughout *Mansfield Park*, Fanny's inveterate modesty makes it impossible for her to display her pleasure in Edmund's company and her displeasure in Crawford's.

Modesty ostensibly protects women from the hazards of vulnerability, from avowing love without first securing a return. But as Austen's redefinition in *Northanger Abbey* suggests, strict modesty bars women not simply from avowing their love first but also from dreaming of love first. Women must, then, guard both their outward behavior and, more onerously, their inward wishes. *Emma Courtney* stunned readers because it entertained female-initiated choice in matrimony as a serious social possibility. In Austen's novels, however, as in most others, women simply do not have "the advantage of choice" (NA 77) which Emma Courtney seizes. They can only wait for proposals. They can scrutinize their suitors' gestures, review their every word, differentiate acts of civility from acts of particular affection, and form all manner of conjectures about the likelihood of receiving proposals. But finally they can only wait. As bold as they are in every other respect, even Emma and Elizabeth Bennet can only wait. And of course waiting is practically all that Fanny Price and Anne Elliot ever do. Because their passivity makes them more vulnerable to the anxieties of hope and disappointment, women must be careful not to dream too much too soon. From the outset Marianne and Mrs. Dashwood are not particularly careful on this point. In Elinor's words, "what Marianne and her mother conjectured one moment" about Edward's plans to marry her "they believed the next—that with them, to wish was to hope, and to hope was to expect" (SS 21). But the wariness Elinor is enjoining does not obtain. *Sense and Sensibility* is a novel of secrets and surprises that continually frustrate expectations which no degree of modesty, no becoming refusal to love or even to hope and to dream first, could have prevented. Not only do neither Elinor nor Marianne have any access to knowledge about their suitors' pasts, but they have no grounds even for suspecting that they lack such knowledge, and their suitors, respected gentlemen known to the neighborhood, engage their affections, despite prior engagements. In *Sense and Sensibility* female modesty is no guarantee of female safety. It makes no difference whether one holds back with Elinor's modest caution or hurries forward with Marianne's dauntless ardor, for both are, in Elinor's words, "led away . . . to fancy and expect *what*, as [Willoughby and Edward] were *then* situated, could never be" (SS 368).

Whether or not women ought to reveal, let alone feel or act upon, sexual attraction was, as we have seen, a hotly debated topic in the fiction of Austen's time. For conservatives, proper ladies do not form attachments until a parentally approved partner declares himself, and the moral autonomy of women urged by Wollstonecraft and Hays promotes unfeminine eagerness. The many debates in *Sense and Sensibility* about openness and about the submission we owe to the opinions of our neighbors thus intersect with contemporary political fiction. Marianne advocates self-expression unhampered by conventional restraints. When Elinor, for instance, chides her for speaking to Willoughby without reserve about all her favorite subjects, Marianne's retort outlines the cramped boundaries of acceptable conversation: "I have been too much at my ease, too happy, too frank. I have erred against every common-place notion of decorum . . . had I talked only of the weather and the roads, and had I spoken only once in ten minutes, this reproach would have been spared" (SS 48). For Marianne, the defiance of "common-place notion[s] of decorum" is a matter of principle:

> Marianne abhorred all concealment where no real disgrace could attend unreserve; and to aim at the restraint of sentiments which were not in themselves illaudable, appeared to her not merely an unnecessary effort, but a disgraceful subjection of reason to common-place and mistaken notions" (SS 53).

Far from basing her actions on impulsive, purely subjective feelings, Marianne employs a rational argument to justify her behavior, one that illuminates the essential arbitrariness of established standards. To a conservative, "common-place notions," like the one recommending reserve and concealment to young ladies, deserve their honored status because generations have ratified their wisdom and usefulness. To the authority of customary practice, Marianne, by contrast, opposes rational analysis: "restraint" is only necessary if the sentiments custom would have her conceal are "in themselves" illaudable; "real disgrace" and "real impropriety" (SS 68) are thus distinguished from the false shame we feel when we attend too closely to the judgments of our censorious neighbors. As we recall, the relentless satire on Bridgetina Botherim in *Modern Phi-*

losophers enables Hamilton to plea for the moral dignity of women elsewhere. But on the subject of modesty, Hamilton is strict. A glance at her presentation of Bridgetina's opinions about commonplace maxims can help us appreciate the sympathy Austen evinces for Marianne's position. When Bridgetina's friend urges her to restrain her tender effusions about Henry Sydney until they can discuss them in private, Bridgetina bursts out,

> "You would have me basely conceal my sentiments, in conformity to the pernicious maxims and practices of the world. But what so much as the dread of censure has cramped the energy of the female mind? . . . What are the censures of the world to me? . . . Do you think I have not sufficient philosophy to despise them."[5]

Austen has omitted in Marianne's case the prohibited protofeminist emphasis, but the principled determination to scorn the unworthy practices of the world stays the same. What is grotesque and ludicrous in Hamilton's novel is sensible in Austen's, for though Marianne's openness is sometimes criticized, it is never really scorned, or even fully dismissed. Clearly, Austen can, in a sense, get away with a character like Marianne because she suppresses her antecedents—Marianne reads Scott and Cowper, not Hays or Wollstonecraft—and projects a fictive world that supports many of Marianne's contentions. A horrified onlooker in *Modern Philosophers* warns, "I never knew any one that began in despising the censures of the world, that did not conclude in deserving them," and in Hamilton's novel such a warning makes sense.[6] The fact that Bridgetina and her ridiculous friends boast the superiority of Hottentot society to what they call the "distempered civilization" of England shows us how seriously we are to take their social criticism. But the "maxims and practices" of the worldlings in *Sense and Sensibility* deserve no such deference. Far from recommending maidenly reserve or any manner of moral delicacy, they urge Marianne "to make a conquest," a "common-place phrase" Marianne abhors (SS 45). As Marianne rightly observes, "If the impertinent remarks of Mrs. Jennings are to be the proof of impropriety in conduct, we are all offending every moment of all our lives" (SS 68), and even Elinor with her "doctrine" of propriety does not believe that general civility should entail the "subjection of the understanding" to our neighbors: "All I have ever attempted to influence," she insists, "has been the behaviour. . . . When have I ever advised you to adopt their sentiments or conform to their judgment in serious matters?" (SS 94).

Moreover, in Austen's novel and Hamilton's, the female temerity to disclose desire is received very differently. Bridgetina Botherim's confessions of love are, as her name suggests, entirely unwelcome to her disgusted and previously engaged sweetheart. Bridgetina justifies hounding a man anyway by appealing to moral philosophy: "*Man does right in pursuing interest and pleasure. . . .* My interest, my pleasure, is all centered in your affections; therefore I will pursue you, nor shall I give over the pursuit, say what you will."[7] But while Bridgetina is continually humiliated by her stubborn and unrequited passion, Marianne's fervor melts Willoughby's jaded heart even against his will. Marianne's forwardness to express her attachment is based on an assumption of trust in Willoughby which all observers share. Although Austen threatens to explode the trust that legitimized her openness, in the end it is restored, though its value is diminished. Reading Marianne's letters to Willoughby, Elinor regrets "the imprudence which had hazarded such unsolicited proofs of tenderness, not warranted by anything preceding" (SS 188), but as it turns out the proofs of tenderness were warranted. Marianne insists that Willoughby "*did* feel the same . . . for weeks and weeks he felt it. I know he did" (SS 188). She is right. Marianne's very breach of decorum thwarts Willoughby's ruthless designs and almost brings about a conversion experience that would lead him to renounce his worldly "dread of poverty" (SS 323). Willoughby may not be a particularly worthy object of affection—though Edward, after all, is only slightly more so—but Austen spares Marianne the humiliation of unreturned love, and acquits her of delusion as well as shame.

Unlike her trusting sister, Elinor is careful not to dream of him until she knows—or thinks she knows—that he has dreamed of her. Her modesty governs her drawing room manners as strictly as it does the conduct of her fantasies. Concerning the intentions of Willoughby as well as Edward, she always tries, with various degrees of candor and success, not to assent prematurely to attractive conclusions. To a credulous mother who accepts "probabilities" in place of "certainties," Elinor so "love[s] to doubt where [she] can" (SS 78–79) that she would sooner hang back suspiciously rather than believe what is before her eyes: "If you were to see [Marianne and Willoughby] at the altar, you would *suppose* they were going to get married" (SS 80, emphasis added). But scepticism such as Elinor's seems necessary if one is to avoid constant error. In *Sense and Sensibility* even the least equivocal appearances are profoundly deceiving. With mock portentousness, Austen declares that "the imaginations" of some people "carry them away to form wrong judgments of our conduct, and to decide on it by slight appearances" (SS 248), but the incongruously minute instance in question proves that even ordinary inferences are too audacious: a random visitor in London "allowed her fancy so far to outrun truth and probability" (SS 248) as to suppose that the Dashwood sisters were staying with their brother. If the mere assumption of the Dashwoods' familial decency is based on "slight appearances," certainly the suppositions that Willoughby will marry Marianne or that Edward will wed Elinor are more substantial, yet these too, as we know, are tenuous. Only Elinor is from the start alert to this possibility, and her scepticism is derived not from fussy pedantry or an allegiance to doctrines of propriety, but from a need to protect herself from depending on contingencies, from wishing, dreaming about, and finally needing what may never be. Confused by Edward's reserve, Elinor avoids imagining that her marriage is imminent: "She was far from depending on that result of his preference of her, which her mother and sister still considered as certain" (SS 22). Marianne wonders at Elinor's unromantic refusal to "avoid society, or appear restless and dissatisfied in it" (SS 39), but Elinor is trying precisely not to withdraw into sweet dreams that may be no more than illusions that enslave.[8]

But one of the deepest and most methodically contrived ironies of *Sense and Sensibility* is that not all of Elinor's scepticism can save her from erroneous conjectures, nor all her modesty preserve her from depending upon Edward. When she espies a lock of hair upon Edward's finger, she is "instantaneously" satisfied, "beyond all doubt" (SS 98–99) that it is her own, and proceeds to take hope. But what appears to prove Edward's affection for herself only proves his loyalty to Lucy Steele, of whose existence Elinor is ignorant. And once she learns about Lucy, she quietly harbors the fantasy that Edward will still somehow free himself. After hearing of Edward's supposed marriage, Elinor realizes that "in spite of herself, she had always admitted a hope, while Edward remained single, that something would occur to prevent his marrying Lucy; that some resolution of his own, some mediation of friends, or some more eligible opportunity of establishment for the lady, would arise to assist the happiness of all" (SS 357). Elinor's fantasies here and elsewhere about the "reform" of Mrs. Ferrars and the joyous liberation of fettered inclinations and repressed children (SS 102) have a touch of the visionary about them, but they are no less personal than Marianne's cherished wishes, and her disappointment when they are shattered is no less crushing. True, the upshot is more fortunate for Elinor than for Marianne—Edward is unpredictably but honorably extricated. But Elinor's behavior has turned out to differ from Marianne's only in degree and not in kind. She has neither smothered her dreams nor even, with all her heroic efforts at screening and concealment, really masked her attachment. When Edward returns to Barton after Lucy's elopement, he knows he can count on his glad acceptance: "in spite of the modesty . . . with which he talked of his doubts, he did not, upon the whole, expect a very cruel reception. It was his business, however, to say that he *did*, and he said it very prettily. What he might say on the subject a twelvemonth after, must be referred to the imagination of husbands and wives" (SS 366).

A close examination of Elinor and Marianne does not permit us to conclude that they represent antithetical modes of behavior, as do the staid, exemplary Louisa Dudley and her giddy and selfish sister Marianne in West's *A Gossip's Story*, a novel sometimes cited as an antecedent. But the differences between them are nevertheless significant. *Sense and Sensibility* is Austen's most saliently Johnsonian novel in the concern it manifests everywhere for the therapeutic care of the mind as it lives in time, buffeted by hope, fear, and disappointment. As a sentimental heroine giving herself over on principle to love or to grief with a totality of passion, Marianne actually cultivates an immobilizing obsessiveness. When she and her mother leave Norland, the "agony of grief which overpowered them at first, was voluntarily renewed, was sought for, was created again and again" (SS 7), and later when Willoughby leaves Barton cottage, Marianne similarly ritualizes her unhappiness: "she courted the misery which a contrast between the past and present was certain of giving. She read nothing but what they had been used to read together" (SS 83). To be sure, Elinor has her obsessive moments too. After Edward's departure, Elinor's "thoughts could not be chained elsewhere; and the past and the future, on a subject so interesting, must be before her, must force her attention, and engross her memory, her reflection, and her fancy" (SS 105). But unlike her sister, Elinor does not "augment and fix her sorrow, by seeking silence, solitude, and idleness" (SS 104). The result is no less than a matter of life and death, for Marianne's mania almost kills her. Marianne herself describes her brush with death as "self-destruction" (SS 345). The outright suicide or gradual, often penitent decline of ardent but betrayed women was an ubiquitous and politically sensitive subject, especially after Godwin's *Memoirs* appeared virtually to celebrate Wollstonecraft's suicidal tendencies as somehow appropriate in a heroine of her exquisite sensibility. Suicide, of course, is a common theme in the fiction of the 1790s, and Marianne's brush with "self-destruction" is yet another among the many ways *Sense and Sensibility* retains its character as a nineties novel. Austen's treatment of the subject is distinctive because it refuses to attribute the romantic heroine's near destruction to an (either foolishly or heroically) indulged passion that defies sensible, commonly accepted strictures about conduct, but suggests instead that established codes themselves insist upon and anxiously collude in it. If Marianne's near death is almost suicide, it is almost murder as well.[9]

Women abused in love are expected to die. This is what conventionally happens in sentimental novels, and this is what everyone, with stunning matter-of-factness, expects from Marianne. Like *Northanger Abbey, Sense and Sensibility* challenges fictional conventions, not to show how they are false, that is, to debunk and dismiss them out of a commitment to common sense or reality, but rather to expose how they are true, that is, to determine their logic as myths that function within a larger ideological framework. Once injured, a woman outlives her usefulness: even if she preserves her chastity, she loses her complexion. As John Dashwood puts it, "At [Marianne's] time of life, any thing of an illness destroys the bloom forever" (SS 227). After her "bloom" vanishes, a woman cannot fetch a good husband—as Dashwood says, "I question whether Marianne *now*, will marry a man worth more than five or six hundred a-year" (SS 227). Dashwood, of course, is coyly circling the only issue he really cares about: if a woman can no longer serve herself and her family as an object of exchange in marriage, who knows but that she may burden her brother— or half brother—for subsistence. Privately, he and his wife have already begrudged their widowed stepmother her chances for a long and vigorous life: "People always live forever when there is any annuity to be paid them; and she is very stout and healthy, and hardly forty" (SS 10). For a dependent stepsister of only seventeen, wasting away is almost a matter of good grace. Though appearing as no more than a perfectly natural up- shot of an unfortunate series of events, a heroine's death serves many of the interests of respectably entrenched power.

The betrayed heroine thus interests others as a good, if lugubrious, story, and the closure offered by her decease permits listeners and tellers ritualistically to engage sensations of softening, self-approving pity. The prospect of Marianne's death elicits more in the way of genuine feeling from otherwise narrow or callous people than anything in her life ever did. Though never outright envisioning her death, John Dashwood reaches the upper limits of his capacity for fellow feeling when he meditates upon the pathos of decayed beauty: "One must allow that there is something very trying to a young woman who *has been* a beauty, in the loss of her personal attractions" (SS 237). Having "determined very early in the sei- sure that Marianne would never get over it" (SS 309), Mrs. Jennings is touched by the "rapid decay, the early death of a girl so young, so lovely as Marianne" (SS 313), and even recollects that Mrs. Dashwood must feel for Marianne much as she feels for her own daughter. But these mani- festations of sentimental responses to sad stories, genuine though they are, leave intact the conditions that make them commonplace, conven- tional. Indeed, by turning our unfortunate neighbors into sad stories it is no longer necessary to put ourselves through the inconvenience of deal- ing with them as people. Marianne's sad story prompts the compulsively gregarious Sir John Middleton for a short time to cut Willoughby altogether, but the same capacity for sentiment which makes Sir John pity the supposedly dying Marianne also makes him forgive Willoughby.

But not all stories about the wronged woman provide such uncompli-cated satisfaction, particularly when she takes a long time dying. If se-duced and abandoned, she is an offense to good society, like "natural" children whose mention drives Lady Middleton to converse about the weather. Her person must be sequestered and her story suppressed, for both bring into intolerable light the lapses of a patriarchal society which routinely betrays its trusts in order to secure wealth. If her sad story is to be told at all, then she herself will not be presented as the principal character in it. In *Sense and Sensibility*, Brandon and Willoughby, and not Austen's narrator, are the tellers of heroines' sad stories. Each trans-forms them into his own tales, and Austen sees to it that we will be able to spot the gaps. That man of feeling, Colonel Brandon, opposes what passes for respectability in the world. Though exemplifying the best *Sense and Sensibility* has to offer, he yearns for the safety from further harm which a heroine's death affords. He complains with rather disturbing di-rectness that instead of delicately languishing to an early grave out of disappointed love for him, Eliza survives: "Happy had it been if she had not lived to overcome those regrets which the remembrance of me oc-casioned" (SS 206). Happy for whom? one wonders. Exhibiting untoward resilience, Eliza "overcomes" a romantic attachment that would properly have sunk a more "sensible" and therefore more admirable heroine; she lives on to suffer an abusive marriage, to form an adulterous attachment, to divorce, and finally to degenerate into poverty, sin, and putrescence so unsightly that even before she actually dies Brandon describes her as "the remains of the lovely, blooming, healthful girl, on whom I once doated" (SS 207). Austen pokes a lot of fun at Marianne's purportedly heroic con-tempt for "second attachments," but single women who form second at-tachments—like widows who remarry—are extremely distressing to interested men. A woman's readiness to form second attachments has the appearance of grossness or impropriety, even when blessed as a stroke of good fortune, because it gives her an unladylike parity in the conduct of her emotional and erotic life which challenges conventions assuring the primacy of male choice. How much more endearing Lucy Steele would appear to everyone concerned had she wilted opportunely away upon in-ferring Edward's second attachment instead of sallying forth to form her own. An earlier death would indeed have "happily" spared Eliza future pain, but in placing her where his (bootless) protection is no longer nec-essary, beyond reach of other men, it would have spared Brandon's pain as well, and insured his own immutable status as the hero in her story.

As a would-be predator Willoughby makes himself the hero of Marianne's story even more egregiously. Willoughby treats Marianne's anticipated death as an occasion to solicit sympathy for himself: "If you *can* pity me, Miss Dashwood, pity my situation as it was *then*. With my head and heart full of your sister, I was forced to play the happy lover to another woman!"(SS 327). And Elinor does pity him. Though she recognizes his selfishness, she never appears to observe how his self-reproach smacks of vainglory of a peculiarly prurient sort. As Willoughby (wrongly) imagines, Marianne's dying breaths pay tribute to his potency: "What I felt on hearing that your sister was dying—and dying too, believing me the greatest villain upon earth, scorning, hating me in her latest moments" (SS 330–31). Like Brandon then, Willoughby does not find the prospect of an abandoned woman's death displeasing. Recalling that his departure almost did Marianne in on the spot—"I had seen Marianne's sweet face as white as death" (SS 327)—he fantasizes about his preeminence at a death scene caused and haunted by his absence: "Yet when I thought of her to-day as really dying, it was a kind of comfort to me to imagine that I knew exactly how she would appear to those, who saw her last in this world" (SS 327). Scandalized by his ardor, Elinor reminds Willoughby that he is a married man without claim to Marianne's affections. But a claim to Marianne's devotion, even after he has jilted her to marry another woman for money, is precisely what he wants. Given a society that does not officially condone polygamy, death simultaneously preserves the heroine exclusive to the hero's sentimental dominion and disposes of her tidily when he moves on to his chosen life of horses and sport. Good Sir John appreciates this. Touched by his hunting companion's sentimental pangs for the woman he wronged, he gives him one of Folly's puppies as consolation.

Like many novels of the 1790s, *Sense and Sensibility* asks how the ideal of romantic love serves women if the same charms of sensibility that render them alluring—as Dashwood notes, "There is something in [Marianne's] style of beauty, to please [men] particularly" (SS 227)—also induce febrile morbidity. On this matter conservative and progressive women novelists could agree, although their emphases differed. West, More, and Hamilton, for example, teach daughters to be useful wives and helpmates along life's arduous way. Because they regard passions, in West's words, as "trials of fortitude" rather than "sources for gratification," they oppose romantic notions that sanctify volatile passions and foster a hypersensitivity to earthly infelicities we must endure.[10] Progressive women novelists urge a rationality, usefulness, and fortitude no less strenuous. But for them, cultural injunctions about female manners are subjected to radical social criticism. They attack educational practices promoting women's self-immolating enslavement to their own passions, and they arraign sensibility as a means by which cultural injunctions are internalized and self-executed. Whatever her own susceptibility to sensibility, Wollstonecraft makes an attack on Rousseau's idealization of female sensibility, particularly as it promotes the virtue of men, the centerpiece of *Rights of Women*; and in *Emma Courtney*, Hays dramatizes the nearly deadly corrosiveness of romantic passion and favors rational "esteem" over consuming "love" just as earnestly as Elinor does here.

While the critique of sensibility, then, is not itself politically specific, Austen's treatment of it is progressive insofar as she implicates the assumptions of an entire respectable community in it. The presence of so many characters so casually anticipating a death which never comes about calls attention to the ideological function of this too common and too dangerous convention. And the fact that the tales of dying heroines here are inset stories told by interested men highlights the pornographic, but utterly conventional, ways in which heroine's stories, appropriated by men, are made to suit established social arrangements. Orthodox morality typically denounces acts of suicide, undertaken either from despair or as a reasoned choice. But it countenances, indeed expects, self-destruction in the covert, sentimental form of a wronged woman's self-punishing, typically penitent death. Austen's thrusts at sentiment in *Sense and Sensibility* thus cut in both ways. Just as she had ridiculed the absurdity of Marianne's flighty enthusiasm for nature by subjecting her to a violent storm, which in turn, however, occasioned an actual heroic rescue, she both confirms and denies the convention dictating the decay of the sentimental heroine. Marianne really does get sick after all, and as Mrs. Jennings opines, "the severity and danger of this attack" can be attributed "to the many weeks of previous indisposition which Marianne's disappointment had brought on" (SS 314). Moreover, affliction which testifies to Willoughby's power and Marianne's loyalty serves to reproach the not adequately sensitive Elinor for having underestimated the seriousness of her sister's grief and "trifled with so many days of illness" (SS 312).

But in other respects, Austen's practice as a novelist undermines, even though it cannot entirely elude, conventions about dying heroines. During her illness, for example, Marianne raves not about the still passionately loved Willoughby, as he flatters himself. In fact, Marianne's semicomatose reflections recur to the women in her life, particularly to a beloved mother, a sister she fears she has wronged. Furthermore, Marianne and that other abused heroine, Eliza Williams, do not die after their interest to their seducer gives way to his love of money. Because Eliza is a natural child herself with an illegitimate infant, she, unlike Marianne, is ultimately as embarrassing to Lady Middleton's standards of elegant conversation as she is to the reach of Austen's art. Eliza is consigned to silence and isolation, and Austen does not bring Eliza in from the margins of her proper novel and invite her to tell her own story. Still, as we have seen, Austen could easily have killed Eliza off in the interests of tidiness. But this was the conventional route she does not wish Eliza to take. By the end of *Sense and Sensibility*, Eliza lives on, in obscurity to be sure, but also as enduring testimony to betrayal, and we can only assume that the continuing support of these living "remains" falls to Brandon and his new wife. For her part, Marianne is dangled over the brink of death only to be yanked back into a second and happy attachment which flies in the face of cultural ideals about women's sentimentally self-monitored loyalty to the men who first love them. Perhaps most anticonventionally of all, Austen makes the happy outcome of the novel as a whole contingent upon Lucy Steele's hardhearted but redemptive "second attachment" for Robert Ferrars. Elinor's exertions, only partially successful though they are, receive so much approbation because they help her survive a scenario her culture has inscribed for heroines without obliging her to emulate Lucy's calculation. *Sense and Sensibility*, then, criticizes, not the unseemliness or the rebelliousness of Marianne's emotionality, but rather its horrifying conformity to the social context she lives within. Her anticonventionality turns out to be all too conventional after all, and instead of defying dangerously common expectations, she comes close to capitulating to them.

The critique of conservative ideology in *Sense and Sensibility*, proffered largely though an examination of the morally vitiating tendencies of patriarchy, is extremely trenchant and in some ways extremely radical. The competency the two couples achieve at the end—whose fortunes range from downright cramped to modest—is a badge of their independence from the power that in *Sense and Sensibility* corrupts. Here, in bold contrast to *Pride and Prejudice*, isolation from the patriarchal family is a precondition for honest liberty: Edmund duly apologizes to his incensed mother, but he stoutly refuses to make any "mean concessions" (SS 372) that might restore him to an eldest brother's rights. Reconciliation and the money grubbing it serves is left to such moral nullities as Lucy, Robert, and the John Dashwoods. But Austen's social criticism here goes even further. Opposition of the patriarchal family is a precondition for the development of moral imagination itself: Brandon gives a living to a friend of a friend, a man he is not related to (at the time, at least), and solely because Edward is behaving honorably in defiance of family interests.

Brandon himself is in a position to offer modest patronage only because
his own days of subjugation to a corrupt father and older brother are happily behind him.

In leveling her criticism against the most cherished unit of conservative
social structure, however, Austen has not omitted to provide us with some
tenuous alternatives, impressive despite their failures. *Sense and Sensibility* is also a novel of "matriarchs": widows, sometimes with, sometimes without money, who exert influence over the gentlemen who wreak
so much harm.[11] Mrs. Ferrars, of course, is utterly collusive with patriarchal interests. Like an anxious father, she wants to see her firstborn son
involved "in political concerns, to get him into parliament, or to see him
connected with some of the great men of the day" (SS 16), and to that
end she uses the only power she has over him—her purse strings. Against
her, detail for detail, Willoughby's aunt stands in perfect opposition as a
model of radical authority attempting unworldly and morally corrective
coercion. For Mrs. Smith, morality is not a function of family interests,
as it is for the John Dashwoods, and the enhancement of family fortune
takes second place to the fulfillment of obligations to basic decency, particularly towards seduced and abandoned women. Accordingly, she
threatens to use her power to disinherit Willoughby in order to persuade
him to behave honorably and marry the woman he has wronged. The
defiant Willoughby considers her attitudes almost amusingly quaint, and
he reports her attempt to rein him in with sullen self-pity, as though she
were being a fussy and unreasonable old bore: "The purity of her life,
the formality of her notions, her ignorance of the world—every thing was
against me" (SS 323). From the radical point of view, of course, it is Mrs.
Smith's very refusal to abet what passes as commonplace in "the world,"
particularly insofar as it is injurious to the Elizas of it, that makes her an
exemplary version of authority.

Finally, there is Mrs. Dashwood herself, who has no money to enforce
her policies and whose authority is entirely noncoercive. Generally viewed
as an excessively lax parent, little more than one of the girls herself, Mrs.
Dashwood actually presides over a remarkable little establishment. Barton Cottage is a small dwelling on a tiny corner of a gentleman's estate,
and Mrs. Dashwood and her three daughters have taken refuge there in
genuine financial distress. Yet one of the novel's most painful ironies is
that what has meant hardship and dispossession for them has meant
something very much like regeneration to the shiftless men who retreat
there now and then. Because these men belong to the world, the cottage
is subject to their efforts at sentimentalization. In *Sense and Sensibility*,
country cottages are like dying heroines. Idle and selfish gentlemen here
take a spectatorial delight in the uncomfortably confined life to which the

Dashwood ladies have been reduced, a delight which forestalls concern for the injustices which have placed them there to begin with. For Robert Ferrars, this "species of house" is the latest fad. His notion of cottages, like Mrs. Elton's of gypsy parties, is a vapidly fashionable appropriation of Rousseauvian ideas about retirement:

> "For my own part," said he, "I am excessively fond of a cottage; there is always so much comfort, so much elegance about them. And I protest, if I had any money to spare, I should buy a little land and build one myself, within a short distance of London, where I might drive myself down at any time, and collect a few friends about me, and be happy." (SS 251)

People like Robert will bring their jeweled toothpick cases, their "sterling insignificance" (SS 221), and all the corrupting sophistication of their worlds with them wherever they go. But though Edward has been vitiated by the world, he is not the worldling his brother is. For him, accordingly, Mrs. Dashwood's cottage does present an alternative society where he can, as Robert blithely puts it, "be happy," where friends assemble, and where the known cares of Norland, and of secret care at Devonshire, lose their hold: "he grew more and more partial to the house and environs— never spoke of going away without a sigh. . . . He had no pleasure at Norland; he detested being in town. . . . He valued their kindness beyond anything, and his greatest happiness was in being with them" (SS 101).

Isolated from the world and its accustomed dissipations and artificialty, Barton Cottage has the same impact on Willoughby. There, the professions of sensibility he carelessly strews about solely in order to ensnare Marianne blossom into an ardor he never felt before. For this, he holds responsible not merely Marianne's charms, but also the society Mrs. Dashwood provides. Mrs. Dashwood, he insists, must never alter or enlarge her quaint cottage:

> "You would rob it of its simplicity by imaginary improvement! and this dear parlour, in which our acquaintance first began, and in which so many happy hours have since been spent by us together, you would degrade to the condition of a common entrance, and every body would be eager to pass through the room which has hitherto contained within itself, more real accommodation and comfort than any other apartment of the handsomest dimensions in the world could possibly afford. . . . Tell me that not only your house will remain the same, but that I shall ever find you and yours as unchanged as your dwelling." (SS 73–74)

It is small wonder Mrs. Dashwood should be charmed by sentimental declarations such as these, but she and her cottage have charmed Willoughby as well, and her trust in his honor is partially vindicated. Of course Willoughby turns out to be too attached to the world to embrace what to him are the redemptive possibilities of retirement at Barton Cottage. But he has been capable of feeling the capacity of Mrs. Dashwood's "dear parlour" to transform him, and of understanding his refusal to let them do so to result from "false ideas of the necessity of riches" which "expensive society" perpetuates (SS 323). Mrs. Dashwood and Mrs. Smith alike are painfully singular in their superiority to mercenary interests. But if neither woman is formidable enough to effect any change in the world of "false ideas," they are formidable enough to show where that change ought to begin.

Sense and Sensibility has always been Austen's least-beloved novel, and it has never been allowed its full weight in Austen's canon. But once its force is acknowledged, Austen's oeuvre looks very different. The sobriety of *Mansfield Park* will appear less distinctive, and its scepticism about the family will be more familiar. The venturesomeness of *Persuasion*, what with its weariness of bootless prudential maxims and its impatience with country neighborhoods, will look more like a continuation rather than a reversal. And Austen's most popular novel, *Pride and Prejudice*, will seem exceptional among all the novels in the perfectly comedic harmony and extravagant felicity it accomplishes. *Sense and Sensibility* promises no such concord. It is only by recourse to outrageous acts of chance that Austen marries her heroines off with some measure of muted felicity, and that happiness is marked by a refusal of social integration and the moral compromises it entails. *Sense and Sensibility* is unremitting in its cynicism and iconoclasm. Marianne changes her opinions about second attachments, but she is never obliged to surrender to the "commonplace," "gross," and "illiberal" (SS 45), and in permitting her to withdraw from the world, *Sense and Sensibility* grants her the highest happiness it can imagine.

CHAPTER FOUR

PRIDE AND PREJUDICE AND THE PURSUIT
OF HAPPINESS

If we can judge from her few surviving comments about her work, Jane
Austen did not appear to have liked *Pride and Prejudice* nearly as much
as we have. To her its "playfulness and epigrammaticism" appeared excessive and unrelieved: "The work is rather too light, and bright, and
sparkling": the novel lacked "shade," and required "a long chapter of
sense" or even "of solemn specious nonsense, about something unconnected with the story; an essay on writing, a critique on Walter Scott, or
the history of Buonaparté" in order to interrupt, qualify, or somehow
contrast with its remorseless high spirits (*Letters*, 4 February 1813). But
the deficiency of shade, so far from ranking as a fault, has been the novel's
chief recommendation to general readers and critics alike, who find in the
marriage of the exuberant heroine and her manly hero the comedic promise of personal fulfillment as well as social harmony. While the novels of
Austen's contemporaries, with very few exceptions, are given over to crises
of social and marital disintegration, *Pride and Prejudice* is a categorically
happy novel, and its felicity is not merely incidental, something that happens at the end of a novel, but is rather at once its premise and its prize.

In its readiness to ratify and to grant our happiness, *Pride and Prejudice*
is almost shamelessly wish fulfilling. The fantasies it satisfies, however,
are not merely private—a poor but deserving girl catches a rich husband.
They are pervasively political as well. If *Pride and Prejudice* legitimizes
a progressive yearning for pleasure, it also gratifies a conservative yearning for a strong, attentive, loving, and paradoxically perhaps, at times
even submissive authority. At no other time in Austen's career would she
indulge a fantasy of this magnitude to this degree, for it is Darcy himself
who secures the happiness the novel celebrates. As an authority figure,
"a brother, a landlord, a master" who holds, as Elizabeth remarks, "many
people's happiness . . . in his guardianship" (PP 250), Darcy is singularly
free from the faults that underline comparable figures elsewhere—General Tilney's repressiveness, for example, or Sir Walter's foolishness. *Pride
and Prejudice* is thus a profoundly conciliatory work, and of all Austen's
novels it most affirms established social arrangements without damaging

their prestige or fundamentally challenging their wisdom or equity. Whereas *Sense and Sensibility* excoriates the traditional family and *Mansfield Park* subjects characters of Darcy's stature to disabling satire, on the surface at least, *Pride and Prejudice* corroborates conservative myths which had argued that established forms cherished rather than prohibited true liberty, sustained rather than disrupted real happiness, and safeguarded rather than repressed individual merit. Its hero accordingly is a sober-minded exemplar of the great gentry, a dutiful son and affectionate brother. Its villain is an ungrateful upstart who, by attempting to elope with a female of good family, seeks not simply to enrich himself but also to sully the scutcheons of legitimate male power—as Darcy puts it, "Mr. Wickham's chief object, was unquestionably my sister's fortune, which is thirty thousand pounds; but I cannot help supposing that the hope of revenging himself on me, was a strong inducement" (PP 202). And its turning point is the heroine's contemplation of the household of a private gentleman. Prepared to find Pemberley a grandiose estate designed expressly to overbear subordinates with awe, Elizabeth finds instead an unpretentiously elegant manor, and rather than testimonials to the insolence of power, she hears tributes to a kind master, a beloved landlord, tributes which moreover are not tainted by "prejudice," that ultimate progressive pejorative.

To some, *Pride and Prejudice* has a markedly fairy-tale-like quality which, while accounting for much of the novel's enduring popular success, is politically suspect. One of Austen's recent critics observes that the novel's wishful, though aesthetically satisfying, "romantic conclusion" fudges the ideological contradictions uncovered earlier between the "individualistic perspective inherent in the bourgeois value system *and* the authoritarian hierarchy retained from traditional, paternalistic society."[1] By this account, the happy ending of *Pride and Prejudice* is an "aesthetic solution" that cannot really address the "social problems" the novel itself uncovers, and indeed that actually conceals their depth. But while these objections are partly true, we should not let our own rather modern preference for ideological conflict predispose us to undervalue Austen's achievement in *Pride and Prejudice*. To imagine versions of authority responsive to criticism and capable of transformation is not necessarily to "escape" from urgent problems into "romance" and to settle for politically irresponsible "consolations of form" which offer us a never-never land and leave the structures of the "real world" unchanged.[2] When we recall that Austen's preceding novel could locate her protagonists' contentment only in a retreat from and renunciation of power, Austen's decision here to engage her exceptionally argumentative antagonists in direct, extensive, and mutually improving debates can just as well be viewed as a step towards, rather than an "escape" from, constructive political commentary.

While it is thus indeed true that the happy ending of *Pride and Prejudice* "dismisses the social and psychological realism with which the novel began"—dodging, for example, such dire issues as the destitution we are told the Bennet sisters would otherwise expect after their father's death—nevertheless the novel as a whole certainly does not evade or neutralize social criticism out of a fond or unquestioning allegiance to established forms and the attractive men who embody them.[3] In fact, the "conservatism" of *Pride and Prejudice* is an imaginative experiment with conservative myths, and not a statement of faith in them as they had already stood in anti-Jacobin fiction. To be sure, by using these myths, even to hedge, qualify, and improve them, Austen is also, as we shall see, unavoidably used by them. But throughout the course of the novel those myths become so transformed that they are made to accommodate what could otherwise be seen as subversive impulses and values, and in the process they themselves become the vehicles of incisive social criticism.

Darcy may conform to conservative requirements for one of his rank and sex, but Elizabeth emphatically does not, and many social and political issues cluster around her characterization. Austen's conviction that Elizabeth was "as delightful a creature as ever appeared in print" was well-founded, for, as she could not have failed to realize, no heroine quite like Elizabeth Bennet had "ever appeared in print" before (*Letters*, 29 January 1813). Standing where we do, we tend either to overlook or to underestimate Elizabeth's outrageous unconventionality which, judged by the standards set in conduct books and in conservative fiction, constantly verges not merely on impertinence but on impropriety. As if to call attention to this point, Austen has Mr. Collins drone Fordyce's *Sermons to Young Women* "with very monotonous solemnity" (PP 68) to the assembled Bennet sisters. Originally published in 1766, the *Sermons* were steadily popular throughout the rest of the century, but enjoyed particular currency between 1790 and 1810, when they were frequently reprinted in England and Ireland. Collins's approval of such "books of a serious stamp" (PP 69) in and of itself signals Austen's disaffection with the rules about women promulgated in them. Austen could hardly recommend behavior to her readers through anyone so morally stunted as Collins, a fact not sufficiently reckoned with by critics who argue that Austen's inflexibly orthodox morality is anchored in, if not actually derived from, volumes he enjoys.

Although it would appear that Lydia Bennet might actually benefit from Fordyce's teachings on "shamefacedness in women," many of his recommendations, like More's, could only confirm her in her thoughts after the officers, as when he suggests that rather than reading books, women's "business chiefly is to read Men, in order to make yourselves agreeable and useful."[4] But once granted moral authority, Fordyce's injunctions to modesty and humility damn Elizabeth's behavior every bit as decidedly as they do Lydia's. His reproof of "briskness of air and levity of deportment" would fall harshly on a heroine famed for "a lively, playful disposition, which delighted in any thing ridiculous" (PP 12). His disapproval of women who "betray a confidence in [their] charms" would reflect ill on one who assures her modest sister, "Compliments always take *you* by surprise, and *me* never" (PP 14, emphasis Austen's). And his rule that in dress, as in all matters, women ought "never to go beyond their circumstances, nor aspire above their station" would damage a woman who refuses to dress down in order to respect Lady Catherine's fondness for preserving "distinction of rank" (PP 161).[5] Fordyce's commendation of the "amiable reserve" of "elegant females," together with his underlying assumption that women's primary desire and duty is to please men, especially through the affectation of modesty, may show us where Collins derives *his* notions of female conduct, but they do not provide us with standards flexible and intelligent enough to evaluate Elizabeth.

Not that Mr. Collins is the only one to take seriously the standards set in conduct books. With some justice and with some degree of concurrence from the sensible Mr. Darcy, Miss Bingley censures Elizabeth's "country town indifference to decorum" (PP 36). Elizabeth's wit is occasionally marked by an unabashed rusticity bordering on the vulgar—"I expected at least that the pigs were got into the garden, and here is nothing but Lady Catherine and her daughter" (PP 158). But this "indifference to decorum" does not stop with an independent vivacity of thought and conversation, as it does with the engaging heroines of Restoration comedy to whom she is often compared. Elizabeth's celebrated liveliness is vigorously physical as well, verging sometimes on unladylike athleticism. Whereas Millamant, as we recall, "nauseates walking," Elizabeth not only treks for miles *alone*—something the propriety-conscious Emma would never do—but she also runs, jumps, springs, and rambles. Austen's manifestly self-conscious achievement in Elizabeth Bennet thus consists precisely in having made her "creature" so "delightful" despite her continual infractions of the rules of propriety. Lydia's offending presence in the novel makes this possible. Even though, as a husband hunter patterned after her doting mother, she has nothing in common with the feminist ideologues of turn-of-the-century fiction, she serves in much the same way they do in the novels of moderate social critics. Instead of standing as living proof that young ladies must be disciplined into "shamefacedness," as Fordyce would term it, Lydia is a decoy who attracts the disapproval to which Elizabeth herself could otherwise be subject, and by lamenting Lydia's glaring excesses, Elizabeth is cleared for her less egregious but still "improper" rambles, conceit, and impertinence without arousing our discomfort or incurring our censure.

By linking Elizabeth and Lydia, Austen eludes rather than reiterates conventional moral codes, and the carefully elaborated cross-referencing of other characters, qualities, and relationships throughout the book functions in the same way: not to serve some neoclassical taste for balance, but rather to impede generalization. Austen has contrived *Pride and Prejudice* in such a way that virtually every argument about it can be undercut with a built-in countervailing argument, a qualifying "on the other hand" which forestalls conclusiveness. Take, among numberless examples, the important issue of education. Mr. Collin's bullyish obsequiousness is attributed largely to the "subjection" he experienced at the hands of his "illiterate and miserly father" (PP 70). On the other hand, Darcy's snobbery is attributed to a father who indulged his self-importance. Yet as antithetical as their educations are, both men are similarly conceited and inattentive to the feelings of others. On the subject of female education too, Austen orchestrates opposites and analogues, not to clarify, but rather to embarrass judgments. The same parental neglect that somehow turns Lydia into a thoughtless flirt turns Jane and Elizabeth into independent and responsible moral agents. By contrast, no pains are spared in the education of Miss Anne de Burgh, but she, comically enough, is the novel's reigning nonentity who never utters a single word on her own behalf. In none of these cases does Austen prescribe a symmetrically poised middle way, or imply some formula for moderation. On the contrary, the very method of the novel obstructs the impulse to make a tidy moral. Instead of opposing "good" liveliness to "bad" liveliness, "good" education to "bad" education, the intricately counterbalanced construction of *Pride and Prejudice* obliges us to regroup and reassess characters and issues, to broaden our judgments and to accept contradiction.[6]

Austen leaves it to Mary Bennet to compile precepts about human nature and female delicacy. Elizabeth, for her part "was not formed for ill humour" (PP 90), much less for sober moralizing. Elizabeth regards as unmerited censure Caroline Bingley's suggestion that she "has no pleasure in any thing else" but books, and assures the company on the contrary "I have pleasure in many things" (PP 37). Indeed, Elizabeth's "temper," we are assured, is "to be happy" (PP 239), and it is her readiness for happiness, enjoyment, and pleasure, words which ring on virtually every page, that makes her and her novel so distinctive. In marked contrast to counterrevolutionary literature, *Pride and Prejudice* is a passionate novel which vindicates personal happiness as a liberal moral category, rescuing it from the suspicion into which it had fallen. Elizabeth Hamilton counted on her readers' unhesitating dismissal of Bridgetina Botherim's at once ridiculous and dangerous doctrine, "And is not happiness and pleasure the only true end of our being. . . . These are the sublime principles of philosophy."[7] But in *Pride and Prejudice*, Elizabeth can explain to Darcy a "philosophy" (PP 369) not categorically different from Bridgetina's without sounding absurd or licentious. Whereas conduct-book moralizers would urge reviews of past conduct as means for earnest self-examination, to be followed by vows of reformation, Elizabeth says simply, "Think only of the past as its remembrance gives you pleasure" (PP 369). Darcy, of course, insists on heeding "painful recollections" of his own past errors, not because he finds Elizabeth's philosophy of pleasure objectionable, but rather because he gallantly wishes to show her how much he is willing to change for her sake.

In making the wish for and experience of happiness and pleasure central to her novel, Austen is no less than redeeming a tradition of liberal moral and political philosophy which antedates the postrevolutionary controversies that called it into question. Her acceptance of happiness as a morally acceptable goal proves not that she was a closet radical but rather that she and progressives were drawing on a shared tradition. Austen's relation to Samuel Johnson can help illustrate this point. Because readers have known ever since the "Biographical Notice" of 1818 that Johnson was Austen's favorite moral writer in prose, Johnson has always been acknowledged as an important factor in her intellectual development.[8] Indeed, owing to what has been a longstanding tendency to disparage or overlook the perspicacity of the women writers whom Austen read and admired, he has generally been considered the only formidable figure on Austen's conscious literary horizon, and as a result has been credited as a source for all her ideas or, more to the present point, as a political mentor, as that great "Tory conservative" from whom she drew her ideological inspiration.

But it by no means follows from Johnson's privileged status as Austen's favorite prose moralist that she regarded him as an archauthoritarian, and on this point Austenians have not kept abreast of the Johnsonians. Some turn-of-the-century conservative novelists indeed do look to Johnson as a mentor. His belief that happiness is not attainable endeared him to counterrevolutionary writers who saw their opponents as quixotic projectors vainly attempting to perfect society or increase the lot of human happiness. In *Tale of the Times*, the heroine's first step towards ruin is made to coincide with her disenchantment with *Rasselas*. Because she has believed her Jacobin seducer's suggestions that Johnson is an "enemy to levity and simplicity, a lover of discipline and system," Lady Geraldine can no longer receive the support from the sage who would reconcile us to the infelicity we must endure here below.[9] Soon thereafter, Lady Geraldine lets herself feel discontented with her husband, and she comes to tolerate—note, not to approve—Fitzosborne's heterodox talk about relaxing divorce laws, because he seems to her sincerely concerned for "the improvement and happiness of the world."[10] A wish for personal as well as public happiness is thus seen as a disastrously seductive dream from which the supposedly stoic Johnson, given the chance, could save us. In conceiving Johnson as a stern moralist warning us to sacrifice happiness to duty, West, it must be emphasized, is not drawing on, but is herself actually creating, literary history, for there is an important distinction to be made between the moralist and the moralizers—the self-confessed regulators of manners—who recurred to him in order to enhance their own undertakings. Writing from her own conviction that women are the sacred guardians of morals, particularly in an age swarming with noxious ideas, West often prescribes standards of right behavior which Johnson of all people—what with his peculiar domestic life and in his notoriously singular, even repulsive manners—could not attain.[11]

Throughout the nineteenth century until recently in our own, readers more or less shared Fitzosborne's view that, "averse to those rights which man inherently possesses, tenacious of those bulwarks which society forms," Johnson was in fact "repulsive in his politics, uncomplying in his morality, and austere in his religion."[12] But not all of Johnson's contemporaries and near contemporaries considered him to be the forbidding and bigoted Hercules of Toryism whom Boswell described in his biography and whom West and More, among others, venerated. While they were busily writing him out of a political tradition from which they had much to fear, many progressive writers perceived in Johnson a potentially, if not actually, sympathetic figure. Among those who anticipated twentieth-century scholars in esteeming Johnson's feisty and rebellious sympathy with the underdog, his reluctance to be prescriptive, and his impatience with metaphysical cant that obfuscates or sentimentalizes political realities were early feminists, such as Macaulay, Hays, and Wollstonecraft, who admired him despite their awareness that he often—and with what Macaulay considered to be perverse inconsistency—stood on the other side of political questions.[13] Johnson has no difficulty endorsing an ethic of pleasure later generations could brand hedonistic; even in a religious context he does not hesitate to declare that "Every man is conscious, that he neither performs, nor forbears any thing upon any other motive than the prospect, either of an immediate gratification, or a distant reward."[14]

And if he did not think that happiness was attainable, he still insisted that the desire for happiness—or pleasure, or gratification—was our sole motive for action, whence the distinctive tension of his vision: "We desire, we pursue, we obtain, we are satiated; we desire something else, and begin a new pursuit" (*Rambler* 6). In considering Austen's relation to Johnson and to the political discourse of what was for her the recent past, we must remember that Johnson's legacy could, and did, go two ways. For some writers he served as a leonine champion of authoritarianism, but for Austen he served as a philosophic psychologist, a writer who legitimized the energy generated by our desire for happiness, and who, unlike his later, anti-Jacobin admirers, was less interested in prescribing rules of behavior than in exploring the never-concluding dynamic of desire, hope, and disappointment set into motion by our pursuits of happiness.[15]

In all of Austen's novels, but especially in *Pride and Prejudice*, pursuing happiness is the business of life. Austen trots character after character before our attention so that we may consider what pleases or, conversely, what vexes and mortifies them, thus inviting us to assess the quality and durability of their happiness. At the outset, at least, Darcy's sense of self-consequence is characterized by a haughty determination to be mortified by everyone outside his small circle. Unlike the easygoing Bingley, who has an agreeable disposition to be pleased anywhere, Darcy is much as the neighborhood around Meryton first perceives him: "proud . . . above his company . . . above being pleased" (PP 10). But if this refusal to be pleased is a serious moral failing, as Darcy himself later admits, a determination to be imperturbably agreeable is little better. Knighthood has given Sir William Lucas license to spend all his time thinking "with pleasure of his own importance" (PP 18), and he feels this pleasure most acutely by being pleased—quite indiscriminately—with everything, smiling graciously even as Darcy snubs him with quips about the savagery of dancing, or even as Mrs. Bennet insults the claims of his daughter to marry Mr. Collins. With her "high animal spirits" (PP 45) Lydia Bennet, by contrast, finds her boisterous pleasures in redcoats and balls. Because she has never been taught that "her present pursuits are not to be the business of her life" (PP 231), a visit to the encampment at Brighton "comprised every possibility of earthly happiness" (PP 232). Mrs. Bennet's grip on happiness is considerably weaker, and she is hardly able to take any pleasure at all. Though marrying off her daughters is the chief "business" of her life, so firmly is she convinced that the world conspires to irritate her "poor nerves" (PP 5, 113) and thwart her wishes that she passes most of her time in vexation.

Austen's care to establish the standards of her characters' happiness provides us with an index to their moral imaginations, tempers, and resources that enables us to engage in judicious moral evaluation without resorting to the conclusive moralizing characteristic of some of her contemporaries. By leaving censorious reflections on Lydia's elopement to the "spiteful old ladies in Meryton" (PP 309) and to the pompous Mary, for example, Austen distances herself from prescriptive pronouncements on this subject, and no specifically authorial moral opprobrium is ever attached to Charlotte's frankly mercenary marriage to Collins. It is enough instead that Lydia's abrupt lapse into conjugal indifference and pecuniary want shows just how little her previous ideas of "earthly happiness" comprehended after all, and that Charlotte's choice of and apparently successful adjustment to Mr. Collins as a husband indicates where she rates the exigencies of physical maintenance relative to the pleasures of rational society. Thus, although Austen's refusal to settle the differences in what her characters seek as desirable—in *Persuasion* Admiral Croft likes and Anne Elliot dreads the prospect of "future war" (P 252)—implies a toleration of some ethical relativity which some of her contemporaries could have found disturbing, she nevertheless does not leave us bereft of rational means for ethical discrimination.

The attention devoted to happiness in *Pride and Prejudice* does not stop with characterization. Happiness itself has distinctive social and political ramifications which the novel carefully develops. First of all, in keeping with the liberal tradition of moral philosophy to which *Pride and Prejudice* is affiliated, happiness is something many of the characters feel they have a basic right to. Darcy's central fault, after all, is to have been careless about pleasing other people, to have had what Elizabeth stingingly terms "a selfish disdain of the feelings of others" (PP 193), and Lady Catherine and he both are judged wanting precisely because their own pride renders them incapable of regarding the happiness of their inferiors. In ways which illuminate Austen's agenda in *Pride and Prejudice*, Johnson, himself touchy about this subject, reproves the overbearing disdain with which the high and mighty can torment their inferiors:

> Some, indeed, there are, for whom the excuse of ignorance or negligence cannot be alledged, because it is apparent that they are not only careless of pleasing, but studious to offend; that they contrive to make all approaches to them difficult and vexatious, and imagine that they aggrandize themselves by wasting the time of others in useless attendance, by mortifying them with slights, and teazing them with affronts.
>
> Men of this kind, are generally to be found among those that have not mingled much in general conversation, but spent their lives amidst the obsequiousness of dependants, and the flattery of parasites; and by long consulting only their own inclination, have forgotten that others have a claim to the same deference.
>
> Tyranny thus avowed, is indeed an exuberance of pride. (*Rambler* 56)

Lady Catherine, as Collins assures Elizabeth, "likes to have the distinction of rank preserved" (PP 161). Rather than make others feel at ease, she patronizes Elizabeth so superciliously that even Darcy looks "a little ashamed of his aunt's ill breeding" (PP 173). But Elizabeth also takes him to task for a carelessness of pleasing, and when he lamely pleads shyness with strangers, she taxes him with the same ugly failure of civility Johnson describes: "Shall we ask him [Darcy] why a man of sense and education, and who has lived in the world, is ill qualified to recommend himself to strangers?" (PP 175). Fitzwilliam, who happily does possess "the readiness and ease of a well-bred man" (PP 171), answers in Darcy's stead: "It is because he will not give himself the trouble" (PP 175). Just as Lady Catherine takes every "occasion of dictating to others" (PP 163), Darcy too, as Elizabeth puts it, enjoys "the power of doing what he likes" (PP 183), without troubling himself with the consideration that others have what Johnson calls "the same claim to deference."

Nowhere is Darcy's failure of deference to others clearer than in his proposal, bearing as it does an appalling resemblance to that of Collins. To Collins only one person is worthy of deference. Accordingly, he expects Elizabeth to be gratified to learn that he is proposing to her on Lady Catherine's advice that he choose "an active, useful sort of person, not brought up high, but able to make a small income go a good way" (PP 106). But as deferent as Collins is to Lady Catherine, his principle concern is with himself, and consequently he expresses no wish to contribute to Elizabeth's happiness but rather only a conviction that matrimony will add to his own. Even after he must accept the reality of Elizabeth's negative, Collins believes that a refusal of himself can derive only from a "defect of temper" on Elizabeth's part, rather than a failure to please on his own. Like Collins, Darcy also parades hollow gallantries that do not veil his assurance of immediate success and that tax Elizabeth with her unfavorable fortune and connections. So little is Darcy concerned for Elizabeth's happiness that he does not hesitate to inform her of the damage he is doing to his own self-consequence by proposing marriage to her in the first place, expressing his "sense of her inferiority—of its being a degradation—of the family obstacles which judgment had always opposed to inclination" (PP 189).

Considered with respect to the liberal ideas about personal happiness, Darcy's failures of politeness are quite momentous, and Johnson once again elucidates them with a morally fervent solicitude for the unempowered that shows us why progressive social critics liked him, his approval of subordination notwithstanding:

> Though all are not equally culpable with Trypherus, it is scarcely possible
> to find any man who does not frequently, like him, indulge his own pride

by forcing others into a comparison with himself, when he knows the advantage is on his side, without considering that unnecessarily to obtrude unpleasing ideas is a species of oppression; and that it is little more criminal to deprive another of some real advantage, than to interrupt that forgetfulness of its absence which is the next happiness to actual possession. (*Rambler* 98)

Although Johnson does not go so far as Hume in vindicating vanity, he employs politically charged language which describes the offensiveness of hauteur as just short of criminal, a theft of that self-approbation to which, he implies, we all have a right. Johnson's remarks can suggest how Elizabeth's initial pique with Darcy ought to be considered as more than "merely" injured vanity, an implicitly rearguard construction which places the problems squarely in Elizabeth's court. Elizabeth effortlessly concurs with Charlotte's opinion that Darcy "has a *right* to be proud," but she believes that she has a right to pride as well: "I could easily forgive *his* pride, if he had not mortified *mine*" (PP 20). Readers who contend that *Pride and Prejudice* is a didactic novel consistent with the orthodox morality expounded in sermons and conduct books typically observe here that Elizabeth is guilty of the "sin" of pride, either in her all-too-fallible private judgments or in her personal attractions, for both of these wounds to her self-esteem render her susceptible to Wickham's flattery.[16] Yet *Pride and Prejudice* invites us not to chide Elizabeth with threadbare morality about original sin, but on the contrary, if not actually to flatter people's pride as Wickham and Collins do, then at least to honor it. In Johnson's words, "unnecessarily to obtrude unpleasing ideas" onto people about themselves is almost criminally to take their happiness away. Defending the honesty of his proposal, Darcy insists that "reason" vindicates him in confronting Elizabeth with painful truths about her circumstances (PP 192), but to Johnson it is no excuse that "reason" may be on the side of the offender: "a thousand incivilities may be committed, and a thousand offices neglected, without any remorse of conscience, or reproach from reason" (*Rambler* 98).

Unless we acknowledge that Darcy's pride is a "criminal" assault on Elizabeth's happiness, we will not appreciate the profundity of his eventual transformation. Darcy himself later explains that Elizabeth taught him "how insufficient were all my pretensions to please a woman worthy of being pleased" (PP 369). The "most certain way of giving any man pleasure," as Johnson explains the economy of social pleasures, "is to persuade him that you receive pleasure from him" (*Rambler* 72), and this is precisely what Darcy cannot do when he still thinks "meanly of all the rest of the world" (PP 369) outside his family circle. Elizabeth can easily account for Colonel Fitzwilliam's visits at Hunsford: he "came because he had pleasure in their society, a persuasion which of course recommended him still more." But Darcy's visits remain a puzzle: they seem "the effect of necessity rather than of choice—a sacrifice to propriety, not a pleasure to himself" (PP 180). When Darcy improves his manners, however, he becomes "desirous to please" (PP 263) Elizabeth, and "determined, to be pleased" (PP 262) by her, and it is this finally which impresses her with grateful desire that their happiness depend upon each other. Austen's concern with good manners, then, has decidedly political underpinnings: to be guilty of hauteur is to deprive people of a pleasing sense of self-esteem that it is legitimate for them to have.

Because no one else can be happy for us, the pursuit of happiness privileges private judgment and invites a degree of autonomy of which more conservative novelists were suspicious. Although Elizabeth is merely articulating the principle which, as we have seen, actuates everyone's behavior in the novel, among Austen's contemporaries perhaps only declared radicals would have a sympathetic character defiantly aver as she does, "I am only resolved to act in that manner, which will, in my own opinion, constitute my happiness, without reference to *you*, or to any person so wholly unconnected with me" (PP 358). Admittedly, Austen does not push her luck, here or anywhere else in *Pride and Prejudice*. Elizabeth can say this and retain her credibility because we know that her happiness, unlike Lydia's, is not constituted by illicit sex. Further, she does not carry her determined autonomy so far as to rule out the wishes of people *not* so wholly unconnected with her, such as her parents. But whereas Hamilton, West, and More, for example, oppose the duty of filial obedience to the vagaries of private judgment, Austen, as critics have long recognized, typically removes her heroines from the parental abode altogether precisely in order to free them from this necessity and to oblige them to think and act for themselves. Except in *Mansfield Park*, Austen tends to skirt the whole issue of filial obedience. The conflict momentarily evoked when Elizabeth must decide whether forever to alienate her mother by refusing Collins or her father by accepting him is comically dissipated when Mrs. Bennet's rage dwindles into impotent peevishness. Elizabeth would presumably not defy concerted parental opposition, although everything we have seen of her mother's folly and her father's negligence plainly shows that they need their young daughter's advice more than she needs theirs. But if Elizabeth does not specifically rule out the possibility of consulting with her parents before acting in that manner which will, in her own opinion, constitute her happiness, her omission specifically to rule it in here as an obligation is just as striking.

If Austen tends to avoid considering how and when the independence she clearly values conflicts with those sensitive imperatives of duty as would apply between parent and child, her novels devote a lot of attention to coercion, bullying, and advice among friends, and all of these are problematic to an ethic championing personal choice and self-responsibility. Austen clearly highlights such issues when Elizabeth and Darcy debate the merits of adherence in a personal decision versus persuadability to a friend's opposing advice:

> "To yield readily—easily—to the *persuasion* of a friend," [Elizabeth observes,] "is no merit with you."
> "To yield without conviction is no compliment to the understanding of either." (PP 50)

Johnson had pointed out that giving advice is gratifying because of the "temporary appearance of superiority" (*Rambler* No. 87) it gives us, and conversely, receiving advice is typically painful because it "interrupts our enjoyment of our own approbation" (*Rambler* No. 40). Austen matches Johnson's awareness of how the love of power and claims of pride complicate the giving and receiving of counsel. Indeed, Bingley rather offends his friend when he impatiently divulges that, claims to persuade by conviction rather than by coercion to the contrary, what Darcy really likes is to box him around: "I assure you that if Darcy were not such a great tall fellow, in comparison with myself, I should not pay him half so much deference. I declare I do not know a more aweful object than Darcy, on particular occasions, and in particular places" (PP 50–51). As it happens, the ideal of enlightened counsel and freely reasoned assent is achieved notably *not* in his own relations, but rather in those of women. Mrs. Gardiner's offer and Elizabeth's acceptance of advice not to encourage Wickham, for example, is "a wonderful instance of advice being given on such a point, without being resented" (PP 145) because both persons here are equal and unreserved parties in a rational friendship, where domination plays no part.

Elizabeth has cause later to reproach Bingley for the sweet-tempered ductility she praises here. The same amiable disposition which conduces so to his happiness also jeopardizes that happiness. Elizabeth finds it hard to think "without anger, hardly without contempt, on that easiness of temper, that want of proper resolution which now made him the slave of his designing friends, and led him to sacrifice his own happiness to the caprice of their inclinations" (PP 133). Austen puts a high premium on self-responsibility and stability of purpose even with her female characters—many of whom have little truck with the deference and hesitancy dictated to them as sex- differentiated virtues. But for her male characters, dependence on the wishes or the purses of others, if sometimes exonerated as a necessity, is never admirable, as we have already seen in *Sense and*

Sensibility. Thus if the "fire and independence" (PP 121) evinced by Mr. Collins's abrupt shift from Jane to Elizabeth to Charlotte show, among other things, an unattractive confidence that the ladies are standing in line for him, Bingley's converse readiness to doubt his judgment and to withdraw a suit so essential to his happiness shows, as Elizabeth's politically potent metaphor suggests, a slavish failure to live by the principles of dignity and self-respect Elizabeth herself formulates to Lady Catherine. *Pride and Prejudice* backs off somewhat from the subversive potential of its material here. Bingley recovers from these heavy charges: what looks at first like a feeble surrender of self-direction into "the custody" of stronger friends later looks more like plausible modesty; Darcy's officious interference looks more like friendly, even sensible, advice. And Bingley's easy temper works out for the best after all: the reformed Darcy turns him towards Jane once again just as sure-handedly as he had earlier turned him away. But even though Elizabeth no longer has grounds to resent Bingley's readiness to let Darcy "determine and direct in what manner" he "was to be happy" (PP 186), she still observes that he is more compliant to Darcy's judgments than assertive of his own. Unwilling to rile her prospective husband too much too soon with corrective ridicule, Elizabeth remarks ironically to herself that "Mr. Bingley had been a most delightful friend; so easily guided that his worth was invaluable" (PP 371).

As we have seen, Austen's valorization of self-responsibility causes her to be somewhat evasive on the score of parental authority, and highly qualified even about the appropriateness of friendly advice. But concerning the meddlesomeness of social superiors she is fairly clear. Elizabeth believes, and Darcy himself later bears her out, that Lady Catherine has "certainly no right" (PP 357) to interfere in Elizabeth's decisions. But in demanding that Elizabeth forswear Darcy and keep to the "sphere" in which she was brought up, "this great lady" is exercising what she believes to be her authority to dictate to others, just as she takes it upon herself to settle differences among her cottagers and "scold them into harmony and plenty" even though she is not in "the commission of the peace for the county" (PP 169). Lady Catherine appears to consider it a matter of public importance that ancient families such as hers not be sacrificed to the "upstart pretensions of a young woman without family, connections, or fortune" (PP 356). Moreover, to her mind the interests of great families and the imperatives of morality itself are one and the same. As a result, Elizabeth's refusal to recognize the legitimacy of her application seems like a headstrong repudiation of "the claims of duty, honour, and gratitude" (PP 358). Lady Catherine's argument would have been familiar to any reader of Hays's, Inchbald's, or Smith's novels. In Smith's *The Young Philosopher*, for example, Mrs. Crewkhearne similarly contends that it is a matter of national importance that her noble nephew not degrade his family by forming a low connection, and her position is avidly seconded by toadies, particularly by a doltish clergyman who advances his own worldly position by catering in this manner to the "prejudices" of his well-born patrons.[17]

Austen's simultaneously bold and delicate handling of the confrontation between Elizabeth and Lady Catherine typifies her entire relationship to the novelistic tradition of social criticism under discussion here. The treatment is decisively progressive because Elizabeth does not consider the interests of the ruling class to be morally binding upon her: "Neither duty, nor honour, nor gratitude," Elizabeth holds, "have any possible claim on me, in the present instance. No principle of either, would be violated by my marriage with Mr. Darcy" (PP 358). Defending her love of laughter from charges of cynicism, Elizabeth proclaims, "I hope I never ridicule what is wise or good" (PP 57), and this promise of principled restraint differentiates Elizabeth's laughter from Lydia's animal glee. But at a time when Hannah More, among others, was writing conduct books for the middle classes and tracts for the lower, enjoining both not to question the wisdom of Providence in placing them in humbler spheres, Elizabeth's disclaimer is not quite as innocuous as it may appear, for the point of contention is exactly what or who *is* "wise or good," and Elizabeth appears not to doubt her own qualifications to decide for herself, and has no trouble censuring a Lady's officious airs or ridiculing a pompous patrician with his failure to behave like a gentleman. As far as Elizabeth is concerned, "extraordinary talents or miraculous virtue" will always command her respect, but the "mere stateliness of money and rank" (PP 161) will not awe her. Convinced that they occupied high ground, progressive novelists seize on the same kinds of distinctions and exploit them for all they are worth, contending, more systematically and more conspicuously of course, that the defenders of money and rank marshal speciously ethical artillery—such as Lady Catherine's "duty," "honour," and "gratitude"—in order to sustain their hegemony, and that it is only by force of "prejudice" that we are either bullied or duped into equating our moral imperatives with their interests.

Although this much is clearly true, the conflict between Elizabeth and Lady Catherine nevertheless remains exceedingly discreet in that even as it demarcates this politically volatile issue, it circumnavigates it at the same time. Austen dramatizes social prejudice, and her revised title highlights that buzzword. But people lower on the social scale can be prejudiced too, and the disputants themselves stand well back from polemical jargon. *Pride and Prejudice* thus alternately verges on and recoils from radical criticism: Lady Catherine is not quite so extreme as to claim outright that the well-being of the kingdom depends on the purity of her family line. And for her part, Elizabeth claims not that she has the right to quit the "sphere" of her birth, but rather that in marrying Darcy, she would be staying within that sphere: "He is a gentleman; I am a gentleman's daughter; so far we are equal" (PP 356). To the extent that this assertion of equality demystifies the great gentry, it serves reformist ends, for it deprives men like Darcy of any rationale for their pride. But in the meantime, it leaves the social structure radicals had assailed substantially intact. Elizabeth, after all, changes her mind about Darcy when she realizes how conscientiously he tends to the happiness of those in his charge as a good master, landlord, and brother: "How many people's happiness were in his guardianship!—How much of pleasure or pain it was in his power to bestow" (PP 250–51).

The challenge Elizabeth poses to the power of rank and wealth is further diminished when we consider Lady Catherine's sex as well as her utter ridiculousness. Unlike Mrs. Smith in *Sense and Sensibility* and Lady Russell in *Persuasion*, who both figure as alternatives to male authority, women such as Lady Catherine and Mrs. Ferrars are parodies of male authority. As such, although they defend and collude in the interests of the patriarchal family, they themselves obviously are not the most formidable embodiments of it. Because these surrogates are easier to assail than, say, fathers and uncles, they make it possible to show what is oppressive about the power of rank and wealth, and what is overbearing about their assumptions of superiority. Further, they also make it possible to represent rebellion against the claims of familial authority, because in Austen's novels, at least, female authority figures are invariably defied by their young male relations. Though they may hold some purse strings, they hold virtually no moral sway. Because they cannot enforce obedience, their imperiousness is risible. This need not have been so. Austen could have endowed Lady Catherine with some of the daunting majesty Burney extends to Mrs. Delvile in *Cecilia*, for example, a figure who for similar reasons makes similar appeals to the heroine's honor and gratitude, but who does command the respect and voluntary obedience of both her son and Cecilia. But far from being dignified, Lady Catherine is in her own way every bit as ludicrous as Mrs. Bennet. If Austen's use of a weak and ridiculous female authority figure makes it possible to dramatize effectual resistance, it is at the cost of minimizing the extent and perhaps even obscuring the object of that resistance. Quite simply, it is left unclear whether all attempts on the part of the high and mighty to meddle in the autonomous choices of others are to be deemed insufferable, or whether it is merely that Lady Catherine's attempts to wield power are incompetent, inappropriate and eccentric.

Elizabeth's and Darcy's defiance of Lady Catherine exemplifies the balancing act everywhere in evidence in *Pride and Prejudice* and indicates the advantages as well as the limitations of complying, even critically, with conservative myths about the gentry as Austen does in this novel. The figure of Lady Catherine invites as well as dispels a critique of authority, for she receives all of the opprobrium we are never permitted to aim directly at Darcy or his parents, or at great gentry families in general. Though Darcy assures Elizabeth that his parents were "good themselves (my father particularly . . .)" [PP 369], they evidently share the same sentiments which prompt Lady Catherine to assert her authority on their behalf: solicitude for the "shades of Pemberley" (PP 357) demands it. Conflict with the aunt thus averts a more politically potent and sentimentally complicated conflict with parents. Here, the family is spared a frontal attack. We have to read closely in order to discover that Darcy's own parents taught him to "care for none beyond my own family circle, to think meanly of all the rest of the world" (PP 369), and by the time we learn this, it does not matter any more, for they are deceased, and Darcy is too touched by filial piety to dishonor their memories. But even though the "shades of Pemberley" are finally "polluted" by Elizabeth, her middle-class relations, a steward's rascally son, and the barely respectable Lydia, the majesty of Pemberley itself is still affirmed, and any suspicion on our part that it may have been been tarnished is soon set to rest by our confidence that the now properly proud Darcy would never permit any real compromise of its integrity. Austen thus disclaims and exploits mythology about the gentry that counterrevolutionary writers employ. The insolence of rank and power has been chastized, but never radically enough to make us doubt their prestige or wonder whether it really would be "something" after all, as Elizabeth says, "to be mistress of Pemberley" (PP 245). The same worldly advantages that have not been allowed to bully Elizabeth into respect have still been allowed to exalt her in the end.

Austen's attempt to reform gentry myths in *Pride and Prejudice* entailed consenting to most of their basic outlines. The resulting tension is just as conspicuous in her treatment of marriage and family as it is in her treatment of class relations. To most readers, Austen's allegiance to conservative social values is proven by the inevitability of marriage in her novels, for it is marriage that at all times confirms and reproduces established social arrangements, and marriage that, at this particular time, was seen as the best possible arrangement in an imperfect world and, moreover, the sole arrangement by which we can nurture precious moral affections. On some counts, as we have already seen, Austen clearly parts company with the conservative apologists of her own time. Family affections are so far from being considered sufficient or essential to the development of rectitude here, any more than in *Sense and Sensibility*, that Darcy cannot be an acceptable husband until his moral imagination has been broadened enough to respect the dignity of those outside his "family circle." Furthermore, the wish to subordinate unruly individual passions to prescribed social duties prompts conservative novelists such as Hamilton and West to minimize and even dismiss the importance of love as a precondition of marriage. Austen, on the other hand, puts a premium on it. Not without a touch of self-mockery which seems to imply an awareness that she is the heroine of an extraordinary novel, Elizabeth boasts that the marriage of Darcy and herself can "teach the admiring multitude what connubial felicity really was" (PP 312). At least one reason why she is right is that unlike Charlotte's marriage to Collins, her marriage, as well as Jane's, promises "rational happiness" as well as "worldly prosperity" (PP 307).

But there is more. Unlike Jane's marriage to Bingley, Elizabeth's relationship with Darcy resonates with a physical passion the milder couple lacks. The rapport between these two from start to finish is intimate, even racy. Even as he disapproves, Darcy, for example, admires "the brilliancy which [Elizabeth's] exercise had given to her complexion" (PP 33). Furthermore, their exchanges are marked either by playful invitations to aggression—Elizabeth's semiearnest "Despise me if you dare" (PP 52), and Darcy's gallant "I am not afraid of you" (PP 174)—or by mutual accusations, the eventual acrimoniousness of which both proves and advances their intense intimacy: their arguments about personal motives or family embarrassments leave them more and more exposed to each other, and as a result more and more implicated in each other's trust. The fact that Darcy and Elizabeth form and pursue most of their relationship in secret and alone not only electrifies this intimacy, but also pushes it to the verge of an impropriety unique in Austen's fiction. As a rule, Austen's lovers must contrive excuses for their tête-à-têtes: Henry Tilney's dissembled wish to visit the Allens wins Catherine and himself a walk alone together; when Wentworth and Anne Elliot find themselves at an evening assembly together, they can only review their emotionally fraught history in a series of joyful but "short meetings" during which both pretend to be "occupied in admiring a fine display of green-house plants" (P 246). Often described with an attention to physical details which conservative novelists omit and with an indifference to the rules about proper parental guidance and the public supervision they recommend, the relationship between Elizabeth and Darcy, as Donald Greene has memorably written, is sure to comprehend more than the sober and cooperative companionship conservative novelists approved.[18] Austen's implicit approval of erotic love, here and elsewhere in her fiction, suggests how she endorses the "affective individualism" that anti-Jacobin novelists were trying to quell.[19]

These departures from orthodox injunctions about marriage aside, marriage is still the only destiny for women that Austen ever dramatizes at any length. True, marriage seems at times to be the way an author ends her novel, not the way she represents what could or recommends what should happen in life. In *Northanger Abbey*, for example, Austen's eleventh-hour fabrication ex nihilo of a husband for Eleanor Tilney is a self-conscious repudiation of the verisimilitude of her own ending, as well as a swipe at gothic procedure. Austen's acute interest in probing and manipulating the conventional import of fiction, announced as early as the juvenilia, should make us chary about inferring that the marriages concluding her novels constitute an unequivocal ideological statement about marriage itself, considered either as a goal for women, or as a boon to society. But even if marriage in Austen's novels is not always described realistically as a woman's purpose in life, nothing else is, and because *Pride and Prejudice*, unlike all of the other novels, actually celebrates marital felicity as an ideal, it has been particularly vulnerable to cogent feminist critiques. Unlike Edgeworth, Burney, and West, for example, Austen does not extensively consider female friendship as an important alternative or even supplement to the marital relationship, and considering her own circumstances as well as the accessibility of fictional alternatives, this omission has seemed like either a failure of nerve, or—worse perhaps—a failure of imagination.[20] When Elizabeth, for example, is trying to negotiate a tea-table tête-à-tête with Darcy, someone described only generically as "one of the girls" interposes herself with an untoward assertion of female solidarity: "The men shan't come and part us, I am determined. We want none of them; do we?" (PP 341). But indeed we do want "them" to come and part "us," and the success of this passage depends on our agreeing that it is folly to suppose that female bonding can or should displace men in the minds of sensible women.

Although Austen cannot completely recuperate from such criticism, some of its sting must be softened. *Pride and Prejudice* does subscribe at least partially to myths about the glamour of social status and the fulfillment ideally offered by marriage, all of which progressive novelists had challenged, but only so that it can proceed to modify and repossess them from within. One of the most important reasons Elizabeth's marriage to Darcy is so wholly satisfying is that it requires no sacrifice of the two friendships Elizabeth has actually placed before Darcy all along. When he first proposes, he does not dream that Elizabeth's loyalty to her disappointed sister could possibly prevent Elizabeth from jumping gratefully at the chance to marry him, and to his immense mortification, he is mistaken: "Do you think that any consideration," Elizabeth retorts, with a mixture of indignation and incredulity, "would tempt me to accept the man, who has been the means of ruining, perhaps for ever, the happiness of a most beloved sister?" (PP 190). Darcy later makes himself desirable by righting the wrong done to Jane, thereby fostering rather than curtailing Elizabeth's attachment to her. Similarly, during her first survey of Pemberley, Elizabeth is saved "from something like regret" (PP 246) by recollecting that her uncle and aunt, a particular friend, would not be welcome there, and when the chastened Darcy does meet them, he is visibly surprised and relieved to perceive that they would be acceptable guests and relations after all.

While much eighteenth-century fiction, as Janet Todd has demonstrated, ridicules women for sacrificing the purities of disinterested friendship to the treacheries of husband hunting, Austen's novels do not in my view join the chorus. They do not present female community as an "oppressive blank" to be dispersed only by the relieving "solidity of marriage." Nor do they suggest that the marital relationship ought to take precedence over rational friendship or the dictates of self-respect.[21] Marriage is an unquestioned necessity in Austen's novels, but it is never the first or only necessity, and the women, as well as the men, who pursue it as though it were never enjoy the full benefits of authorial approval, even if they are spared the burden of specific censure. Elizabeth Bennet is not any less haunted than Charlotte Lucas is by the spectre of poverty, and she wins our respect by refusing unsuitable proposals anyway, fully conscious that, as Mr. Collins does not scruple to assert in the recommendation of his own suit, "it is by no means certain that another offer of marriage may ever be made" (PP 108) to her. Pride and Prejudice is a work of wish fulfillment precisely because it does not bring Elizabeth's refusal to put marriage first to the test: it happily averts a showdown between survival and self-respect, or love and friendship, for the two principal marriages at the end settle potentially competing claims without conflict or sacrifice. Like Sense and Sensibility, Pride and Prejudice widens the family circle beyond the narrow boundaries to which counterrevolutionary writers had implicitly or explicitly confined it. Its conclusion preserves the heroines' friendships and promises the mutual regard of husbands and relations. The band of good friends is all related by marriage in the end, but they are not good friends because they are related—as conservative apologists would have it—rather they are good relations because they were good friends first.

The celebrated balance of Pride and Prejudice is less a triumph of conviction than a provisional experiment, an effort to work through established forms—a conservative enterprise, after all—in order to transform them into the purveyors of ecstatic personal happiness. But although Austen would work through received forms throughout her entire career, we will certainly misrepresent her accomplishment if we posit this singular novel as the typical one against which the others are to be judged, for in no other novel, not even in *Emma*, would Austen allow us to believe that structures of authority could be assailed without irreparably tarnishing their luster. The aura of hyperbole permitted to glamorize Darcy is so powerful that we typically extend it to all of Austen's novels. But Austen's next novel would immediately retrench and strip institutions of the obfuscating and seductive myths with which conservative apologists had invested them. Mr. Rushworth is richer than Darcy by far, and yet he is never more than a booby squire, oddly deserving the disgrace of cuckoldry to which he is treated in the end. In *Pride and Prejudice* patricians may be laughed at, and even brought low, but that is only to purge them from the insolence that makes them oppressive, not the dignity that makes them desirable. In *Pride and Prejudice* alone Austen consents to conservative myths, but only in order to possess them and to ameliorate them from within, so that the institutions they vindicate can bring about, rather than inhibit, the expansion and the fulfillment of happiness.

CHAPTER FIVE

MANSFIELD PARK: CONFUSIONS OF GUILT
AND REVOLUTIONS OF MIND

Critics of *Mansfield Park* have been at once the most naive and the most ambitious, sometimes retreating to the homey comforts of biographical fallacy, and at other times soaring into the specious grandeur of "zeitgeist" criticism. The former generally contend, with high displeasure, that in *Mansfield Park* Austen turned her back on the health and high spirits of her previous novel and gave her blessing instead to a heroine beleaguered, retiring, and militantly dour. For years, the sobriety of *Mansfield Park* prompted the question, "What's wrong with Jane Austen?"[1] This disturbing and essentially Janeite formulation not only suggests that Austen's earlier work is superior because it is frothy; it also implies that her responsibility is to delight us by creating a heroine we would all like to marry, and that a "failure" to have done so reflects a personal crisis, a conversion to evangelicism, a refusal of marriage, a bitter accession to middle age. But Austen's undertaking in *Mansfield Park* was nothing if not lucid and premeditated: "Now I will try and write something else, & it shall be a complete change of subject—ordination" (*Letters*, 29 January 1813). Of course the extent to which the novel Austen completed can or even should be described in the terms she intended for it at the outset has been extensively debated, but her confident and self-consciously experimental approach to its composition is unequivocal. Austen did not want to write another "rather too light, and bright, and sparkling" novel.

While Janeites confessed and unconfessed have lamented the ungratifying humorlessness of *Mansfield Park*, watchdogs of seriousness have preferred it precisely because it does not resemble a frivolous silver-fork novel. In fact, the momentousness of the novel has been gauged in direct proportion to the incapacity of it and its little heroine to delight us. As one critic has aptly put it, "once a heroine is divested of her power to please, she is granted an import beyond her apparently modest sphere. . . . Elizabeth and Emma live for readers as personal presences, but never as the Romantic, the Victorian, or the Modern *Zeitgeist*. Failing to charm, Fanny is allowed in compensation to embody worlds."[2]

Of course there is something to be gained by viewing *Mansfield Park* as the heavy of Austen's canon. It is the first novel belonging exclusively to her adulthood, and in the density of its texture and the surpassing complexity of its detail it openly discloses its ambition. But there is something to be lost as well. If *Mansfield Park* has met with approval because it is more than a ladies' novel, the price has been the neutering of many of its most pressing issues. To Lionel Trilling, for example, grasping the "innerness" and "largeness of import" in Austen's novels meant suppressing their distinctive emphasis on female experience. Accordingly he praises Richard Simpson for claiming that Austen's concern "does not reach its limit at particular female destinies but extends to an object no less general than 'man,' to man in society and to the complex process of his self-realization through society."[3] When Trilling deploys Rousseau to elucidate Austen's ostensible critique of acting, he first does not notice how Rousseau's own attack dwells with particular indignation on the subject of female actresses, and he next ignores how Sir Thomas's anticipated objections are restricted specifically to young ladies in his care, young ladies who must not compromise their modesty by calling attention to themselves.[4] Edmund considers the prospect of women acting so unthinkable that he simply assumes that male actors will be enlisted to act in their stead: "But what do you do for women?" (MP 139). When the theatrical goes forward despite bickering, Edmund criticizes not the subversiveness of the histrionic impulse in general, but the impropriety of female exhibitionism in particular—the unashamed display of their speech, their persons, their talent, and the dangerous intimacies all these encourage: "My father wished us, as school-boys, to speak well, but he would never wish his grown up daughters to be acting plays. His sense of decorum is strict" (MP 127). Similarly, when Trilling recurs to T. E. Hulme's thoughts on the relationship of the "divine" to the "anti-vital" in order to account for Fanny's virtuous debility—she "cannot cut a basket of roses without fatigue and headache"—he universalizes, that is degenders, Austen's analysis of manners, and consequently misses an entrée to her social criticism.[5] Turn-of-the-century female conduct books copiously demonstrate that the extreme physical delicacy which Trilling considers so distressing and so striking in Fanny is the most conventionally feminine thing about her. Far from being considered a feature of Christian virtue in general, which all mankind, including Sir Thomas and Edmund, should cultivate, it is a quality exclusively recommended to daughters of good families.

To insist on the importance of such distinctions is not to engage in irritably partisan quibbles. For conservatives especially, it was a given that gender is a constitutive element of political life. The orderliness of the world cherished by Sir Thomas and Fanny is closely linked to imperatives of female propriety. Like *Pride and Prejudice*, *Mansfield Park* tests the parameters of conservative mythology about the august gentry family. But if in the former Austen shows herself willing to transform that mythology into its best, in the latter she exposes not only the hollowness but also the unwholesomeness of its moral pretensions. The language of disease permeates *Mansfield Park*, and the problem is not with perniciously "new" people like the Crawfords—these citified siblings are stock figures—the problem is within the great house itself.[6] Austen accomplishes her critique of the gentry family by registering its impact on a heroine who, though a model of female virtue and filial gratitude, is betrayed by the same ethos she dutifully embraces. If there is something anomalous about this work, it is not its political position or its moral and religious orientation. What is unusual instead is its exploration of the viewpoint of a heroine ideologically and emotionally identified with the benighted figures who coerce and mislead her. This painful and richly problematic identification makes *Mansfield Park* Austen's most, rather than her least, ironic novel and a bitter parody of conservative fiction.

Although not begun until early in 1811, *Mansfield Park* is animated by the preoccupations of the 1790s. On the face of it, *Mansfield Park* looks even more than *Pride and Prejudice* like the flower of conservative mythology. Sir Thomas seems to perform the duties proper to a father of his station with scrupulous decorum. He is ponderous, it is true, but not unbecomingly so. Whether adopting poor relations, repairing the family's flagging fortunes, or pontificating about the moral necessity of single incumbencies, Sir Thomas always minds his dignity. In his musings about his daughters, he thinks exactly as he ought, to use the phrase so important to him: "His daughters he felt, while they retained the name of Bertram, must be giving it new grace, and in quitting it he trusted would extend its respectable alliances" (MP 20). Such, of course, are the classic aspirations of the father of a good family: he strives to adorn his name by cultivating everyone attached to it, and to extend his benevolence outwards through marriage until the neighborhood and eventually the nation itself become a web of amiable relations, stable and loyal because wrought from the fabric of familial affections. But just as notable as Austen's effort to establish the stereotypical outlines of Sir Thomas's character is her tendency simultaneously to sully his probity with deadpan insouciance. The instances of paternal rectitude cited above, for example, are each tainted: Fanny is charitably admitted to Mansfield, but only on Sir Thomas's specific condition that she be made always to remember she is not "a *Miss Bertram*" (MP 10, emphasis Sir Thomas's); the family fortunes he rescues depend on slave labor in the West Indies; he approves

Edmund's ordination during an uncanonical season and later procures for him a multiple incumbency of the very sort he had earlier disparaged.[7]

Austen's enterprise in *Mansfield Park* is to turn conservative myth sour, as she surely need not have done were her allegiances to the world of the country house as assured as is generally argued. This effort is evidenced, not simply in the inobtrusive profusion of ironic details, but also in the central and most conspicuous donnée of the novel, the characterization of the family at Mansfield Park. From the first pages on, Austen is at pains to employ the Burkean vocabulary of the political sublime in order to describe the sexually differentiated dynamics of the Bertram household.[8] Everything from Sir Thomas's arched brow to his inflated diction marks him as a figurehead for the sublime. The sway this redoubtable patriarch is supposed to hold over his children is commensurate with his ability to awe them, to strike them with terror lest they offend. If we were to judge his children solely by their sensations upon his return from Antigua, this model might appear accurate. The exceptionally timorous Fanny almost faints with terror as her "former habitual dread of her uncle was return-ing," but the brassier Bertram children, not less affrighted, share her "excessive trembling" and "fearful thoughts" (MP 176). They too are seized with "absolute horror" (MP 176), and a "terrible pause" (MP 175) ensues as they listen for his footsteps.

But the conservative description of paternal authority invoked here and throughout the novel remarkably fails. Sir Thomas's gravity operates only as an external check, not as an internal inhibition, upon the behavior of his children. He quiets but he does not quell lawlessness; his children tremble at the detection, rather than the commission, of wrongs. Their sneakiness is quite successful. One of the first things we learn about Sir Thomas, after all, is that he is in the dark about his daughters' disposi-tions, and that his own forbidding airs have made this so: "Sir Thomas did not know what was wanting, because, though a truly anxious father, he was not outwardly affectionate, and the reserve of his manner re-pressed all the flow of their spirits before him" (MP 19). The dutifulness Sir Thomas assumes he has secured by his paternal sublimity is thus his own delusion. His dignity is undercut by the ignorance it gives rise to and further diminished by the pity it inspires in the perceptive but pow-erless Fanny.[9]

Austen's scepticism also extends to the beautiful, that is to say, the feminine. As soon as she comes to Mansfield, Fanny observes that Lady Bertram "by the mere aid of a good-humoured smile, became immedi-ately the less awful character of the two" parental figures (MP 12). Fan-ny's perception rehearses debates about the aesthetic properties of sexual difference that had already been recognized to serve political agendas, for while the sublime arouses passions of dread and respect, the beautiful softens and endears. Although many political allies and opponents alike objected to Burke's gallant taste for helplessly distressed females, Wollstonecraft was the first to attack the link between Burke's aesthetic and political preferences for women. Before her *Vindication of the Rights of Woman*, Wollstonecraft assailed Burke's *Reflections* along with his *Enquiry* for holding that "*littleness* and *weakness* are the very essence of beauty" in women, and thus encouraging in them a helpless enervation that unfits them for the exertions of moral agency. The homage Burke would have men feel towards women of delicacy, Wollstonecraft sneers, "makes those beings vain inconsiderate dolls, who ought to be prudent mothers and useful members of society."[10] Austen's treatment of the vitiating tendencies of female manners follows along the same lines, for in Lady Bertram's case female delicacy becomes pampered somnambulance. Being beautiful—a "vain inconsiderate doll," as the severer Wollstonecraft would put it—engrosses her wholly: "To the education of her daughters, Lady Bertram paid not the smallest attention. She had not time for such cares. She was a woman who spent her days in sitting nicely dressed on a sofa" (MP 19).

The feminine vulnerability approved by Burke and denounced by Wollstonecraft does not by any means promote simple subjection. Indeed, it is quite empowering in its own way, provided that we, unlike the "cruel ruffians" assaulting Marie Antoinette's bedchamber, continue to cherish chivalrous opinions about women and refuse to believe "a queen is but a woman; a woman is but an animal, and an animal not of the highest order."[11] Under these circumstances, female weakness promotes amiable and civilizing sentiments of protectiveness. Beauty thus enforces submission and inhibits unruliness, not by any unseemly assertion of imperiousness—such would trespass on the manly domain of the sublime and excite discordant passions of dread—but rather by arousing a melting solicitude.[12] Without her husband, Lady Bertram is, as Mrs. Grant puts it, a "cipher" (MP 162), and she is as content to be "guided in every thing important by Sir Thomas" (MP 20) as he is to guide her. Though Sir Thomas is irked to note that while he is away his wife will not be "quite equal to supply his place . . . or rather to perform what should have been her own" (MP 32), he nowhere objects to the delicacy and dependence that make up part of her attraction to begin with or wishes her to be more able. As it is, Lady Bertram's duties are transferred to the busy functionary, Mrs. Norris, who inspires neither pity nor terror, and whose very activity is finally denounced as perversely encroaching.

In Austen's hands, of course, the beautiful does not work the way it is supposed to any more than the sublime does. Lady Bertram's serene vacuity renders chivalrous solicitude unnecessary. Far from embodying a nicety her children tremble to offend, she is so oblivious to their affairs that they carry on under her very nose. Instead of being alarmed with womanly fears for her husband's safety during his voyage, Lady Bertram is blissfully unaware that Sir Thomas is imperiled at all. The indulgent concern that Tom pretends to feel on her behalf during Sir Thomas's absence is only a ploy to justify his darling project, *Lover's Vows*. Rather than fidget in wakeful anxiety, Lady Bertram sinks "back in one corner of the sofa, the picture of health, wealth, ease, and tranquillity," falling every so often "into a gentle doze" (MP 126). Clearly, the Burkean models of parental authority go awry in *Mansfield Park*. Dread of the potent father and fond concern for the delicate mother are just as likely to conceal or promote wrongdoing as they are to foster the capacity for generous feeling which in Austen's novels is possessed only by moral people.

Conservative apologists pitched their flag on the claim that the patriarchal family nurtured moral sentiments, and that the same affections that make us dutiful children and feeling siblings make us obedient subjects and responsible members of our neighborhoods. But in *Mansfield Park*, confidence in the moral tendencies, not simply of parental figures in particular, but of the family in general, is woefully misplaced. *Mansfield Park* is set in motion when the thoughtless extravagance of an eldest son drives his entire family into debt. Sir Thomas, a sometime man of feeling, scolds his heir with every expectation that he will be susceptible to sentimental arguments: " 'I blush for you, Tom,' said he, in his most dignified manner; 'I blush for the expedient which I am driven on, and I trust I may pity your feelings as a brother on the occasion. You have robbed Edmund for ten, twenty, thirty years, perhaps for life, of more than half the income which ought to be his' " (MP 23). But good Sir Thomas blushes in vain. A tender regard for familial dependents evidently does not come with the heir's territory. In fact, "with all the liberal dispositions of an eldest son, who feels born only for expense and enjoyment," Tom never musters much in the way of magnanimity towards any one beyond giving Fanny "some very pretty presents" and laughing at her, acts of "kindness" which are "consistent with his situation and rights" (MP 17–18).

Such discrepancies between the pretenses and the substance of conservative myth remind us that *Mansfield Park* is no less a parody, though much less a comedy, than *Northanger Abbey*, and that fissures in social and political discourse can be examined as methodically as those in the discourse of gothic fiction. By questioning the moral efficacy Burkeans attach to familial figures, *Mansfield Park* engages in progressive, though muted, social criticism.[13] In some of the most famous purple patches of the *Reflections*, Burke hailed chivalric respect for the sacredness of paternal authority and patriarchal family relations as the "decent drapery of life," tailored through the ages to cover our "naked shivering natures" —not as fixed and immutable truths, but rather as "pleasing illusions" and "superadded ideas" which serve our wishes for dignity and raise us in our own esteem.[14] Burke's attack on the demystification of authority structures in France, like his defense of prejudice, was often adopted in women's fiction of the period, and sometimes in novels Austen certainly knew, such as Edgeworth's *Belinda* and Brunton's *Self-Control*. Where the process of demystification appears in Austen's fiction, by contrast, it is generally infused with a positive charge. Even though *Pride and Prejudice* spares Darcy's position from demystifying satire, Darcy and Elizabeth themselves angrily tear off "pleasing illusions" about each other, and this measured but satiric stripping is essentially educative. Mr. Knightley's success as a character depends on the fact that, despite the chivalric provenance of his name, he is continually presented as a plainspoken man (another mystification in itself, certainly), who gets vexed, who flushes as he buttons his gaiters, and who never does learn the worst about the woman he marries.

More than any other novel by Austen, *Mansfield Park* is a work of demystification, and here that process is conceived, not in Burkean fashion as a brutal assault upon a naked queen, and with that a challenge to the power of the king, but rather as an inquiry into the moral wardrobe of the venerable father himself. Invariably careful to say the right thing, the authority figures at Mansfield Park all don the drapery of decency. But authorially underscored differences between profession and deed invite us to consider whether their drapery is not more indecent than that which it purports to obviate by concealing. The to-do over the staging of *Lovers' Vows* should call our attention to more than the disorderly passions of the young people at Mansfield. Their enactments of illicit or improper desire are actually among the least deceptive instances of acting in the novel, for every major character is acting all the time. Lady Bertram's acts are perhaps the least offensive, deriving as they do from innocent vacuity rather than deceit. If she has nothing to conceal, she does not exactly have anything to show either, even when she feels she should. Her letters on the "dangerous illness of her eldest son" (MP 426), for example, are a "medley of trusts, hopes, and fears . . . a sort of playing at being frightened" (MP 427). The "playing" of the others, however, is marked by a greater degree of subterfuge, consisting not of a ludic engagement of impulses or energies, but rather of a more strategic production of obfuscating displays, designed as much for themselves as for others. Mrs. Norris plays the self-sacrificing sister and aunt, Maria and Julia the parts of proper young ladies, and Edmund the highminded priest, ever vigilant if not ever successful in maintaining what Fanny calls his "moral elevation" (MP 158). However spontaneously thoughtless he may appear, even Tom himself does not hesitate to play up the role assigned to him. Displeased with Edmund's insubordinate objection that acting will ruin their sisters' reputations, Tom maintains that the womenfolk are not a younger brother's business: "I'll take care that his [Sir Thomas's] daughters do nothing to distress him. Manage your own concerns, Edmund, and I'll take care of the rest of the family" (MP 127). To the extent that Tom's remark is consistent with his "situation and rights," it is a legitimate assertion of his prerogative. But insofar as it is belied by Tom's manifest obliviousness to his family's concerns and his sisters' good names, it is yet another instance of the double-talk characters in *Mansfield Park* employ when they wish to invest their self-will in the sanctity of social form.

Sir Thomas is the most assiduous of actors at Mansfield Park, and his shows are designed to satisfy himself as well as others of his paternal judiciousness. Like Tom, of course, Sir Thomas is committed to "taking care of the family," and this primarily entails looking after the womenfolk. Sir Thomas plainly perceives that Maria despises Rushworth. But his offer to call off a marriage "so unquestionably advantageous," one which moreover would form a "connection exactly of the right sort; in the same county, and the same interest" (MP 40), is halfhearted at best and disingenuous at worst. Sir Thomas stops well short of the candor that could have brought Maria to think twice. As we learn in formulations that slowly unfold his bad faith, he is too "satisfied" with her perfunctory avowal of esteem for Rushworth, "too glad to be satisfied perhaps to urge the matter quite so far as his judgment might have dictated to others. It was an alliance which he could not have relinquished without pain" (MP 201). When we read just a little later that Sir Thomas is "very happy to think any thing of his daughter's disposition that was most favourable for the purpose" (MP 201), the scrupulous gestures of concern we just witnessed are unmasked as parade.

Sir Thomas's shows of kindness to Fanny are more deceptive. When he "advises" her to retire to bed after the ball, he employs a discourse of benevolence the narrator proceeds to strip: " 'Advise' was his word, but it was the advice of absolute power" (MP 280). Lest we assume that "absolute power" exercised on behalf of a ward's frail health is permissible, if not indeed desirable, we are obliged to think again, as the narrator leads us through a sequence of suppositions which exposes Sir Thomas's motives: "In thus sending her away, Sir Thomas perhaps might be thinking merely of her health. It might occur to him, that Mr. Crawford had been sitting by her long enough, or he might mean to recommend her as a wife by shewing her persuadableness" (MP 281). Eager to dispose of his niece with unexpected advantage in the marriage market, Sir Thomas stages this drama for Henry Crawford's benefit, and it will later become even more painfully clear how little Fanny herself has to do with Sir Thomas's "act" of solicitude. Though Sir Thomas's acts on behalf of the moral welfare of his family are more polished than Tom's, though he is always careful to don the drapery of decency, his probity is just as specious as Tom's, and his exertions just as coercive.

Mansfield Park never permits paternalistic discourse completely to conceal or to mystify ugly facts about power. Instead it turns back onto itself into incoherence, one of the novel's principal stylistic devices. Maria is not the only one to be confounded "from listening to language" which "actions contradicted" (MP 193). The "persuadableness" Sir Thomas wishes to appear to recommend, for example, is in fact a logical impossibility: since "absolute power" is, as we are told, what is really at play, the option of dissent which persuasion implies is not available to Fanny, here or elsewhere. Like Mrs. Norris, who with his authorization instructs Maria and Julia, "if you are ever so forward and clever yourselves, you should always be modest" (MP 19), Sir Thomas too is caught between the promptings of decency and acquisitiveness, and so lapses unreflectively into the same sort of self-contradiction. He "fancies," for example, that the best way of showing Henry Crawford to be a "model of constancy" is "by not trying him too long" (MP 345). This kind of double-talk is also typical of Tom. Having just been railroaded into playing whist, Tom fumes against polite formulations that give with one hand what they take away with the other: "A pretty modest request upon my word! . . . And to ask me in such a way too! without ceremony, before them all, so as to leave me no possibility of refusing! *That* is what I dislike most particularly . . . to have the pretence of being asked, of being given a choice, and at the same time addressed in such a way as to oblige one to do the very thing—whatever it be!" (MP 119–20). Tom is not aware that when he states "in an languid way, 'If you want to dance, Fanny, I will stand up with you' " (MP 118), he commits the same offense. But the "pretense" of choice Tom resents is essential to the paternalistic discourse represented in *Mansfield Park* because it enables people to compel others without having to regard themselves as bullies. When Mrs. Norris announces that she is not "going to urge" Fanny to act, "but I shall think her a very obstinate, ungrateful girl, if she does not do what her aunt and cousins wish her" (MP 147); when Edmund pressures Fanny to read *Lov-*

ers' *Vows* by manipulatively pleading "Do Fanny, if it is not *very* disagreeable to you" (MP 171); or when Sir Thomas himself damns Fanny's refusal of Crawford as "self-willed, obstinate, selfish, and ungrateful" (MP 319), while at the same time insisting "You cannot suppose me capable of trying to persuade you to marry against your inclinations" (MP 330–31), they each hang onto the drapery of decency just barely held together by impressive-sounding but incoherent formulations such as these.

The system of female manners is supposed to eliminate the need for the nakedness of coercion, and the embarrassment this entails, by rendering women so quiescent and tractable that they sweetly serve in the designs of fathers or guardians without wishing to resist and without noting that they have no choice. In most of Austen's novels, of course, fathers are not inclined to tyranny, nor are daughters trained to such ductility. But the women of Mansfield Park *are* held to a code of female propriety. The subject of femininity is a matter of great concern to virtually all the male characters. Still a bit queasy about authorizing Maria's marriage, Sir Thomas consoles himself with the (inaccurate) observation that Maria's disposition is, like his wife's, so placid that she will never be unhappy with the lot to which he is anxious creditably to assign her: "Her feelings probably were not acute; he had never supposed them to have be so" (MP 201). Of course Sir Thomas's confidence that Maria will cooperate in an alliance advantageous to himself without any ill effects is preposterous: she never really attended to lessons in female modesty in the first place, nor is her disposition so placid as he wishfully fancies. Studious to conceal rather than sublimate the rebelliousness of her temper, Maria suffers petulantly but desperately from restraint: "I cannot get out, as the starling said" (MP 99). For her, marriage to Rushworth is not voluntary service to a new man, but "independence" from Mansfield and "escape" from Sir Thomas (MP 202). But lessons in modesty did take on Fanny. She consistently strives to feel and do as she ought, to entrust herself to guardian males without presuming to act *"in propria persona"* (MP 398). But modesty so extreme has intolerable costs. Refusing the unseemliness of self-assertion, Fanny trusts that guardians will think for and of her, only to discover instead that they are too full of their own, invariably wrongheaded, plans to think much about her at all. When she finds herself neglected or abused, then, she has no other recourse than to consider herself somehow at fault for having nursed an implausible sense of consequence. When Sir Thomas, Edmund, and Lady Bertram collude in Crawford's unwelcome suit, Fanny may be surprised to learn just how little is set store by her wishes, but we cannot be, because she has always denied or concealed having any wishes of her own in the first place. Fanny's efforts to be modest, then, are every bit as frustrating and corrosive as Maria's efforts simply to appear so. Between the two of them the confounding bind in which the code of propriety places women is laid bare.

Maria's status as Sir Thomas's daughter entitles her to at least the decent appearance of matrimonial choice. As an indigent niece, however, Fanny is not granted the same consideration. When Sir Thomas discovers to his amazement that Fanny has no intention of accepting Crawford's proposal, he rails at what he understands to be pernicious doctrines of the day which have infected even Fanny:

> "I had thought you peculiarly free from wilfulness of temper, self-conceit, and every tendency to that independence of spirit, which prevails so much in modern days, even in young women, and which in young women is offensive and disgusting beyond all common offence. But you have now shown me that you can be wilful and perverse, that you can and will decide for yourself, without any consideration or deference for those who have surely some right to guide you—without even asking their advice."(MP 318)

By this time, of course, Sir Thomas's term, "advice," can no longer deceive us, since we have already learned that his is "the advice of absolute power" (MP 280). What he expects from Fanny is a cheerful readiness to be guided, so that the nakedness of force will never be necessary. Her resistance implies an assumption of self-responsibility that challenges his authority, and he is alarmed. Unlike Austen's other country gentlemen, who typify the mores of their station without much self-reflexivity, Sir Thomas is alert to revolutionary ideology. His violent antipathy to the "independence of spirit" and the determination to "decide" for oneself prevalent in modern females is anchored in much of the postrevolutionary discourse we have already reviewed, where the merits of thinking for oneself were widely debated. Sympathetic young men in Opie's *Adeline Mowbray* and Smith's *Young Philosopher*, for example, get into trouble precisely because they are committed to the principle of thinking, judging, and deciding for themselves, rather than conforming slavishly to the dictates of authority or convention. By contrast, in her *Letters Addressed to a Young Man*, Jane West denounces self-conceited independence in favor of a Burkean "concurrence" to "established forms" that have emerged over time.[15] Counterrevolutionary writers looked upon "independence of spirit" in a woman with even more alarm. In "The Unsex'd Females," the ne plus ultra of the period's antifeminist rhetoric, Richard Polwhele denounced literary ladies in England for their sexual immodesty and republican sentiments, equally unclean violations of natural law. Less grossly, but no less fervently, Letitia Hawkins elaborated the commonplace equation between the government of the passions and the government of England, when she opposed radical sophisms about "equal rights, the abjectness of submission, the duty of every one to think for themselves," because they diminished "the respect formerly paid to authority" and encouraged a tendency to regard a "husband as an unauthorized tyrant," a tendency which could only culminate in promiscuity and adultery.[16]

All the worst crimes pursuant upon female immodesty—illicit sex and adultery—come to pass in *Mansfield Park*. But here such effects proceed from causes contrary to what conservative writers conceived. The only character in *Mansfield Park* whose hands remain clean has to think for herself and to defy the figureheads of social and religious authority in order to remain guiltless. It is symptomatic of Sir Thomas's breathtaking impercipience that he attributes radical agendas and ungovernable passions to the dutiful and mild Fanny. Sir Thomas's interviews with Fanny and Maria on the subject of feminine choice mirror each other, for just as he attributes Maria's wish to marry a man she does not love to a commendable, because easily governable, serenity of temper, so he attributes Fanny's refusal to marry a man she does not love to a "young, heated fancy" (MP 318) and a "wild fit of folly" (MP 319), to headstrong passions unbecoming in themselves and inconvenient to parents or guardians, whose "advantage or disadvantage" depends on her. Fanny's hope that "to a man like her uncle, so discerning, so honourable, so good, the simple acknowledgement of settled *dislike* on her side would have been sufficient" (MP 318) to end Crawford's suit is disastrously disappointed. Indeed, it is the very assumption that her "settled *dislike*" matters that so affronts Sir Thomas. Sir Thomas can be a man of feeling when it comes to pitying the disappointment of a younger brother deprived of his patrimony. But as Fanny herself later recollects, he cannot entertain the sentiments of girls given in marriage to undeserving husbands: "He who had married a daughter to Mr. Rushworth. Romantic delicacy was certainly not to be expected from him" (MP 331).

Taking the opposite approach, rather like that of the good cop, Edmund tries to persuade Fanny to let Henry "succeed at last" precisely because she is so modest. He too, then, appeals to her wish for sexual approval: "You have proved yourself upright and disinterested, prove yourself grateful and tender-hearted; and then you will be the perfect model of a woman, which I have always believed you born for" (MP 347). Being a model woman, by this account, entails several responsibilities. Fanny has already *seemed* to fulfill some of them by not forming romantic attachments independent of parental supervision—Edmund has no idea she is carrying a torch for him—and by not being a fortune hunter. But to be a model woman, Fanny must do yet more. Now that her guardian sanctions the match, she must feel so thankful to have been asked at all and so anxious not to disappoint the feelings of a man who has favored her with his attention that she must, in short, say "yes." Here even Fanny rankles, contending in the manner of Elizabeth Bennet that "it ought not to be set down as certain, that a man must be acceptable to every woman he may happen to like himself" (MP 353). But Fanny goes yet further in questioning the antithetical duties exacted from modest women. First they are required not to desire at all, and next they are enjoined to feel desire on proper command: "How then was I to be—to be in love with him the moment he said he was with me? How was I to have an attachment at his service, as soon as it was asked for?" (MP 353).

There is no adequate way to answer Fanny's questions, for the paradox of female modesty is not simply that the same purity which is supposed to place them above the suspicion of sexual desire actually inflames male desire.[17] It is also that female purity itself is simultaneously demanded as natural and disbelieved as affected. From the outside, Fanny's refusal of Henry looks like the coquettish "no" Mr. Collins has learned to expect from "elegant" females before hearing their inevitable, grateful "yes"—in short, like another of the many acts people in *Mansfield Park* stage for propriety's sake. Fanny is dismayed to find that Henry persists in his unwelcome suit despite all her entreaties. But her pleas appear even more disingenuous to him than Mrs. Norris's "acts" of liberality or Sir Thomas's show of kindness in sending Fanny to Portsmouth do to us:

> Fanny knew her own meaning, but was no judge of her own manner. Her manner was incurably gentle, and she was not aware how much it concealed the sternness of her purpose. Her diffidence, gratitude, and softness, made every expression of indifference seem almost an effort of self-denial; seem at least, to be giving nearly as much pain to herself as to him. (MP 327)

Fanny's own language is made to inform against her: A modest "no" is heard as a coy "yes." Diffidence, gentleness, self-effacement—the same attributes of modesty which should relieve her from the attention and consequence she shuns—turn on her even more insidiously than her "protectors" Sir Thomas and Edmund do, depriving her of the credibility Elizabeth Bennet describes when, eschewing sexual distinction, she asks to be treated like a "rational creature" worthy of the "compliment of being believed sincere" (PP 109). Modesty, then, dispossesses Fanny of her meaning by reversing her own assertions. As such, it legitimizes and guarantees domination by providing it with a "decent" rationale.

Another way to describe a modest young woman whose function it is to oblige the wishes of fathers, uncles, and brothers without exhibiting any "independence of spirit" or any "perverse" and "disgusting" desires to decide for herself is to say that she is a slave. Surprisingly, until very recently the subject of slavery as it bears upon Austen's novels has received little critical attention, an omission that must derive at least in part from the time-honored premise of Austen's indifference to matters of "public" interest.[18] Fanny herself is curious about slavery. But even though she appears to favor writers famous for abolitionist sympathies, such as Johnson and Cowper, there is no reason to assume that when she asks Sir Thomas "about the slave trade" (MP 198) she is critical of the institution or uncomfortable with his role in it.[19] Austen does not provide us with details about Sir Thomas's treatment of slaves in the West Indies, but the fact of ownership itself serves not simply to reveal the source of the income which supports the Bertrams' stateliness, but also more importantly to illuminate the nature of Sir Thomas's kindness to Fanny. If his treatment of Fanny can be a guide, Sir Thomas is like the model paternalist Mr. Edwards, in Edgeworth's "The Grateful Negro" (1802), a man who believes that the emancipation of his slaves would not make them happy, who sees his guardianship as an act of kindness on behalf of dependents who cannot act for themselves, and who renders his slaves orderly and obedient by developing their capacity to feel grateful for his own kindness. Sir Thomas exacts compliance from Fanny in the same way, by virtue of his position not as a parent but rather as a benefactor: "You do not owe me the duty of a child. But, Fanny, if your heart can acquit you of *ingratitude*—" (MP 319).

Sir Thomas's emphasis is unmistakable. What is at issue in the allusion to slavery and the stress on gratitude is the propriety of benevolence itself, the power structure on which it is premised, and the confidence one is inclined to place in the interests and reliability of those empowered to be benevolent. Conservative apologists for the beneficent, mutually moralizing effects of hierarchical relationships united in opposing the Jacobin critique of gratitude as a purely personal and obfuscating sentiment rather than a general rational moral principle, and as we have already seen, novels as well as conduct books insisted upon the importance of gratitude to the survival of the nation. Set immediately after the French Revolution, Edgeworth's story "Madame de Fleury," for example, treats the capacity for gratitude towards benefactors as the litmus test not only for the right (i.e., royalist, politics) but also for morality itself. The "good" girl proves herself so by announcing proudly, " 'I do not pretend to know any thing of the rights of men, or the rights of women,' cried Victoire; 'but this I know, that I never can or will be ungrateful to Mad. de Fleury.' "[20] In contrast to conservative writers such as West, More, and Edgeworth, Austen explores the sinister aspects of benevolence and the burden of gratitude it places on a recipient. In *Emma*, for example, Jane Fairfax suggests a similarity between the "governess-trade," or "the sale" of "human in-tellect," and the "slave-trade," or the sale of "human flesh," even though "the guilt" of those who engage in either trade is "widely different" (E 300). Mrs. Elton, however, misses Jane's point, exposing the uneasiness of the nouveaux riches about being identified with ungenerous causes: "You quite shock me; if you mean a fling at the slave-trade, I assure you, Mr. Suckling was always rather a friend to the abolition" (E 300). But the emphasis of Jane's analogy implies a heartfelt protest, not simply against slave traders, whose guilt is taken for granted, but rather against the of-ficiousness of benefactresses such as Mrs. Elton and Emma, whose dic-tatorial acts of kindness satisfy their own fondness for dominion more than another's wish for happiness.

As could be expected from a character who takes the code of modesty so much to heart, Fanny is not in the least inclined to question Sir Thom-as's authority to dictate to her. Informed ever since her arrival that "an extraordinary degree of gratitude and good behaviour" is expected from her in return for her "wonderful good fortune" (MP 13) in being invited at all, Fanny finds nothing improper about Mrs. Norris's admonition that she be "the lowest and last" wherever she goes. Fanny rates "her own claims to comfort as low even as Mrs. Norris could" (MP 221). Believing the grey mare more entitled to consideration than she is herself, Fanny regards even rather minimal attentions—Sir Thomas's greeting upon his return, or his wish for her to use the carriage on a cold evening—as ex-travagant kindnesses. Rather than wonder why Sir Thomas had never ordered a fire to burn in the east room before, when she finally finds one there, for the first time in eight years, she is so impressed that he "could have leisure to think of such a trifle" that she regards his attention as "too much," as "an indulgence" beyond her intrinsic deserts. To her, ingra-titude is a particularly heinous offense—" 'I must be a brute indeed, if I can be really ungrateful!' said she in soliloquy; 'Heaven defend me from being ungrateful!' " (MP 322–23)—and like a grateful slave she lets par-ticular and small acts of kindness overshadow a larger act of cruelty.

The grateful submission of women is of such consequence to begin with because their sexual modesty alone guarantees the continuing au-thority of their guardians. With the exception of Tom Bertram, whose passion for horses prevents him from noticing any of Mary Crawford's attempts to ensnare him, the men in *Mansfield Park* are nervous about female sexuality. Edmund, for example, is alternately spellbound and horror striken by Mary Crawford, and poor Mr. Rushworth is at ease only with his mother. Though Henry Crawford is, of course, the major of-fender on the score of illicit sex, he is also, by his own admission, "of a cautious temper" (MP 43) about women. This only makes sense, since he learned his "lessons" (MP 43) from his uncle the admiral. Still assuming that the sisterly Austen, like Fanny, idealized the navy and extolled the manly integrity of all its officers, commentary has attended very little to Admiral Crawford, "a man of vicious conduct" (MP 41) whose particularly sordid domestic behavior intrudes upon the central narrative here. It is, after all, the rank indecency of this paternal figure that brings the Crawfords to Mansfield. Upon the death of his much-abused wife, the admiral shows his hostility to his niece and his contempt for social rules by bringing a mistress under his roof. With such experience behind him, as he jocularly confesses, Henry is understandably "unwilling to risk [his] happiness in a hurry" (MP 43). His commendation of the virtues he expects Fanny to practice as a wife discloses the nature of his risk:

> Henry Crawford had too much sense not to feel the worth of good principles in a wife, though he was too little accustomed to serious reflection to know them by their proper name; but when he talked of her having such a steadiness and regularity of conduct, such a high notion of honour, and such an observance of decorum as might warrant any man in the fullest dependence on her faith and integrity, he expressed what was inspired by the knowledge of her being well principled and religious. (MP 294)

Henry's dependence on Fanny's steadiness, honor, decorum, faith, and integrity adds up to the singularly important confidence that she will be above the temptation of adultery. However careless he is about violating the domestic sovereignity of another man, Henry has "too much sense" to omit forfending against this disgrace in his own home, even though he has been taught to consider this disgrace virtually inevitable. Evidently as the admiral would have it, every woman is a rake at heart, and as a result marriage is "never pardonable in a young man of independent fortune" (MP 292). With her surpassing modesty and rectitude, Fanny is "exactly the woman to do away every prejudice of such a man as the admiral, for she is exactly such a woman as he thinks does not exist in the world. She is the very impossibility he would describe" (MP 293).

If the other male characters do not share the admiral's penchant for illicit sex, they do share his suspicions about the "impossibility" of female modesty and his unwillingness to let a wife's infidelity compromise his social identity. Austen makes this clear by the staging, of all possible progressive plays, *Lovers' Vows*. The radical agenda of Kotzebue's play announces itself, not simply in its characterization of the worldly baron who wishes to sell his daughter off in marriage to a rich lout, but also in its sympathetic presentation of female desire.[21] Fanny disapproves of both female roles—"the situation of one, and the language of the other, so unfit to be expressed by any woman of modesty" (MP 137): a deserted unwed

mother and a lively young woman frankly enamored with the shy clergyman who has "formed" her mind both presuppose the independence
of female sexuality. Defenders of the patriarchal family were particularly
horrified by the "indecent" woman who, like Emma in *Emma Courtney*,
might consider herself as entitled as men are to declare her love and to
propose marriage, or who, like Julia in *Memoirs of Modern Philosophers*,
feels free to enact her desires without male authorization. In *Lovers' Vows*,
however, such indecency is presented amiably and without reproach, and
in the original, Amelia's declaration of love verges on an outright proposal. Herself sympathetic to, but prudently detached from, the
Wollstonecraft-Godwin circle, Inchbald was sensitive to the uneasiness of
her increasingly reactionary audience on the subject of female sexuality.
Recognizing that "the forward and unequivocal manner in which she
[Amelia] announces her affection to her lover, in the original would have
been revolting to an English audience," Inchbald softens the blow in her
translation, rendering Amelia's declaration of love "by whimsical insin-
uations, rather than coarse abruptness" (MP 478). Enough indelicacy remains, however, to scandalize Fanny even as it discloses her own unenacted
desires for the clergyman who has formed *her* mind. Austen calls further
attention to the anxiety prompted by the acknowledgement of female desire within the play when Mary Crawford's uncommonly bold question
about casting—"What gentleman among you am I to have the pleasure
of making love to" (MP 143)—meets with stunned silence.

Mary's question poses the temptation of sexuality as well as the threat
of social disorder, and Edmund responds to both from the start. Austen
uses sexualized details more extensively here than in any other novel,
and they attest to Edmund's susceptibility to erotic enchantments. He not
only approves but encourages Mary's horseback riding. Her "pure genuine pleasure of the exercise" (MP 66–67) is engaging to him, and his
own pleasure in being "close to her . . . directing her management of the
bridle" (MP 67), Fanny rather resentfully observes, is glaringly apparent.
As Fanny is made once again to witness, Edmund would sooner forego
contemplating the harmony of the stars than miss a few bars of the decidedly *un*celestial music of Mary at her harp. But if Edmund can accept
Mary's unblushing vigor, he cannot tolerate what Darcy, so much the
larger figure, finds so attractive in Elizabeth Bennet: her freedom of speech.
Mary Crawford does not stand in "awe" of her own uncle the admiral, or
live, as Fanny does, in "dread of taking a liberty with him" (MP 436).
Nor does she venerate Edmund "as an example of every thing good and
great" (MP 37). His approbation is as little essential to her self-definition
as the support his arm is to her brisk walk (MP 94). She speaks without
the respect for decorum on which Edmund insists. When Mary complains

about a matter as innocuous as the admiral's messy improvements at Twickenham, Edmund is "silenced" by a freedom with her uncle that "did not suit his sense of propriety" (MP 57). When she indulges in irreverent and salacious puns at the expense of the navy—the "*Rears, and Vices*" (MP 60) one encounters at her uncle's house—she arouses the same degree of disapproval: "Edmund again felt grave" (MP 60).

Disturbed by these infractions, Edmund quizzes his pupil Fanny on what was "not quite right" (MP 63) in Mary's conversation. Fanny could wish that her own loyalty and modesty could make her desirable, and as a result she is a sterner judge of female propriety than he is. Of course both agree that Mary "ought not have spoken of her uncle as she did" (MP 63). But to Edmund, the fault is superficial: "I do not censure her *opinions*; but there certainly *is* impropriety in making them public" (MP 63, emphasis Edmund's). Tacitly courting Mary himself, Edmund is uneasy about a prospective wife's propensity to talk without inhibition about so formidable a figure. A man's bad character should stay behind closed doors, and a woman's character as a woman is subject to review whenever she fails to respect his character in public: "She," he assures the dubious Fanny, "is perfectly feminine, except in the instances we have been speaking of" (MP 64).

Whereas the dimsighted Edmund wishes Mary to engage in the same kind of decorous concealment that makes Maria dangerous, Fanny insists rigorously on a totality of felt respect for male authority figures. But if Edmund's position is disturbing because it recommends double-talk, Fanny's is disturbing because it has ceased to take note of the indecencies that the drapery of position can conceal. The scurrility of the admiral is not significant to Fanny, except as an inconvenience a sister should gladly endure for a brother's sake. To her, it is not merely Mary's expression of criticism about the admiral that is wrong but the sentiment itself: "whatever his faults may be," she insists, he "is so very fond of her brother" (MP 63) that he ought to be respected. So complete is Fanny's credence in the moral puissance of patricians that she does not stop merely with reproaching Mary's "ungrateful" (MP 63) sentiments. Indeed, she does everything she can to exculpate the admiral himself and blames his wife instead: Mary's "impropriety is a reflection itself upon Mrs. Crawford. . . . She cannot have given her [Mary] right notions of what was due to the admiral" (MP 63–64).

The plot of *Mansfield Park* corroborates Fanny's severity with Mary Crawford, but at the same time it also explodes her confidence in the dispositions of patriarchal figures. Edmund ends this conversation about Mary's failings all-too-typically oblivious to Fanny's dissent—"I am glad you saw it all as I did" (MP 64)—and assured of his own wisdom. But he

will soon learn that the "feminine lawlessness" (MP 94) he finds charming when it comes to the laws of time and distance is intolerably menacing
when it comes to the other laws patriarchy establishes to order the world.
In reference to Tocqueville's fear of the female, Catherine Gallagher has
aptly observed, "The assumed sexual propriety of women underlies both
property relations and semiotics in the world Tocqueville inhabits, a world
in which property is acreage and the important self-representation is still
the name of the father."[22] *Mansfield Park* halts with the commission of
not one but two separate and distinctively female crimes which jam the
patriarchal codes of property and speech alike: Maria's act of adultery
with Henry and Mary's unruffled and hence, as it appears to Edmund,
wanton way of discussing it. In asserting the volatility of female desire
outside established modes of social control, both acts of immodesty subvert the law of the father in Mansfield Park.

Mansfield Park adumbrates a phenomenon which has preoccupied
modern feminists: the dependence of certain kinds of masculine discourse
on feminine silence. Mansfield Park runs smoothly only so long as female
dissent can be presumed not to exist. Lady Bertram, of course, has nothing
to say for herself; her daughters never voice their noncompliance, and
while their rebellion is obvious enough to Fanny, she herself can never
say what she knows, and when she tries she is not listened to; even Mary
Crawford's blatant liberties with paternal figures are unheard for as long
as possible. But when women's defiance of patriarchal codes can no longer
be ignored, men here are utterly stymied, and their confusion gives another, quite dizzying turn to the political sublime. Sir Thomas is "astonished" (MP 314) even by mild Fanny's unexpected and "very strange"
act of resistance, interrupting as it does, not only his command of her, but
also his command of his own understanding: "There is something in this
which my comprehension does not reach" (MP 315). But when Maria
commits her even more confounding crime, Sir Thomas reportedly falls
just short of paralysis—"My father is not overpowered. More cannot be
hoped. He is still able to think and act" (MP 442)—while Mrs. Norris,
his mistress-at-arms, is thoroughly deprived of her faculties of speech and
reasoning, "quieted, stupified, indifferent . . . benumbed" (MP 448). As
the case of Mary Crawford attests, however, chastity alone is not enough
to assure and ensure the interests of patriarchy. Silence too, at least on
some subjects, is also required to place that chastity beyond suspicion,
even though, paradoxically, that silence, like modesty itself, will also and
always be liable to doubt. Finally it is Mary's ability to speak about illicit
sex that seems so audacious and perverse that Edmund's very power of
speech is taken away: "To hear the woman whom—no harsher name than
folly given!—So voluntarily, so freely, so coolly to canvass it!—No re-

luctance, no horror, no feminine—shall I say? no modest loathings! . . .
I was like a man stunned" (MP 454–55).

Edmund is silenced by the same "———" that silenced that other
younger son and clergyman, Henry Tilney: obliging young ladies blithely
framing and uttering thoughts which they cannot so much as consider,
let alone speak. Mary is dismissed from Mansfield Park, but not because
she, like Marianne or the female philosophers of turn-of-the-century political novels, consciously holds an opposing ideological position—though
this too, of course, would be intolerable. Rather, she is dismissed because
she never has considered what the issues are in the first place, and as a
result does not even realize that a modest silence on the subject of sex and
grateful veneration of the moral prestige of patriarchal benefactors are
required of her. At times, this obliviousness to the exigencies of gentry
mythology reflects back unfavorably onto the Bertrams themselves. After
all, on some subjects, such as the pursuit of wealth through the formation
of advantageous marriages, Mary and the Bertrams see eye to eye. She
and Sir Thomas alike reinforce Lady Bertram's admonition to Fanny that
"it is every woman's duty to accept such a very unexceptionable offer"
as Henry's (MP 333), and so they form an alliance which denudes Sir
Thomas of the dignifying moral pretensions he is at such pains to maintain. But Mary makes no such pretensions, and that is what damns her.
She covets the trappings of social prestige and respects the dictates of
worldly wisdom—including that portion of it which requires female
chastity—but she does not recognize the mystique of social institutions
and the people who embody them, and thus does not appreciate the enor-
mity of Maria's crime. Fanny, needless to say, knows better. To her, Maria's is "a sin of the first magnitude" (MP 441). Whereas Edmund had
earlier insisted that Mary's faults consisted in manner alone, he eventually agrees with Fanny that they result instead from "a perversion of
mind which made it natural to her to treat the subject" (MP 456) lightly
as a folly which is dangerous only where it is known, rather than as sin
in itself, which loyalty to a patriarchal social structure should prevent her
even from naming. About this there must be no mistake: the Bertrams
view Maria's offense as a crime against fathers of good families. In Sir
Thomas's opinion, any palliation of Maria's action would entail "an insult
to the neighbourhood" and a danger of "introducing such misery in another man's family, as he had known himself" (MP 465).

It is small wonder that, having been charged with "blunted delicacy
and a corrupted, vitiated mind" (MP 456), Mary Crawford should next
appear to Edmund as a siren, flashing "a saucy playful smile, seeming to
invite, in order to subdue" (MP 451) him and emasculate his moral indignation: after all, the ability to think and speak of the violation of do-

mestic trust lightly is tantamount to confessing a failure to be awed by it. From the Bertrams' point of view, the novel closes with a vengeance of reactionary formulas derived from conservative fiction: the demon aunt is cast out as a betrayer of the good man's trust, and the offending daughter banished to the hell of her perpetual company; the impious seductress is righteously spurned by the man of God, and her reprobate brother forever barred from happiness; the giddy heir apparent is sobered by instructive affliction, and the modest girl, in a triumph of passive aggression, is vindicated and rewarded with everything she wanted but never presumed to ask for. But the wicked are not merely segregated from the virtuous. Sir Thomas, "anxious to bind by the strongest securities all that remained to him of domestic felicity" (MP 471), repents his ambitions, blesses the marriage of Edmund and Fanny, and stations them both next door, so that the good themselves can huddle even closer within the hallowed ties of marriage.

But *Mansfield Park* erodes rather than upholds conclusions which comprise a conservative reading of the novel. Austen calls attention to the parodic elements of her denouements here much as she does in *Northanger Abbey*, where a dubious surplus of conventionalized material and a "tell-tale compression" of pages (NA 250) hurrying characters to tidy destinies lurches the novel into fantasies we are not permitted to credit. When Edmund finally gets around to asking Fanny to marry him, the narrator intrudes with an unwontedly Sternean garrulity that obliges us to consider their alliance as a perfunctorily opted anticlimax the narrator washes her hands of, rather than a properly wished-for and well-deserved union towards which the parties have been moving all along: "I purposely abstain from dates on this occasion. . . . I only intreat every body to believe that exactly at the time when it was quite natural that it should be so, and not a week earlier, Edmund did cease to care about Miss Crawford" (MP 470).

Convention is flaunted in a more ominously problematic fashion with the bitter expulsion of Mrs. Norris as the villain of the piece. Throughout the novel, of course, Mrs. Norris has been treated with a peculiar superabundance of opprobrium: no occasion passes that she is not debased with sarcasm. What is less conspicuous, however, is that her offenses are authorized, indeed sometimes are even requested, by Sir Thomas himself. He directs her to cooperate with him in maintaining the superior "rank, fortune, rights, and expectations" (MP 11) of his daughters at Fanny's expense; he approves Maria's marriage with a great family. Mrs. Norris, then, is less a villain in her own right than an adjutant. In her, we see his officiousness, his liberality, his family pride, and even his parsimoniousness—after all, his anxieties about money make him wish

Mrs. Norris would take Fanny off his hands—without the drapery of decency. When she denounces Fanny's "little spirit of secrecy, and independence, and nonsense" (MP 323), he does not notice, as the narrator points out, that "he had been so lately expressing the same sentiments himself" (MP 324). His unwillingness to ponder the similarity here exemplifies that failure of self-reflection he and his family everywhere betray. Though he finally acknowledges his kinship with her, seeing her as "a part of himself" (MP 465–66), her banishment relieves him from the necessity of examining the mutuality of their responsibility in the ruin of his family. The restoration to Sir Thomas of some semblance of moral dignity depends on Mrs. Norris's eruption into mythic loathsomeness, the likes of which is nowhere else to be found in Austen's mature work. The hyperconventional outlines of Mrs. Norris's villainy alert us once again to Austen's uneasiness about assailing authority figures too directly. In *Mansfield Park*, as in *Evelina*, for example, such figures are abased, for a while at least, and made to acknowledge their trespasses to dutiful girls. But while Burney accomplishes this openly, though in manifest contradiction to professions of servility, Austen makes it possible for the father, as well as any reader so inclined, to save face by palming his offenses onto a female surrogate from the realm of fairy tale.

The doubts we are obliged to form about the moral stature of Mansfield further compromise the satisfaction typically proffered by a happy ending. Throughout the novel, the moral welfare of the great house has been subject to the self-will, the bad judgment, or the mercenary projects of those appointed to govern it, and every time Fanny has had to struggle with uncertainty "as to what she *ought to do*" (MP 152–53), it has been because such figures urge her on to what she knows she ought *not* do. And although Fanny has been independent enough to resist them, she has never been lucid enough to recognize what is problematic about their authority even as she sees them err, even as she is obliged inwardly and outwardly to resist them. After Sir Thomas tries to force her into the arms of the man who disgraces his family, Fanny still sees him as her "rule to apply to," and stands in "dread of taking a liberty with him" (MP 436). Edmund is yet worse. If it is true, as he proudly declares, that "as the clergy are, or are not what they ought to be, so are the rest of the nation" (MP 93), then woe to England, for Edmund shares his father's tendency to invest personal desires with the dignity of moral imperatives. Yet to Fanny, Edmund remains "an example of every thing good and great" (MP 37), even after he urges her to settle in with Mrs. Norris, to take part in *Lovers' Vows*, and to marry Henry Crawford.

The most unsettling irony of *Mansfield Park*, then, is that the failures of conservative ideology fall, not exclusively, but still most heavily, on the only member of the household to believe in and act by it fully to the very end. From the squalor of Portsmouth it seems to Fanny that "all proceeded in a regular course of cheerful orderliness" at Mansfield, that "every body had their due importance; every body's feelings were consulted" (MP 392). But Fanny's trip "home," as Sir Thomas designed, taught her how to value the advantages of wealth and comfort Mansfield provides, not how to see past its dignity. The stately household she pines for from afar is about to explode; as we well know, it has never been "cheerful" or orderly, and "every one's" feelings there are *not* consulted, Fanny's least of all. To be "mistress of Pemberley," as Elizabeth Bennet puts it, might indeed "be something" (PP 245), but Mansfield Park has no such luster. A conventionally happy ending which ensconces Fanny there, indispensable at last, and still adulating now enervated figures whose discernment has been radically impeached, sustains rather than settles the problems the foregoing material has uncovered.

Finally, *Mansfield Park* parodies the structures of conservative fiction most subversively, though in some ways most obliquely of all, in its presentation of family itself, the ostensibly sacred bonds the weary Bertrams form at last. Conservative novelists typically set up uncomplicated moral oppositions—good girls and bad girls, good marriages and bad marriages, good parents and bad parents—to reinforce their political ideals. To the extent that the illicit liaison between Henry and Maria contrasts with the lawful marriage of Edmund and Fanny, *Mansfield Park*, of course, appears to do the same. But this polarity collapses under close examination. Although Austen writes nothing that can be construed as a palliation of adultery, the narrator shows no ladylike impulse to recoil in shame from the greatest insult that can be made to a man of Rushworth's prestige, and no inclination to moralize in the manner of Sir Thomas, Edmund, or Fanny. On the contrary, the narrator's comments discourage us from regarding Maria's offense as a "sin of the first magnitude," as Fanny would say, or even as a heinous crime against an estimable personage. Not only does the narrator imply that Rushworth had it coming—"The indignities of stupidity, and the disappointments of selfish passion, can excite little pity. His punishment followed his conduct"—but she also suggests that the good-natured dolt may be betrayed again—"if duped, to be duped at least with good humour and good luck" (MP 464).

If the novel's instance of illicit sex cannot rouse much indignation, its instance of licit sex is less than exemplary as well. The marriage of Edmund and Fanny savors of incest. It is superfluous to remind ourselves that postreformation England lifted laws prohibiting marriage between first cousins, or that Austen's own brother married a first cousin, for the legality of the marriage between Fanny and Edmund is not in question.

What is important instead is how a match so close is presented within the novel, and from the start it is matter of great concern. In the opening chapter Sir Thomas's express opposition to "cousins in love, &c." (MP 6) militates against bringing a girl child to Mansfield at all. Only after concurring with Mrs. Norris's assurance that it is "morally impossible" for cousins to marry who have been "always together like brothers and sisters" (MP 6) does he agree to send for Fanny. Convinced of the independence of fraternal and erotic love, the ever-contriving Sir Thomas later arranges Henry's abrupt departure in order to compel Fanny to feel his absence and to cry "con amore" (MP 282). Cry she does, but "it was con amore fraternal and no other" (MP 282), for Fanny's heart is really with her brother William. But the difference between fraternal love and the "other" is far from clear. Her "heart was divided" (MP 23) between William and Edmund, but as distinct as these sorts of love are in the minds of some characters—one remembers Mr. Knightley's "Brother and sister! no, indeed" (E 331)—in Fanny's case they jump tracks very easily. To Mary Crawford, the tie of blood between the cousins is close enough to put them beyond the possibility of erotic involvement. Unsuspicious of Fanny's interest in the role, Mary assumes that Fanny could read Amelia's lines in *Lovers' Vows* without self-consciousness: "he is your cousin, which makes all the difference" (MP 168). For his part, Edmund recognizes this difference. To Fanny's persistent mortification, cousin Edmund's expressions of affection always preclude the romantic. He surveys her body, to be sure, but only "with the kind smile of an affectionate brother," and he approves of her white dress only to remark, "Has not Miss Crawford a gown something the same?" (MP 222). We and Fanny alike, then, are always reminded that the love she silently bears is not exactly legitimate, even though it is finally opposed to illicit sex elsewhere in the novel. After Maria and Julia appear lost forever to Edmund as siblings, he presses Fanny to his heart and cries, "My Fanny—my only sister—my only comfort now" (MP 444).

A good deal of *Mansfield Park* is devoted to examining the intimacy of fraternal love, and though acknowledging at one point that, far from being innate and immutable, "the ties of blood were little more than nothing" (MP 428) when family members are divided, the narrator elsewhere opines that the bond that can form between "children of the same family, the same blood, with the same first associations," is of a strength "in which even the conjugal tie is beneath the fraternal" (MP 235). Though *Mansfield Park*, like Austen's other novels, has its share of siblings and cousins who are mutually indifferent at best or hostile at worst, it is precisely because familial love, here at least, appears to be the only legitimate arena for strong feelings that it is prone to incestuous permutations. The sight of Fanny's love for William convinces Crawford that Fanny will prove an erotically interesting partner, and thus confirms his designs upon her heart: "[T]he sensibility which beautified her complexion and illumined her countenance, was an attraction in itself. . . . She had feeling, genuine feeling. It would be something to be loved by such a girl, to excite the first ardours of her young, unsophisticated mind!" (MP 235–36). Operating under the assumption that erotic and fraternal love are not intrinsically different and that as a husband he will simply transfer Fanny's promisingly intense passion for William to himself, he shrewdly negotiates his suit for the "conjugal tie" immediately after announcing his benefactions for William. With still less propriety, other characters blur the distinction between erotic and fraternal love in order to screen their improper flirtations. Julia and Maria compete to play opposite their would-be lover in *Lovers' Vows* as his mother, and Mary Crawford reassures Rushworth that the affection Maria-Agatha showers upon Henry-Frederick during the rehearsals of *Lovers' Vows* is "so *maternal*" (MP 169, emphasis Mary's).

Nor is *paternal* affection exempt from an aura of erotic implication. Sir Thomas never much notices Fanny at all until she develops into womanhood. To Edmund, his warm admiration for Fanny's blossoming "complexion," "countenance," and "figure" is altogether in the normal course of affairs. But the modest Fanny feels its prurience. She is abashed and pained—"Nay, Fanny, do not turn away about it—it is but an uncle" (MP 198)—to learn that her physical maturation has been the subject of such minutely discriminating discussion between her uncle and her cousin. Few details in this novel are quite so disturbing as those which disclose the very similar observations of Fanny's father on his daughter's emergent sexuality. Seeing Fanny again after a long separation, Mr. Price "observed that she was grown into a woman, and he supposed would be wanting a husband soon" (MP 380). Later he notices her when he is inebriated, only "to make her the object of a coarse joke" (MP 389), the tenor of which would appear too gross to specify. But when Mr. Price announces how he would punish Maria, the sexual undercurrent of his paternal affection becomes all too explicit: "But by G—— if she belonged to me, I'd give her the rope's end as long as I could stand over her" (MP 440).

The coarseness of these sentiments may seem out of place in the world of Austen's fiction, but *Mansfield Park* deals more with this delicate subject than any of her other novels, and Mr. Price's grossness is but one element in a sustained body of detail that invites us to reconsider conservative political arguments which idealize familial love. Approaching reactionary ideology from a decidedly Freudian point of view, Ronald Paulson has contended that the bottom line of the conservative agenda was to preserve paternal authority by quelling the disruptive oedipal energies of children. Seen in this light, the family itself tames sexual energy, and provides a safe arena for the nurturance of strong affections, free from the perilous volatility of concupiscence.[23] In the process of domesticating such energies, however, Mansfield Park has made them domestic. And thus rather than consolidating already existing alliances, as in *Emma*, or forming new ones which extend the ties of family outward, as in *Pride and Prejudice*, the principals in *Mansfield Park* gather together in a tighter knot of consanguinity because the larger world outside has always proved more than they could manage. This has been clear from the start. In *Mansfield Park*, the family is not a corridor to wider social affection, as promised in Burkean social thought. Anthropologists argue that women serve in many cultures as the currency of exchange between men, and by using Maria to form an alliance with a man of Rushworth's stature, Sir Thomas would seem to agree that this is what his daughters are for. But on the contrary, as we have already seen, Maria seemed a good investment to Sir Thomas precisely because he would have to lose her to her husband: "A well-disposed young woman, who does not marry for love," Sir Thomas comforts himself, "was in general but the more attached to her own family" (MP 201).[24]

Mansfield Park is marked by an isolation unmatched in Austen's novels. Here are none of the talkative servants, unpaid merchants, opinionated tenants, and "spiteful old ladies" whose ever-rumored judgments constitute the formidable, if not always reliable, force of opinion in *Pride and Prejudice*; absent too are the various sets we find in Highbury and its environs with which Emma must come to terms. When Sir Thomas announces his fancy to give a ball, we are startled to learn that anyone exists outside the great house and the parsonage, for his oft-proclaimed preference for "the repose of his own family circle" (MP 196) has led to an exclusion of the neighborhood altogether. The concluding assertion of familiality that could look like righteous good sense at last is really only a retrenchment, not an alternative. The Bertrams end where Darcy begins—with the family circle which Austen's more attractive patricians learn to outgrow, and which people of good will abandon altogether in *Persuasion*.

To readers who have been readier than Austen is to privilege the viewpoint of the dutiful father and the unassuming girl who idolizes him, *Mansfield Park* has generally seemed doctrinaire. But the novel is not so placid. The highly conventionalized moral oppositions touted in the conclusion—the narrator's pronounced determination to quit "guilt and misery," to restore the good to "tolerable comfort," and "to have done with all the rest" (MP 461)—will not bear the scrutiny Austen's own style is always inviting. When desolated at Portsmouth, Fanny feels her gladness to receive Mary Crawford's letters as "another strange revolution of mind" (MP 393). Throughout the course of her story, when she has found that the wicked Mary can be kind, that the rakish Henry can be desirable, that the awesome Sir Thomas must be opposed, and the sterling Edmund is weak, Fanny has had to undergo revolutions of mind which lead to the kind of "confusion of guilt" and "complication of evil" (MP 441) she and the Bertrams would like to assign and confine to the Crawfords or to Mrs. Norris. But we need not read their story the same way they do, any more than we need to think about Henry Tilney or his father the same way the deferent Catherine does. Revolutions of ideas invite the kind of reflection which the most stereotypically sage characters, including Fanny, cannot follow through with, and which disturb the coziness of the conclusion by subverting the moral polarities on which it seems to rest.[25] In contrast to *Pride and Prejudice*, if *Mansfield Park* appears to let conservative ideologues have it their way, it is only to give them the chance to show how little, rather than how much, they can do, and so to oblige them to discredit themselves with their own voices.

CHAPTER SIX

EMMA: "WOMAN, LOVELY WOMAN REIGNS ALONE"

There was a time, and not too long ago, when Austen was considered to be above—or was it really below?—the anxieties of authorship. For Richard Simpson, as for many of Austen's Victorian admirers, it was necessary to presume an "unconsciousness of [Austen's] artistic merits" in order to regard her, in his own words, as "dear Aunt Jane," a kindly spinster who never minded being interrupted while at work because her "powers were a secret to herself," and who was gratefully surprised to earn even the little money she did because she rated her own abilities too low to expect acknowledgment.[1] Encouraged by members of Austen's own family, who in the "Biographical Notice" and the *Memoir* protest with obtrusive defensiveness that Austen put her family before her art, such views have survived well into our own century. Taking particular care to "redeem" Austen from "any possible suspicion of superiority or conceit," R. Brimley Johnson asserts that Austen's "taste was strong against any parade of authorship, and her affection would have accused herself of both conceit and selfishness, had she required privacy for work, or allowed herself to be so absorbed as to neglect any social or domestic duty." R. W. Chapman later affirmed that "the sweetest reward of her labours" was nothing more ambitious or independent than "to have pleased her family." And as late as 1957, in the biographical sketch prefixed to his widely available edition of *Emma*, Trilling's stress on Austen's commitment to a charmed family circle assures us that Austen never upset the parlor or the dining room with overweening authorial preoccupations as unladylike as they are egotistical.[2]

For our current recognition of Austen's artistic self-consciousness we have to thank, not the discovery of any new information, but rather a disposition to pay attention to what has always been before us. Austen's account of the profits generated by her novels, for example, is now acknowledged to indicate an interest in matters as vulgar as commercial success. Her somewhat testy preface to *Northanger Abbey* is now permitted to betray lingering mortification at the refusal of Crosby & Co. to print this, her first formally submitted novel, and to convey a wish that readers properly consider the historical provenance of her work. And of course the remarks scattered throughout the letters and her collection of opinions about *Mansfield Park* and *Emma* plainly attest to an intense curiosity about responses to her novels outside the family circle. To all appearances, she deemed no opinion about her novels too stupid or malapropos to copy out and preserve for future reference.

Austen's concern about the fate of her novels with the public was deeply felt and often manifested itself in decidedly personal attitudes towards her heroines, about whose popularity with the public she was a good judge. Elizabeth Bennet, she was certain, was so delightful a creature that if readers did not like her, it was no fault of her own. But with Emma, Austen knew she was taking a risk. Authorial solicitude on her behalf, however, has proved a mixed blessing. Her statement "I am going to take a heroine whom no-one but myself will much like" has been treated more as an invitation to search out what is objectionable about Emma than as a calculated challenge to the judgments of her audience, for the criticism of Emma is freighted with alarming animosities.[3] Concerning this Austenian heroine, more than any other, commentary conspicuously gives the lie to the naive assumption that literary criticism is the business of disinterested professionals whose discussions evolve from ideologically neutral historical, aesthetic, or merely commonsensical criteria. If Austen enters the canon because she seemed to deny or devalue her authority, Emma has been the heroine critics have loved to scold precisely because it never occurs to her to apologize for the control she takes over the destinies of others. Because Emma is often charged with the same transgressions—being "arrogant, self-important, and controlling" or "narcissistic and perfectionist"—from which critics diligently attempted to exempt Austen, it is worth considering them at some length.[4] The absolution of one and the arraignment—sometimes indulgent and sometimes not—of the other alike derive from a profound discomfort with female authority, and female authority itself is the subject of *Emma*.

Determining the common denominator in much *Emma* criticism requires no particular cleverness. Emma offends the sexual sensibilities of many of her critics. Transparently misogynist, sometimes even homophobic, subtexts often bob to the surface of the criticism about her. Even those critics who do not specifically address the subject of gender employ loaded oppositions about moral and social values, supposedly endorsed by the author herself, which imply a sexual hierarchy reified in marriage. For example, A. Duckworth's contention that "Emma in the end chooses society rather than self, an inherited order rather than a spontaneous and improvised existence," implicitly opposes and prefers the orderly, patriarchal, rational, masculine, and, above all, right to the disorderly, subjectivist, imaginative, feminine, and self-evidently wrong.[5] In much *Emma* criticism, however, psychosexual concepts are not merely implicit. To many of this novel's most distinguished critics, Emma's want of feminine softness and compliancy is her most salient and most grievous shortcoming. Mudrick's assertion that Emma is a "confirmed exploiter" is an erotic complaint disguised as a moral one. His "Emma has no tenderness" really means that she is not sexually submissive to and contingent upon men: hers is "a dominating and uncommitting personality." Curiously enough, though, because he does not notice his own assumption of a masculine monopoly on desirable qualities, Mudrick inadvertently justifies Emma's dereliction from "femininity." If Mr. Woodhouse "is really" that most contemptible of creatures, "an old woman," we can hardly wonder that his daughter opts for the emotional detachment and the penchant for managing that could place her beyond such scorn. But though Mudrick complains that Emma "plays God," what he really means is that she plays man, and he, as well as others, will not permit her thus to elude the contempt that is woman's portion, do what she may. Wilson, who alludes ominously to Emma's "infatuations with women," and Mudrick himself, who darkly hints about her preference of "the company of women" whom "she can master and direct," treat Emma's "coldness" as though it were a culpably perverse refusal of their own sexual advances. To critics at a loss to account for how Emma could like Harriet more than she likes Mr. Elton, what other than an unacceptable attachment to women could possibly account for a failure to be impressed with and "humanly" committed to men?[6]

Readers who have not cared to ponder Emma's sexuality have still entangled her in unexamined and curiously revealing attitudes which are, if anything, more pernicious in their linkage of sex and politics. Blowing the whistle on readers who doubt that marriage will cure Emma, Wayne Booth, for example, declares with the preemptive dogmatism peculiar to outraged decency, "Marriage to an intelligent, amiable, good, and attractive man is the best thing that can happen to this heroine, and the readers who do not experience it as such are, I am convinced, far from knowing what Jane Austen is about."[7] Never implying that this highstrung young lady really needs a good man, Trilling argues that Emma's objectionable behavior derives from a sexual peculiarity more subversive than a mere passing disinterest in marriage: "The extraordinary thing about Emma," he claims, "is that she has a moral life as a man has a moral life." Emma's anomalous status as a moral agent is owing entirely to her self-love, a sentiment which in turn derives from "the first of virtues, the most basic and biological of the virtues, that of self-preservation." Untroubled by the Darwinian premise that nature, in the guise of biology, has in depriving women of the survival instinct, de facto barred them from the moral life, Trilling, it is true, does not chide Emma for her manly trespasses. But this is only because they are so reassuringly uncalculated and exceptional as to deserve his curiosity and his indulgence. Trilling also appeals to the "biological nature of moral fact" in his essay on *The Bostonians*, after all, and in that novel challenges to male hegemony that are based on *principle* meet with a very different response.[8]

In fairness not merely to the aforementioned readers but also to the originality of *Emma* itself, it must be observed that if in detaching herself from the romantic plot Emma neglects the feminine roles twentieth-century critics would assign to her, these roles were insisted upon if anything more self-consciously and strenuously in the fiction of Austen's period. There they appear in a handful of permutations which vary according to the persuasions of the author. In anti-Jacobin novels, bad girls are undone by radical seducers, while good girls are obedient daughters and chaste wives. Even in novels by radical men—such as *Fleetwood, Anna St. Ives*, and *Man As He is*—heroines sometimes prove themselves worthy of courageously progressive suitors or husbands by possessing the same mildness, modesty, and educability which would recommend them to reactionary gentlemen. In novels by radical women, however, they can figure as the victims of a husband's or father's greed, or perhaps even of a radical lover's cold egotism. Emma's very difference makes her and her novel exceptional, for even in the case of that one wholly traditional bond at the center of Emma's life—her tender love for her father—the intellectual, physical, and even moral frailty of this paternal figure necessitates a dependence upon female strength, activity, and good judgment. Possessing these qualities in abundance, Emma does not think of herself as an incomplete or contingent being whose destiny is to be determined by the generous or blackguardly actions a man will make towards her. A caricature of comme il faut propriety, even Mrs. Elton defers, nominally at least, to the rule of her husband, her "lord and master" (E 455). But Emma does not need the mediation of marriage because she already possesses an independence and consequence that marriage to a "lord and master" would, if anything, probably diminish: "I believe few married women are half as much mistress of their husband's house, as I am of Hartfield" (E 84). Further, Emma is so accustomed to rule that, as Mr. Knightley jokes to Mrs. Weston, she has absorbed the office of husband unto herself, giving her governess a "good education" in "the very material matrimonial point of submitting your own will, and doing as you were bid" (E 38).

In Austen's other novels, women independent enough to manage their own estates and dictate to others are widows, like Mrs. Smith and Lady Catherine. By contrast, single rich women, such as Sophia Grey, are prey to roving fortune hunters. Unlike her predecessors, Emma alone has "none of the usual inducements" to marriage: "Fortune I do not want; employment I do not want; consequence I do not want" (E 84). Sometimes held up as evidence of frigidity or some comparably pathological character flaw, Emma's businesslike reasoning about marriage is actually all of a piece with that of other characters in *Emma*, from the lowly Harriet to the mighty Churchills, whose possession or lack of "fortune," "employment," and "consequence" bears on their matrimonial decisions. Knightley himself applauds Miss Taylor's marriage to Mr. Weston precisely because it enables her "to be secure of a comfortable provision" (E 11). And far from feeling insulted by being so regarded, Mr. Weston considers Miss Taylor's lack of fortune and consequence a complementary blessing in its own right. The social and economic superiority of his first wife put him at a sentimental disadvantage. Such was her condescension that his "warm heart and sweet temper made him think every thing due to her in return for the great goodness of being in love with him"(E 15), long after she is cast off by her family, and long after the young couple runs through her fortune. Marrying "poor Miss Taylor" gives him "the pleasantest proof of its being a great deal better to chuse than to be chosen, to excite gratitude rather than to feel it" (E 17)—better as well, we assume, to have someone else feel that everything is due to him for *his* great goodness in having chosen beneath him. There is no call to hint at the sinister here: Mr. Weston is not the less amiable for enjoying his benevolence. Unlike us, Austen is not embarrassed by power, and she depicts it with the quiet pervasiveness and nonchalance that suggest how effortlessly she took it and the sentiments relative to it for granted. What makes Emma unusual, then, is not that she, as Trilling would have it, is a woman freakishly endowed with self-love, but rather that she is a woman who possesses and enjoys power, without bothering to demur about it.

In the animadversions of even the most sympathetic of Emma's critics, then, the political import of sexual difference is clearly exposed, for what they present as pertaining to female nature really pertains to female rule. Emma assumes her own entitlement to independence and power—power not only over her own destiny, but, what is harder to tolerate, power over the destinies of others—and in so doing she poaches on what is felt to be male turf. The royal dedication of *Emma* is often cited to account for the patriotism of its outbursts about English verdure, English reticence, and English social structure. But if it is appropriate to speak of *Emma* as a patriotic novel—and I believe it is—then it must be acknowledged that its patriotism is of a very unusual sort. Austen privately expressed hesitations about the Prince Regent in strong terms, and she inscribed the dedication to him only after realizing she had no choice.[9] When we recall

further that Austen disapproved of His Royal Highness specifically because of his notorious infidelity to his wife, the inscription of a novel pre-
dominated by female power can conceivably look more like an act of quiet
cheek than of humble submission. In stunning contrast with *Mansfield
Park*, where husbands dominate their households with as little judiciousness as decency, in *Emma* woman *does* reign alone. Indeed, with the exception of Knightley, all of the people in control are women: Mrs.
Churchill's whims as well as her aches and pains are felt, discussed, and
respected miles away from her sofa; at least some, if not all, people in the
neighborhood accept Mrs. Elton's ministrations as "Lady Patroness"; and
Emma's consciousness that she is considered "first" in consequence at
Highbury may peeve her critics, but it does not faze her neighbors, and
no one—least of all Mr. Knightley—questions her right to preeminence.

In its willingness to explore positive versions of female power, *Emma*
itself is an experimental production of authorial independence unlike any
of Austen's other novels. As we have seen, the novels up through *Mansfield Park* are textured with highly politicized allusions, themes, plots, and
characters. But the texture of *Emma* is remarkably spare. There is a hue
and cry about an "infamous fraud upon the rights of men and women"
(E 254). But the crime in question is a conspiracy to deprive them of their
dinner, not their dignity as autonomous agents. Austen does not allude
to the tradition of political fiction as regularly in *Emma* as she does elsewhere, but such relative silence does not signify an abandonment of the
political tradition. In fact, the case is quite the opposite. At the height of
her powers, Austen steps into her own authority in *Emma*, and she participates in the political tradition of fiction, not by qualifying or critiquing
it from within, but rather by trying to write from its outsides. *Emma* is
assuredly unlike the anarchistic and egalitarian novels of Godwin, Holcroft, and Wollstonecraft in fundamentally accepting English class structure, and in being able to discriminate positive authority figures. Emma
is frequently brought to task for her "snobbism." But if she offends dem-
ocratic sympathies when she declares that "a farmer can need none of my
help, and is therefore in one sense as much above my notice as in every
other he is below it" (E 29), she is merely describing with unwonted
bluntness a mode of social organization which the most attractive of Austen's heroes—Darcy, for one—thrive on and honor without raising our
dander. Knightley himself opposes Emma's plans to match Harriet with
Mr. Elton, certainly not because Harriet should make up her own mind,
but rather because, though "men of sense" and "men of family" will
rightly scorn to marry her, she is good enough for a farmer such as Robert
Martin (E 64).

But at the same time, *Emma* is a world apart from conservative fiction in accepting a hierarchical social structure not because it is a sacred dictate of patriarchy—*Mansfield Park* had spoiled this—but rather because within its parameters class can actually supersede sex. Thus *Emma* recuperates a world Austen savages in novels such as *Mansfield Park* and *Northanger Abbey*, in order to explore what was precluded in those novels, the place such a world can afford to women with authority. Though it may favor male rule, the social system sustained in *Emma* recognizes the propriety of female rule as well, and it is to this system that Emma, in the absence of any social superiors, owes her preeminence. Now this of course is not to say that Emma's ideas about her social status and the prerogatives attached to it are always sound in themselves or consistent in their application. It is to say rather that Emma's sense of the privileges and duties attached to her station is legitimate. This position has been almost impossible for criticism to accept. Domineering matrons like Mrs. Ferrars or Lady Catherine are bad enough. But we expect heroines to be like Fanny Price, to disclaim power *"in propria persona"* (MP 398) and to attend with admirable patience to the directions of others even when they are wrong. We scarcely notice how, though Edmund pointedly marks the chilliness of Fanny's east room, he never troubles himself to order a fire to burn there, because modest young heroines themselves are not supposed to notice, much less resent, such negligence—and we customarily accept what they see, and what they cannot see, as sound.

Emma's self-assurance—"I always deserve the best treatment, because I never put up with any other" (E 474)—is thus doubly unnerving because it exceeds the purely personal and is reinforced by a social privilege which commands a respect easier to extend to a man of Sir Thomas's stature than to a woman of Lady Catherine's, let alone Emma's. Furthermore, because we tend to read Austen's novels much as Mary Bennet would, as dramas of moral correction—where Marianne is properly punished for impetuosity, Elizabeth for her prejudice (and so on)—Emma's power is generally presented as the problem she must overcome. In no novel are Austen's methods particularly instructional, but *Emma* most conspicuously lacks the clarity of emphasis and the conclusory arguments that mark didactic fiction, omissions that have in fact disturbed many readers. One recent critic has vigorously complained that Emma's humiliation is too brief and too private, and that she is never vigorously "punished" for her wrongdoing; and many readers have been troubled that Emma shows no sign of "reform" by the end of the novel. The leisurely eddying of *Emma*'s pace, combined with the insistent ordinariness—not to say vapidity—of so much of its material, makes strident moralizing sound a bit

strained.[10] As a result, the identification and assessment of the faults which
are supposed to make humiliation and reform necessary have a hyperbolic
ring to them. When one critic lists among Emma's reprehensible "mor-
tifications" of others' feelings her curt refusal of Mr. Elton's inebriated
proposal, one feels this is scraping the bottom of the barrel indeed.[11] Since
the steady absorption of feminist perspectives into the corpus of Austenian criticism, the incommensurateness of action and reaction has been
noted, and some readers, who presumably cannot understand why Mr.
Elton's feelings are deemed worthier of indulgence than Emma's—have
ventured to confess that they could never figure out exactly what Emma
did to merit so much indignation in the first place.

What indeed? Austen anticipates the question as early as the fifth chapter, when Knightley and Mrs. Weston debate the wisdom of Emma's rule
with the maturity and candor of opposition that mark so many of the
disagreements in this novel. Emma has long been the subject of their
quarrels, and Knightley has long been accustomed to monitor Emma with
ready reproof. True to form, he warns that Emma's association with Harriet is "a bad thing" (E 36). But though they proceed from an anxiety for
improvement that we can appreciate only later, even the very worst of
Knightley's criticisms turn out to be fretfully minute: Emma, he complains, has never finished her reading lists; she has not applied her talents
steadily; no one has ever gotten the better of her precocity; her new young
friend will harm Emma by flattering her vanity, and Emma in turn will
harm her by swelling her silly head (E 37,38). Mrs. Weston does not share
Knightley's dire predictions about Emma's projects, because she considers
her judgment worth relying on: "where Emma errs once, she is in the
right a hundred times" (E 40). Here is no blind dependence on the infallibility of Emma's authority, but instead a confidence in its basic sound-
ness: "She has qualities which may be trusted; she will never lead any
one really wrong; she will make no lasting blunder" (E 40).

Emma amply corroborates Mrs. Weston's faith in the fitness of Emma's rule, but often so tactfully as to be almost imperceptible. This tact,
however, is necessary first of all because Emma's best actions are of the
sort which she, unlike Mrs. Elton, disdains to trumpet. A few strokes of
the pen, for example, show that in her attentions to the poor and afflicted
of her parish, Emma is intelligent, generous, compassionate, and—whatever she is in her studies—steady. Further, although Knightley thinks her
"rather negligent" in contributing to the "stock" of Miss Bates's "scanty
comforts" (E 155), Emma's "own heart" ranks visits there an obligation.
She is not shown to fuss over sending that hindquarter of pork to the
Bateses—though her father would mull and send less—and when she does
explain to Knightley that respect for her father's peace prevents her from

making her carriage of use to her neighbors, he smiles with conviction (E 228). Because she nowhere styles herself "Lady Patroness," we can only assume that Emma considers the performance of untold acts of kindness a duty attached to her social position requiring no announcement or praise.

Considering the contrast between Emma and Mrs. Elton can enable us to distinguish the use of social position from the abuse of it, a proper sense of office from a repulsive officiousness; and in the process it offers a glimpse of the conservative model of social control working well. The principle of difference between the two women and their rules is not finally reducible to class. What makes Mrs. Elton intolerable is not that she is new money and Emma is old, and that Mrs. Elton thus only pretends to prerogatives of status Emma comes by honestly. Mrs. Elton's exertions of leadership set our teeth on edge because of their insistent publicity, not because of their intrinsic fraudulence. Emma may be convinced that in attending their party she "must have delighted the Coles—worthy people, who deserved to be made happy!" (E 231), but she keeps the satisfactions of condescension to herself. But by tirelessly asserting her centrality in the minds of others, Mrs. Elton bullies her auditors into frustrated acquiescence: "Nobody can think less of dress in general than I do—but upon such an occasion as this, when everybody's eyes are so much upon me, and in compliment to the Westons—who I have no doubt are giving this ball chiefly to do me honour—I would not wish to be inferior to others" (E 324). Determined to advertise her sagacity, Mrs. Elton furthermore has a vested interest in airing what places others at a disadvantage, uncannily seizing on painful features of others' lives, and forcing them to the center of attention: "I perfectly understand your situation, however, Miss Woodhouse—(looking towards Mr. Woodhouse)—Your father's state of health must be a great drawback" (E 275). But Emma has ready stores of "politeness" (E 157) which enable her to respect what is delicate by leaving it unsaid. She feels gratified when Jane Fairfax divulges the hardships of living at home; but she exclaims "Such a home, indeed! such an aunt!" (E 363) only to herself.

More than nicety is at issue here. Just as the impoliteness Lady Catherine and Darcy evinced towards others in persistently apprising them of their inferiority constituted a socially significant wrong, a theft of the self-satisfaction to which all are entitled, so do Mrs. Elton's bruited exertions of authority triumph improperly in the dejection of others—as when she, intervening as friend as well as patron, hastens Jane's assignment as a governess, or just as bad, when she colludes with her husband to humiliate Harriet publicly for her upstart pretensions. At her worst, Emma transgresses in much the same way when she mocks Miss Bates at Box Hill, or when she discloses her suspicions about Jane Fairfax to Frank Churchill. Shameful though these infractions are, they stand out precisely because they are so infrequent, and if Mrs. Elton's presence on the scene helps us to identify and to deplore them, it also helps appreciate how much better Emma handles herself by comparison. Generally Emma is, if anything, admirably forbearing: she endures page after page of "quiet prosings" and often vexing developments without letting slip the slightest impatience, and she brooks Mrs. Elton's presumption without so much as a sarcasm or protest. Unlike Mrs. Elton, Emma has a proper regard for public opinion that—with a few very important exceptions—restrains her impulse to abuse. Feelings of "pride or propriety" make Emma "resolve on not being the last to pay her respects" (E 270) to the new bride, and when her neighbors celebrate Mrs. Elton's attractions, Emma lets the praise pass "from one mouth to another as it ought to do, unimpeded" (E 281) by her own dissent. Because Emma does not wish to be "exposed to odious suspicions, and imagined capable of pitiful resentment" (E 291), she behaves even more politely than she is inclined, while Mrs. Elton degenerates into the blatancy of incivility. The neighborhood that did not exist in *Mansfield Park* is everywhere in *Emma*. Emma herself defers to its civilizing restraints and in the process shows conservative ideology working at its best. Henry Tilney had pleaded that the watchful eyes of "voluntary spies" whose good opinion we value will repress the insolence of power, but General Tilney, as we recall, did not care how he treated his little guest or who knew it. But Emma is an authority figure responsive to the morally corrective influence of public opinion. This is what makes her feel the truth of Knightley's reproach at Box Hill, and this is what makes her resolute, swift, and feeling in her amends.[12]

Emma is so remarkable a novel at least in part for its ability to include what is politely left unsaid. The excellence of Emma's rule is often disclosed tactfully, because if it were vaunted brusquely à la Mrs. Elton, it would show her father at too great a disadvantage. Mr. Woodhouse's two-fold hostility to disruption and indigestion so unfits him for the duties incumbent upon the head of a respected household that Emma is often obliged to ignore or to oppose him quietly for decency's sake, and in the process she displays powers of delicacy and forbearance which are the more impressive given the vivacity of her own temper and the incisiveness of her wit. When a most unpatricianlike selfishness on Mr. Woodhouse's part would exclude even as old and indispensable a friend as Mr. Knightley from dinner, Emma's "sense of right" interferes to procure him the proper invitation (E 98). Similarly, while Mr. Woodhouse's anxiety for the health of others compels him to take food away from the guests at his table, Emma takes the duties of "patriarchal hospitality" upon her own shoulders without stinting: she "allowed her father to talk—but supplied her visitors in a much more satisfactory style" (E 25). Thus the narrative style of *Emma* shows, but does not call attention to, the courtesy with which Emma manages the household around her. Her diplomacy is characteristically inobtrusive, as when she steers hypochondriacal companions away from topics, such as the insalubriousness of sea air, likely to occasion disputes not the less rancorous for their manifest pettiness; or when she intercedes to separate warring conversants, as when John Knightley indulges in one of his many eruptions of peevishness against Mr. Woodhouse himself (E 105–6).

This kind of superintendence is one of the prerogatives of rule, and it comes as spontaneously to Emma as it does, say, to Sir Thomas. Other than voyaging to Antigua in order to squeeze more money out of his slave plantations—an enterprise which, even if it does highlight his decisiveness, hardly shows him to unequivocal advantage—Sir Thomas's principal activities are much the same as Emma's: he manages his household—with less aplomb—and he oversees the destinies of those around him. This he accomplishes principally by encouraging or discouraging specific marriages. That this is Emma's activity as well, and that this constitutes socially significant activity, are points that merit emphasis. Progressives and reactionaries fought their ideological battles in the arenas of family and neighborhood, and the whos, whys, and why-nots of matchmaking were not the idle concerns of meddlesome women with nothing better to do. In Austen's fiction the making and prohibiting of matches preoccupies country squires like Sir John Middleton and great gentry like Darcy himself just as much as it does well-meaning gossips like Mrs. Jennings; and in this context, Mr. Woodhouse's opposition to marriage—"he lamented that young people would be in such a hurry to marry—and to marry strangers too" (E 177)—is particularly comical. And even though, of all Austen's positive male authority figures, Mr. Knightley is remarkably the least officious and encroaching in this respect, as in all others, his recommendation that Emma mind her own business—"Leave him [Elton] to chuse his own wife. Depend upon it, a man of six or seven-and-twenty can take care of himself" (E 14)—is slightly disingenuous, and he later retracts it. Far from being above applying his own understanding to other people's business, he oversees the personal affairs of his neighbors more closely than Emma does, and his indignation over Emma's "interference" with Harriet Smith is due in part to the embarrassment he feels for his own, now futile, interference with Robert Martin.

Emma is always taken to task for her scheme to improve Harriet, and this disapproval exposes the importance we ascribe to the sex differential in matters pertaining to authority. The satisfaction Emma takes in this

project is surely not unlike the self-approbation generally allowed to reflect well on Sir Thomas when he decides to take Fanny from the squalor
of Portsmouth to the splendor of Mansfield. While he observes Fanny's
comportment at the ball "with much complacency," feeling "proud of his
niece" and "pleased with himself" for the "education and manners she
owed to him" (MP 276), Emma, with the "real good-will of a mind delighted with its own ideas" contemplates the patron-ward relationship
with the same sense of personal gratification: "*She* would notice her; she
would improve her; she would detach her from her bad acquaintance, and
introduce her into good society; she would form her opinions and her
manners" (E 24–25). If anything, Emma's exertions of power on another's behalf are considerably more generous than his. Sir Thomas admits
Fanny into his household only on the condition that she be accorded a
semimenial status, and when she turns on him in defiance of his authority
and to assert her independence from his intentions, he makes her feel his
ire. But Emma realizes that bringing Harriet to Hartfield accords her a
status which Emma herself is now obligated to respect. Accordingly, when
Harriet just as inevitably turns on Emma and threatens to supplant her
in Knightley's affections, Emma's own "strong sense of justice by Harriet" prompts her to admit that Harriet "had done nothing to forfeit the
regard and interest which had been so voluntarily formed and maintained" (E 408), and acknowledging her own responsibility for Harriet's
aspirations, Emma declines to oppose, however heartily she may lament
them.

But Emma's faults with respect to Harriet are imputed to be more serious than mere bossiness. Even granting, as characters in the novel do,
that Emma's wish to improve Harriet's situation is not intrinsically wrong,
Emma is held to be deluded in supposing Harriet worth the trouble at all,
and in treating her as anything more than an irredeemably silly girl who
ought to remain in the set to which she was born. Thus not only are Emma's attempts to "author" people according to her intentions held at fault,
but so are her related efforts to "read" them: Emma is rebuked alternately
as a dominatrix or as an "imaginist" and "female quixote." The categories
of authoring and reading may seem to have an unsuitable (post)modern
ring to them, but historical considerations confirm them in decisively political ways. *Northanger Abbey*, for example, makes it clear that women's
voices as writers and readers affront the moral authority of men—fathers,
brothers, generals, clergymen. Austen's heroines typically bring about
crises when they utter what their more conventional male sweethearts do
not want to imagine or to hear: with the example of gothic fiction before
her, Catherine strikes Henry dumb when she "imagines" his father's
crimes; Mary unnerves Edmund when she speaks lightly of illicit sex, as

a woman ought never to speak. "Imaginism" of Emma's sort, then, is not a private matter; it refuses to rest content with placid surfaces defenders of public order call reality, and it arrogates to itself the right to penetrate— "There was no denying that those [Knightley] brothers had penetration" (E 135)—secrets some would not wish to see brought to light. In the high-Tory antiromance *The Heroine*, Eaton Stannard Barrett, as we have seen, attempted to exorcize precisely this socially disruptive potential of women authors and readers—and not just of gothic novels either, since Burney's *Evelina* does just as much damage as Roche's *Children of the Abbey*—by undermining their authority. To accomplish this, he relegates them from the outset to the realm of insanity. Here Cherubina, crazed from an over-dose of ladies' novels, imagines that she is a warrior poised for battle, that her servants are her vassals, and that her house is her castle. Ceremoniously arming herself, she even rallies her troops with patriotic cant about the degraded aristocracy, oppressed people, and glorious cause of liberty. A young lady who questions her father's paternity is already an outrage, but one who suffers disruptively viraginous delusions of grandeur to which she expects the world to submit cannot be tolerated. As if to underscore the dangerous affinity between the insanity of Cherubina's airs and the insanity of political rabble-rousing of all sorts, Barrett has Cherubina conclude her harangue to her imagined troops with a recognition of her talents as a politician: "I judged that the same qualities which have made me so good a heroine, would, if I were a man, have made me just as illustrious a patriot."[13] For a Tory conservative such as Barrett, female authority and female imagination, unchecked by responsible male authorities, have the power to turn the world upside down. He defuses this threat by defining it as illusory, by invoking a construction of reality which women's novels and women readers challenge every time they distrust the stories their mentors tell them and suggest a connection between their imaginative literature and real life: Cherubina ends up in a madhouse, where she is cured by a commonsensical mentor-suitor who impresses upon her the absolute distinction between romance and reality.

To consider Emma a female Quixote in this tradition is to imply a more simpleminded and transparent distinction between romance and reality than *Emma* anywhere permits. *The Heroine* is a travesty of female writing and reading, while *Emma*, like *Northanger Abbey* before it, is a cagey celebration of it. Such is the consummate mastery of Austen's plotting here that Emma's misapprehensions seem utterly plausible when we read the novel for the first time, and she appears willfully to "mis-read" the sunny clarity of truth only when our own repeated readings of this romance, the stuff of literary criticism, have laid her misconstructions bare. But even more to the point, *Emma* invites us to consider how the two poles of romance and reality, considered so inflexibly discrete in *The Heroine*, actually interpenetrate. In this respect *Emma* recalls and refines the aesthetic self-consciousness of the juvenilia and *Northanger Abbey*. Not surprisingly, given that *Emma* is after all a novel and Emma a character in it, Highbury is teeming with highly conventionalized tales of love, which are often referred to as "histories" and "stories," and which have left their living traces in the orphaned offspring who appear to comprise a rather large proportion of the community. In addition to Harriet herself, to whose "history" we will return, Jane Fairfax herself emerges from a matrix of several "interesting" sentimental histories. The hapless daughter of a love match between a lieutenant who dies in battle and a devoted bride who dies of grief, hers now is a tale of female difficulty. As such, her "history" would not be out of place next to Wollstonecraft's *The Wrongs of Woman, or Maria* and Burney's *The Wanderer, or Female Difficulties*. As Emma rather shrewdly intuits, Jane's covert story is a tale of guilty passion presented amid an assortment of eroticized details that derive from the gothic. Emma considers this "fair heroine" (E 220) as a persecuted, yet guilty nun, "leading a life of privation and penance" (E 217) among family and neighbors, rather than mixing with the world. To Emma, she appears to be steeling herself "with the fortitude of a devoted noviciate" (E 165) for the "mortification" now necessary because she, as Emma infers, has tasted the "dangerous pleasure" of being the beloved of her best friend's husband.[14]

Although their "histories" are not elaborated as methodically, the experiences of other characters have an aura of romance about them as well. Mr. Weston's first marriage appears to have been a romance of high life, in which the dashing Captain takes to wife a high-spirited and spoiled woman who alienates her wealthy relations, obliges her sweet-tempered husband to live beyond their means, who repines at their poverty, and who finally dwindles to a death that melts the hearts of erstwhile resentful relatives. The offspring of this impecunious match, Frank Churchill, is a "child of good fortune" (E 448), and thus his story—like Emma's—is in many respects the reverse of Jane's, for it confounds the dictates of poetic justice and gives him more happiness than he deserves (E 447). Even Miss Hawkins, likewise an orphan whose story ends up better perhaps than she deserves, is given the false history of the social climber, for her credit as well as Elton's require improving the "story" (E 181) of her scanty fortune by rounding it *up* to ten thousand pounds (E 181). Congratulating herself for her success in masterminding marriages, as it would appear for the time being, Emma believes that the matches which form so effortlessly under her guidance must entail a revision of *Midsummer Night's Dream*: a "Hartfield edition of Shakespeare" would require "a long note" on the line, "The course of true love never did run smooth" (E 75). Emma's annotations may be wrong, but in thinking of a text to begin with, and this text in particular, she has not foolishly confounded the disparate categories of romance and reality, for the reality of Highbury is itself constituted by many different stories—adventures, distresses, robberies, rescues—not all of which ever get told or even noticed with the emphasis they could.

Emma's misapprehension of Harriet's "history" (E 23) is generally agreed to be the most conspicuous example of her quixotic preference of romance to reality, and her example discloses why novelists like Barrett, let alone decent young men like Henry Tilney, consider female imaginism worse than foolish, downright dangerous. The "natural daughter of somebody" (E 22), Harriet does indeed present quite a story, and as Austen and her contemporaries well knew, the telling or the suppression of it serves discernible political interests. As a child of a guilty connection, supported with minimal respectability but unacknowledged, Harriet inhabits a story about the failures of responsible paternity, a story which radical novelists, such as Inchbald in *Nature and Art* and Hays in *Victim of Prejudice*, did not let lie. Austen herself folded stories like Harriet's into the center of *Sense and Sensibility*, where the second Eliza, assumed to be the "natural daughter" (SS 66) of Colonel Brandon, is herself about to give birth to yet another natural child after being seduced and abandoned by Willoughby. There, we remember, Lady Middleton could not tolerate even mentioning, much less associating with, a natural daughter, even one of reputedly genteel parentage. Although in 1813 Austen judged the topic sensitive enough to warrant deleting a sarcasm at Lady Middleton's expense from the second edition of *Sense and Sensibility*, Emma is ready enough to accept the breach of marital vows as a fact of life: Mr. Churchill's promiscuous production of "half a dozen natural children" (E 393), she muses, may cut Frank out of his inheritance. In undertaking Harriet's improvement, then, Emma irreverently rocks the boat and refuses to mind her own business. Like Mrs. Smith in *Sense and Sensibility*, she wishes to exert morally corrective authority, and her attempt appears more impressive when we remember the prevalence and the potency of attitudes like Lady Middleton's.

To hold that Emma has quixotically "mis-read" Harriet's history, or that she herself "created what she saw" out of whole cloth instead of accepting the less interesting definiteness of "objective" truth, is thus to beg a lot of questions about the equity of the social system and the position of women generally in that system. It is to imply that Emma ought to have believed that her neighbors commit no sexual indiscretions and to assume that Harriet has no story. But even though it apotheosizes "true gentility, untainted in blood and understanding" (E 358), *Emma* doesn't make matters quite so easy, for reality in *Emma* is not organized along the same lines and in accordance with the same interests Barrett had projected in *The Heroine*. To be sure, Emma *has* in some ways misread Harriet's story: Harriet turns out not to have been the daughter of a gentleman, as Emma had insisted. But Emma herself undercuts much of the import of this realization. When she admits that "even" Mr. Elton would not deserve a wife who lacks "the blood of gentility" (E 482), she also, in a typically Austenian twist, avers that Harriet's blood was "likely to be as untainted, perhaps, as the blood of many a gentleman" (E 482). If the gentility of "many a gentleman" is a fiction as well, Emma's imaginative trespass in Harriet's case proves to be not so egregious.

In some ways, then, *Emma* suggests that Emma has not misread Harriet after all, and that, on the contrary, other people have. Though initially the solitary and outspoken opponent of Emma's schemes for Harriet, Knightley ends up making some powerful concessions: "you would have chosen for him better than he has chosen for himself.—Harriet Smith has some first-rate qualities which Mrs. Elton is totally without" (E 331). Although Elton's own pride would balk at this acknowledgement, Knightley's observation proves persuasive. Having been so imperturbably confident of his power to tempt a woman of Emma's fortune to change her situation, he is stung by Emma's plan for him: "I am not, I think, quite so much at a loss" (E 132). But the bride he triumphantly brings to Highbury belies this indignant claim: while his mate is perfectly suited to him in conceit and mean-spiritedness, her "history" of gentility turns out to be only slightly less spurious and "romantic" than Harriet's, although it is rapidly gaining the privileged footing of reality.

The same flexibility in the social fabric that makes Harriet a legitimate subject for Emma's solicitude has already accommodated Mr. Weston, and is now, alas, giving place to the clergyman's wife—whose father, like Harriet's and Mr. Weston's, was also in trade. What is accepted as real and what is dismissed as imaginary, under these circumstances, then, is a matter of social position, which is always itself in the process of changing. But if this consideration vindicates Emma in one quarter, it turns against her in another, for the fluidity of social boundaries confounds the authoritarian readings of a Barrett, and to some extent, in a different way, of an Emma as well. Emma herself has always been spotty in recognizing this feature of her society. Even as she considers the Coles to occupy a different level of being than herself and observes their steps up the social ladder with some resentment, she recommends Mr. Weston as a model of gentlemanliness without blinking; even as she taxes Robert Martin with the onerous charge of being a coarse farmer, she readily makes exceptions of his educated sisters. If Emma's ideas about the disposition of social status in her world are none too consistent, it is with good cause. The same mechanisms which make rises possible make falls possible as well, and therefore can threaten Emma with the loss of her own authority. The women in *Emma* who do not and cannot reign bring Emma to this humbling consciousness. During her penitent visit to Miss Bates, Emma pauses in sobered contemplation, not of the condition of mankind in general, but of woman's situation in particular: "The contrast between Mrs. Churchill's importance in the world, and Jane Fairfax's, struck her; one was every thing, the other nothing—and she sat musing on the difference of woman's destiny" (E 384).

Emma's exclusion of men from her reverie indicates her readiness not to omit herself from that category of persons whose status as "every thing" or "nothing" seems gratuitous and so undependable. The penultimate chapters of *Emma* present a different heroine from the one who at the outset appeared to assume the permanence of her power and in that assumption had become a rather unfeeling reader. Pondering the difference of woman's destiny, however, Emma remorsefully relinquishes "all her former fanciful and unfair conjectures" (E 384) about Jane and Mr. Dixon well before she actually learns about their untruth. Figuring forth the vulnerability of handsome, clever, and accomplished young ladies to the indignities of powerlessness, penury, and dependence, Jane's story, unlike Harriet's, is not a gratifying one to Emma, and Jane's unwillingness to impart it makes her a closed book that keeps others, most notably Emma herself, at an unflatteringly inaccessible distance, and one even Mr. Knightley, who loves an "open temper" (E 289), cannot like. By preferring to read Jane's story as a tale of guilty passion, Emma had maintained for herself the prerogative either of censure or of generous exoneration that placed her apart from and above Jane. As Emma herself recognizes, in having done so she has "transgressed the duty of woman by woman" (E 231). As a single woman in need of work, Jane must sell herself in slavery, not as human flesh, but as human intellect, she is quick to add. But governesses were typically suspected of an interest in selling their flesh as well. As Mary Ann Radcliffe argued in her *The Female Advocate* (1799), women seeking any sort of livelihood are typically treated like prostitutes, because prostitution is the only sale which they are recognized as capable of transacting, the only thing they have ever really been taught to do. By indulging in precisely these sorts of suspicions, Emma has herself confirmed, rather than opposed, thinking which transgresses "the duty of woman by woman" and betrayed a basic solidarity in order to take up the ugly role of rich and haughty women in tales of female difficulty, whose insolence, neglect, or spite prompt them to exacerbate

the pain of those they should comfort: "Of all the sources of evil sur-
rounding the former [i.e., Jane], since her coming to Highbury, she was
persuaded that she must herself have been the worst. She must have been
a perpetual enemy. They never could have been all three together, without
her having stabbed Jane Fairfax's peace in a thousand instances" (E 421).

But once again, with this history as with Harriet's, the highly qualified
texture of *Emma* makes it impossible definitively to conclude that Emma
had been quixotically wrong. Even the mild Mrs. Weston views Jane's
secret engagement as her "one great deviation from the strict rule of right"
(E 400), and Jane herself considers it an illicit act "contrary to all my sense
of right" (E 419). Curiously enough, however, Emma herself finally sees
Jane Fairfax's story in light of another Shakespearean history, this time
from *Romeo and Juliet*: "If a woman can ever be excused for thinking
only of herself, it is in a situation like Jane Fairfax's.—Of such, one may
almost say, that 'the world is not their's, nor the world's law' " (E 400).
Although Emma's assertion is carefully hedged, it must be noted that she
not only relinquishes the moral authority she had been so quick to wield
at Jane's expense; she also attempts to place stories such as Jane's beyond
the reach of censure which conservative novelists insisted upon when they
vigorously execrated men and women who exempted themselves from the
rules of social control. Austen herself makes the same attempt Emma does
when she imparts to Jane Fairfax "the kindness" of felicity Jane's own
"conscience tells me ought not to be" (E 419), or when she makes careless
characters like Frank Churchill happier than they deserve to be.

Toward the end of the novel, when "the great Mrs. Churchill" quite
abruptly "was no more" (E 387), and when as a result Jane's "days of
insignificance and evil" (E 403) come to an equally unexpected halt, the
arbitrariness and the instability of the "difference of woman's destiny"
is further confirmed, for now the great Miss Woodhouse herself is on the
verge of dwindling into "nothing." As beloved friends around her pair
off and depart to form new ties of intimacy within their own domestic
circles, Emma is left isolated and alone, the mistress of an empty mansion,
her domain painfully contracted. Considering the substance of Knightley's rebuke at Box Hill, the apparent desolation closing in on Emma
seems particularly poignant. Having considered Miss Bates in every respect except celibacy her immutable opposite, Emma had allowed that this
"old maid" was "the proper sport of boys and girls" (E 85). But Miss
Bates too was once significant, "her notice," as Knightley reminds Emma,
once "an honour" (E 375). To a sobered Emma, who fears her days of
insignificance are about to begin, the "difference" between her destiny
and that of Miss Bates is not so great, for the future which seems to stretch
out before both of them consists of the solitary care of an aging parent.

Already Emma can gingerly intimate that the coming death of her father holds forth an "increase of melancholy!" (E 450) she shrinks from facing alone, and the best that Emma is prepared to imagine for her future is a pious cheer altogether worthy of the kindly maiden aunt who bears a similar charge: "[H]owever inferior in spirit and gaiety might be the following and every future winter of her life to the past, it would yet find her more rational, more acquainted with herself, and leave her less to regret when it were gone" (E 423).

The "resources"—beauty, wit, employment, money—which Emma thinks can preserve her from sharing Miss Bates's ignominious destiny as a poor old maid finally amount to very little. It is single womanhood itself, the lack of a circle of people to be "first" with, that turns out to be the evil, and not a powerlessness to "frighten those who might hate her, into outward respect" (E 21). Much to her humbled bewilderment, Emma herself has gone from considering herself the confident author of other people's stories to realizing that she has instead been the hoodwinked and quite powerless subject of another very stale one, the "old story, probably—a common case" (E 427) of an eminently flatterable provincial girl deceived by a duplicitous and mobile man who is pulling all the strings she herself could not. This necessarily reminds us that Emma's "reign" has always been subject to the restrictions common to her sex. Mrs. Elton may be insufferable when she avers that "to those who had no resources" a move from the beau monde of Bristol to Highbury might be a sacrifice; "but my resources," she goes on, "made me quite independent" (E 276–77). But her boast here, as elsewhere, calls attention to a real problem. *Emma* is set into motion by the distinctively feminine boredom Emma suffers after Miss Taylor's departure. The merest "half a mile" (E 6) between Hartfield and Randalls spans an impossibly huge chasm, and not just to Emma either. To her timid father, the distance is too short to warrant the alarming step of ordering the carriage, and to John Knightley, who loathes nothing so much as "another man's house" (E 113), it is great enough to entail a trek no hearth-loving man would want to undertake. Having "ventured once alone" to Randalls, Emma deems it "not pleasant" (E 26) for "solitary female walking" (E 18), and the incidence of gypsy assaults upon unprotected schoolgirls proves her uneasiness to be more than an excess of delicacy. By showing how a matter as simple as getting from one nearby house to another to see a dear friend is for Emma almost prohibitively complicated, *Emma* tactfully shows conditions which make even "the best blessings of existence" (E 5) moot. Considered in this light, Emma's wish to have "a Harriet Smith" (E 26) is not the heavy wrong Mr. Knightley is inclined to think. As Mrs. Weston explains, "perhaps no man can be a good judge of the comfort a woman feels in the society of one of her own sex" (E 36), a woman, moreover, confined to unvarying "intellectual solitude" (E 7). Emma finally terms her fiasco with Harriet "the worst of all her womanly follies" (E 463), not because women are prone to follies in general and therefore will always need the guidance of Mr. Knightleys, but rather because the conditions of isolation and restriction that exposed Emma to danger to begin with are those to which women are uniquely exposed.

If *Emma* begins with the assumption of a broad arena for legitimate and useful female rule independent from masculine supervision, then, it does not end with the assertion of its sufficiency. By the conclusion of her story, Emma is brought low, and marriage saves her. To scholars who see Austen as a political conservative this upshot is particularly grateful because it appears to rein her in. Indeed, Mr. Knightley does look like the benevolent, all-seeing monitor crucial to the conservative fiction of Austen's day. Hovering like a chaperon around the edges of every major scene—the portrait party at Hartfield, the dinner at the Coles, the word game at the Abbey, the outing at Box Hill—he is always on the lookout for wrongdoing and nonsense, always alert in his benefactions for the poor and innocent. Knightley himself confesses that with Emma his role as moral censor has been particularly obnoxious: "I have blamed you, and lectured you, and you have borne it as no other woman in England would have borne it" (E 430), and he is probably right. Alternately beaming with heartfelt approval when Emma acquits herself properly, and frowning with pain whenever she misbehaves, he has been half paternal and half pedagogical in his watchfulness.

But this story is no less a "human disclosure" than any of the other stories in *Emma*. Accordingly, it does not tell all either; something is "a little disguised, or a little mistaken" (E 431). Knightley is not, first of all, above imaginistic misreadings of his own, nor can he be. As his readiness to denounce Frank Churchill as an "Abominable scoundrel" (E 426) attests, Mr. Knightley is just as apt as Emma to misconstrue where his interest is at stake, investing his upstart rival with the extremely literary character of the heartless cad. But Frank goes from "villain" to "not desperate" to a "very good sort of fellow" (E 433) in a matter of moments as soon as Knightley learns that Emma never loved him. Furthermore, Knightley is not nearly so wise and all seeing as he appears to think. He extols "the beauty of truth and sincerity in all our dealings with each other" (E 446), but many things—fortunately—have escaped his monitorship, Emma's worst faults among them. Knightley never learns, for example, that Emma did not stop with Mr. Elton, but proceeded to match Harriet and Frank; nor does he learn that Harriet, for her part, learned enough about gentility to disdain the very idea, and to prefer him instead, which is, after all, more than Emma had the wisdom to do. Emma, of course, must keep at least some of these humiliating little secrets to herself. To do any less would be an Eltonian trespass on Harriet's feelings. But even after Harriet's marriage takes the pressure off, Emma is still disingenuous about the "full and perfect confidence" she can now look forward to practicing as a conjugal "duty" (E 475). She has had more to "blush" (E 446) about than Harriet all along, and only moments later, Emma is blushing again, this time at the name of Dixon: " 'I can never think of it,' she cried, 'without extreme shame' " (E 477). One wonders how Mr. Knightley would judge Emma's readiness not only to form scandalous thoughts about his favorite, but exultantly to impart them as well. But Emma's part in Jane's story is never disclosed, and Emma herself gets by with no more than some private embarrassment whenever she receives "a little more praise than she deserved" (E 475). Austen's refusal to expose and to arraign a heroine reprehensible by conventional standards shows how she parts company with conservative counterparts, and given the morally privileged position monitor figures of Knightley's ilk enjoy in their fiction, Austen's determination to establish a discrepancy between what he knows and what we know about Emma is daring.

But Knightley is a far more extraordinary character than a monitor manqué. He himself does not set much store by his monitorship, and even though he always does lecture and blame, nothing ever comes of it. Monitors like Edgar Mandlebert in *Camilla* and Edmund in *Mansfield Park* enforce their advice by threatening to withdraw affection and approval if they are not immediately obeyed—"advice" being for them, as we have seen in *Mansfield Park*, merely a decent term for "command." They stand as fair-weather friends who may turn on naughty charges at any minute. But Knightley and Emma stand on an equal footing, and this necessarily modifies the dynamic of advice giving, endowing it with more of the friendly directness that marks the advice scenes between Mrs. Gardiner and Elizabeth. For Knightley, advice is not a function of power. He does not assume that the parental liberty he takes in reproaching due him— indeed it is a "privilege rather endured than allowed" (E 374). Being who and what she is, Emma dishes out almost as much as she gets, and when she does not follow his advice—which is almost always—he does not turn away.

Knightley, no less than Darcy, is thus a fantastically wishful creation of benign authority, in whom the benefits and attractions of power are preserved and the abuses and encroachments expelled. As such he is the very reverse of Coelebs in More's *Coelebs in Search of a Wife*. To the extent that *Coelebs* tells young ladies to comport themselves modestly like sweet helpmates if they want to catch a husband, it holds forth the promise to girls across the kingdom that their skill at housewifery and their strenuous exertions of self-subordination will all pay off in the end, making them more desirable to the best sort of men than lively women, wits, and flirts. But *Emma* does the opposite. Here choosy men prefer saucy women—not women who place themselves at the margins, letting themselves be noticed only so they may show that they are not so vain as to crave attention, but women who love even the unflattering limelight, and who do not hesitate to pen themselves the subject of other people's news to Maple Grove and Ireland: "Mr. Frank Churchill and Miss Woodhouse flirted together excessively" (E 368). In the character of Isabella, Austen shows that the good little wife cannot hold a candle to Emma: ". . . poor Isabella, passing her life with those she doated on, full of their merits, blind to their faults, and always innocently busy, might have been a model of right feminine happiness" (E 140). The "might" here does more than underscore the difference between how Mr. Woodhouse deplores the destiny of "poor Isabella" and how more conventional people would envy it. It also places the statement outside narrative endorsement. Chattering vacuously, oblivious to how she and her children endure the same curse of "living with an ill-tempered person" (E 121) which she complacently pities in Mr. Churchill, Isabella has probably fewer claims to ready wit than Harriet herself. And to a man as discriminating as Knightley she presents "striking inferiorities" which serve only to throw Emma's "brilliancy" (E 433) into higher relief. Wifely virtues are not meet for Emma; her hand, as he says somewhat proudly, "is the strongest" (E 297), and he likes it that way.

The conclusion of *Emma* shares the polyvalence characteristic of the endings in Austen's later novels. The tenderness of Emma's filial piety—strong enough to make her hesitate to marry at all—proves her to be reassuringly devoted to precisely those relationships which political conservatives wanted to protect. Moreover, Emma's devolution to marriage with a man seventeen years her senior puts an end to her "reign alone," and brings her back within the confines of that relationship which she had offended so many readers by slighting. But problems still remain. Because Emma and Knightley are social equals, marriage itself does not present the same difficulty it had in *Pride and Prejudice*. There, in order to secure the value of Elizabeth's reward—Pemberley and Darcy—Austen had to preserve the mythic prestige of the same institutions that had earlier depressed Elizabeth's significance. But because *Emma* deals more specifically with female rule, a conclusion like that of *Pride and Prejudice* is inadmissable: it would too conspicuously diminish the social prestige on which the heroine has rightly drawn all along. In order to secure Emma's prestige and the prerogative that comes with it, the ending of *Emma* turns back on the very outlines it seems to confirm. Mr. Knightley himself avers, "A man would always wish to give a woman a better home than the one he takes her from" (E 428), and Mr. Weston's feelings show that such generosity, far from being sublimely disinterested, confers an obligation which later affords "a man" the sweet pleasure of his wife's gratitude. But while Donwell Abbey is surely "a better home" than Hartfield, *Emma* closes by deferring Knightley's wish indefinitely to a time none wish to hasten—that is to say, until Mr. Woodhouse's death. As Emma well knows, Knightley's move into Hartfield is extraordinary considering his own power and independence: "How very few of those men in a rank of life to address Emma would have renounced their own home for Hartfield!" (E 467). The conclusion which seemed tamely and placidly conservative thus takes an unexpected turn, as the guarantor of order himself cedes a considerable portion of the power which custom has allowed him to expect. In moving to Hartfield, Knightley is sharing *her* home, and in placing himself within her domain, Knightley gives his blessing to her rule.

Without working off so many of the politicized texts which commonly undergird Austen's earlier fiction, *Emma* accomplishes the same social criticism as they did, by figuring forth figures of positive and unashamed authority more interested in promoting than repressing satisfaction, and by establishing the priority of social arrangements which, without being revolutionary or anarchistic, nevertheless fall outside the model drearily exemplified, say, in *Mansfield Park*. Their probity being utterly certain, Emma and Knightley do not have to bend to the yoke of conventions that do not suit them, and neither, within limits of course, does Austen. *Emma* ends with a marriage, it is true, but it also celebrates a "small band of true friends" (E 484), and gets away without defining a new domestic circle. Emma and Knightley yet have their separate concerns, their separate realms, their separate rule. This atypicality makes social climbers like Mrs. Elton nervous—"Shocking plan, living together [at Hartfield]. It would never do" (E 469). But eccentricity is one of the privileges of the elite, and in this case it permits the hero and heroine to be husband and wife, yet live and rule together with the autonomy of friends.

CHAPTER SEVEN

PERSUASION: THE "UNFEUDAL TONE
OF THE PRESENT DAY"

Persuasion has always signified more than what it singly comprises: its
two slender volumes have been made to bear the imprint of Austen's entire career. Whereas *Pride and Prejudice* and *Emma* can be and most often
are discussed without reference to Austen's other works, *Persuasion* is
above all else the last novel, the apparent conclusion that determines the
shape of everything that has come before. The critical tradition has des-
ignated *Persuasion* the "autumnal" novel, and this adjective brings with
it a parcel of value-laden and often quite pedestrian assumptions about
both the course of Austen's career and the course of literary history in
general. Wistful and romantically unfulfilled in the twilight of her life,
so the argument goes, the author grows tenderer on romantic subjects
she had disparaged in the confidence and severity of her youth; with her
own opening out onto a new world of emotion, eighteenth-century "ob-
jectivity" yields to nineteenth-century "subjectivity"; the assured, not
to say simple-minded, gives way to the ambiguous and complex.[1] The
underlying assumption that Anne's autumn and Austen's are complementary—in other words, that *Persuasion*, like the other novels, indeed
like all novels by women, is the author's own love story, composed with
little or no aesthetic distance—is of course teeming with fallacies, not the
least glaring of which in this particular case are those which result from
the imposition of specious teleology. *Persuasion* will not look so unequivocally like Austen's last and most mature word about love and the changing world before death stopped her lips if we recollect that *Sanditon*, which
recapitulates the raucous energy and renews the literary debates characteristic of Austen's earliest work, followed so closely on its heels. Austen, unlike her latter-day readers, did not have the benefit of knowing
that her impending death would be imparting a gently resigned, autumnal
melancholy to all her observations. Many prominent, yet seldom-dis-
cussed, elements of *Persuasion* call the youthful *Sense and Sensibility* to
mind—the apparently unfeeling allusion to Mrs. Musgrove's "fat sighings," the conventionalized villainy of William Elliot and the conspicuously artificial means of disclosing it, the overtness of its sarcasms at the

expense of silly and uninformed people. To judge them in terms of the autumnal paradigm, with which they are at odds, these features can only be dismissed as unfortunate lapses in morbid foresight.

This of course is not to say that *Persuasion* gives us nothing new, but only that it should be considered without using the benefit of hindsight to beg so many important questions. Most readers note, for example, that *Persuasion* ridicules the ruling class. This fact appears distinctive, however, only when we assume that it is a departure from the practice of the earlier novels. But surely nothing said in *Persuasion* about the Musgroves or Elliots surpasses the satire to which the Middletons, Palmers, and John Dashwoods are treated in *Sense and Sensibility*. What is different about *Persuasion* is not that it shows how the improvident landowners, proving themselves unworthy of their station, have left England poised on the brink of a new world dominated by the best and the brightest, the Royal Navy. As one historian has observed, foolish and financially embarrassed landowners are nothing new to English social history or to Austen's fiction. Eventually, Sir Walter will reassume Kellynch, and yield it in the time-honored way to his heir William Elliot, a man who, knowing how to serve "his own interest and his own enjoyment" (P 250), will doubtless not, as Sir Thomas had, lose his hold on "the situation in which Providence has placed him" (P 248).[2]

But if in *Persuasion* the landed classes have not lost their power, they have lost their prestige and their moral authority for the heroine. Whereas *Pride and Prejudice* could, with elaborately wrought qualifications and finely modulated discriminations, finally vindicate the highly controversial practice of "prejudice," Lady Russell's "prejudices on the side of ancestry" and "value for rank and consequence" (P 11) are never allowed to be anything more than amiable but groundless articulations of self-interest. Like her idea of what constitutes a "little quiet cheerfulness" (P 134, 135) or, for that matter, Admiral Croft's idea of proper decor, Lady Russell's "prejudices on the side of ancestry" are not favored with any corroborative footing in "objective" reality. As Admiral Croft puts it, "Ay, so it always is, I believe. One man's ways may be as good as another's, but we all like our own best. And so you must judge for yourself . . ." (P 127). *Sense and Sensibility* makes it hard to believe that Austen ever shared Lady Russell's prejudices, yet even there she evinces a heartier tolerance for booby squires than what she somewhat wearily musters here. For all his absurdity, Sir John Middleton's bluff generosity commands some respect. But whether darting eagerly after weasels, defending the claims of eldest sons, or extolling the virtues of "good, freehold property" (P 76), Charles Musgrove has little to recommend himself. His ideas, like his activities, are tediously predictable, and his "old country family of respectability and large fortune" (P 6) has no charm: Anne never regrets her refusal to attach herself to this inoffensive, but unredeemably mediocre gentleman and the long-established kind of domestic life he represents.

Persuasion, then, distinctively minimizes problems which had before been so momentous to the heroines. By centering her novel on a maturer heroine, of course, Austen is free to explore female independence without being obliged to explore the concomitant impertinence which always seems to accompany the self-assurance of younger heroines. The duty of filial piety, for example—Fanny Price's "great rule to apply to" (MP 436)—is nowhere dignified with the status of being at issue here. Even though her "word" has "no weight" within her family circle (P 5), Anne, like Emma, is an autonomous heroine. For this reason, to conceptualize Persuasion, as readers so often do, as a debate between individualism and propriety is not only to employ an opposition already curiously loaded in favor of conservative arguments, but it is also to underestimate the degree of Anne's independence from traditional, paternal authority and to misplace the emphasis of the plot.[3] Starting as early as the second chapter, for example, when we learn that she regards paying one's debts as an "indispensable duty" (P 12), Anne distances herself from an impropriety that is specifically paternal. General Tilney's wrath with Catherine is the catastrophe of Northanger Abbey. But the crisis in Persuasion—Anne's decision to break off her engagement—has little to do with Sir Walter's paternal displeasure. On the contrary, it has everything to do with the advice, not the authority, of a trusted friend, Lady Russell, to whom Anne does not owe the comparable duty of obedience. Such is Anne's filial disposition at nineteen. At twenty-eight she pays Sir Walter even less mind. While Sir Walter pursues Lady Dalrymple, Anne visits a "nobody"—Mrs. Smith—without as much as informing him, let alone seeking his permission, and once his disapproval is expressed, it is ignored without fuss. For Anne, no hard conflict between duty and inclination is implied by defying or simply ignoring her father. Indeed, it is all too easy: "Anne kept her appointment; the others kept theirs" (P 158).

Although Anne's indifference to filial propriety can show us the distance Austen has come since Northanger Abbey, Austen's earlier novel is nevertheless tied up with Persuasion.[4] Published together posthumously in 1817, they seem unlikely companions, but in Austen's mind their partnership was deeper than the accident of their copublication. Persuasion itself speaks to problems that to all appearances pressed on Austen while she was reviewing, perhaps even revising, Northanger Abbey for publication. The "hand of time" may have been "lenient" (NA 201) to Catherine Morland's feelings, but Austen considered it harsh to her novel.

In the "Advertisement" to *Northanger Abbey* she dwells on the "thirteen years" during which "places, manners, books, and opinions have undergone considerable changes," changes which render parts of her novel "comparatively obsolete." The "thirteen years" marked here, of course, are the same thirteen years that cause such dislocation in *Persuasion*. This novel is constantly calling attention to a temporal gap, to the time unwritten, but everywhere felt, to the missing third volume, as it were. Austen's handling of time in her plots is famously exact, carefully coordinated with reference to almanacs. But for all her exactitude, once Austen forges the temporal schemata of her narratives, she generally proceeds to submerge them, and only the most determined of students would wish to note down references to years and dates and then arrange them sequentially. But *Persuasion* is a calculated tangle of years and dates, and the passage of time itself is foregrounded. Here, as in no other novel, we are constantly being pointed backwards—to the knell-like repetition of "thirteen years" (P 6–7) that have left Elizabeth husbandless, to the heavy "eight years" (P 60) that have changed everything but Anne's feelings for Wentworth, to the tolled "twelve years" that have transformed the smart young Miss Hamilton into the poor and crippled Mrs. Smith (P 153); in short, to the inconjurable difference time makes.

The years alluded to in the "Advertisement" to *Northanger Abbey* and throughout *Persuasion* as the occasion of so much change are not just any years which would work changes at any time. With the benefit of hindsight, we look back upon those thirteen years as having sealed the reaction, but as they appear in *Persuasion* they do not present a repressive and politically monolithic aspect. Sir Walter himself seems firmly enough entrenched, to be sure, but he is not all there is. In his related capacities as general, pamphleteer, and stern paterfamilias, General Tilney is the obstacle in *Northanger Abbey* whose authority must be confronted and in some ways, however limited, overcome. But now, some two decades later, defenders of the nation appear under a different guise and are envisioned as alternatives to, rather than representatives of, the establishment. Admiral and Mrs. Croft are not gentry. Far from presiding over a neighborhood, they live most contentedly at sea, unconcerned with the production of heirs or the reproduction of ideologically correct values through the cultivation of local attachments. From some points of view, the differences between Admiral Croft and General Tilney may be minimal. The former, to be sure, nowhere expresses or implies progressive opinion. But to Anne, the difference is great. The years which bring the Admiral into prominence are those which mark off the disparity between the "old English style" of the senior Musgroves, and the "new" English style of their "accomplished" daughters (P 40), and which have brought changes with them accounting for what William Elliot calls the "unfeudal tone of the *present* day" (P 139, emphasis added). But the causes and the processes of such transformation are not themselves the subject of *Persuasion*. Instead they are the pervasive backdrop Austen establishes throughout *Persuasion* in order to consider the psychological impact that social arrangements have on women and the apparent possibilities which the "unfeudal tone of the present day" may hold out for them.

Of all Austen's novels, *Persuasion* is, in point of mere years, the farthest removed from the pressures of political controversy that animate the fiction of her time. And yet, though it is often viewed as a forward-looking novel, it makes a concerted effort to embrace a prerevolutionary context as well. Many of the most basic terms in the novel have a decidedly Johnsonian ring to them, and this should not surprise us, not only because Johnson is so sympathetic a figure to Austen generally, but also because he is probably foremost among the "best moralists" (P 101) Anne recommends to the stylishly melancholy Benwick. *Persuasion* continually contrasts the merits of fortitude, which can be "headstrong" (P 27) or daringly heedless (P 242), with the merits of prudence, which can be "over-anxious caution which seems to insult exertion and distrust Providence" (P 30). The opposition itself, of course, is Johnson's trademark. He frequently juxtaposes "heartless pusillanimity" to "heady confidence" (*Rambler* 25) and opposes the "presumption and arrogance" of expecting sure success to the "weakness and cowardice" of anticipating sure defeat (*Rambler* 43). Although neither Johnson nor Austen definitively resolve this opposition, both writers are self-consciously unconventional in refusing the moral authority of prudential maxims.

Writing when she does, however, Austen cannot treat temerity and timidity as neutral poles in a disinterested debate, nor can she omit scrutinizing their tacit reference to sexual difference. For Lady Russell, they are political attitudes. Lady Russell does not share the mindlessness typical of the squires, ladies, and baronets in this novel. Much to Elizabeth's irritation, in fact, she is always reading "the new poems and states of the nation that come out" (P 215), and as we might expect, her opinions about Anne's suitors bespeak her absorption in and sympathies for conservative apologetics. She aims her approval of William Elliot at Anne in such a way as to show Wentworth's boldness in what she considers to be the worst possible light:

> He [William Elliot] was steady observant, moderate, candid; never run away with by spirits or by selfishness, which fancied itself strong feeling; and yet with a sensibility to what was amiable and lovely, and a value for all the felicities of domestic life, which characters of fancied enthusiasm, and violent agitation seldom really possess. (P 146–47)

Lady Russell's argument is a manifestly sentimental one whose object is to establish the priority of that most basic unit of the social structure, the patriarchal family. She awards the prize for true, as opposed to "fancied," feeling to the man whose sensibility evinces the most responsiveness to women—the "amiable and lovely" being of course their province—and dismisses Wentworthian impetuosity as only fitful in its loyalties and subversive in its effects.

Of course Lady Russell is drastically wrong about Sir Walter's heir. Like all the villainous gentlemen and peers of progressive fiction who manipulate other people's domestic lives in order to secure their own power, he is out for himself, and if a semblance of sensibility to the fair sex is needed to acquire prestige, then so be it. Lady Russell is wrong about Wentworth as well, although in this case her error is plausible, since Wentworth is a complex figure whose own sensibility bears the deep marks of ideological contradiction. The action of *Persuasion* begins eight years before the opening of the novel, when Wentworth angrily spurns young Anne Elliot because he believes she showed "feebleness of character" in relinquishing their engagement. Wentworth's anger deserves particular attention, because it is anything but customary to fault women for diffidence. In another kind of novel by another kind of novelist, Anne's initial hesitation would strike Wentworth and us alike as exemplary and he, like the enthusiastic Henry Crawford glorying in his chains, would, rather than take umbrage at her maidenly doubt, manfully seize an occasion to prove his worth. But Wentworth does not appear to believe that the inconvenient modesty of the maiden will be redeemed by the submission of the wife, or to value the "feebleness" so often held to be part of woman's duty as well as her charm. Conservative fiction and conduct literature tirelessly preach to women about the duty of submission. In her avowedly counterrevolutionary *Letters Addressed to a Young Man,* Jane West assures young men of the kingdom that they have every right to expect their wives to give way, whatever the "pestiferous doctrines" of revolutionaries urge to the contrary. The "wise and beautiful subordination which Providence has instituted to avoid domestic contention" dictates precisely the kind of persuadableness in women that Wentworth scorns: "submission is the *prescribed* duty of the female; peace must be preserved, and she must yield."[5]

Maria Edgeworth was, as we shall see, a careful reader of the very passages of *Persuasion* which specifically address how the different social conditioning of men and women creates differences in their psychological makeup. The political agenda of her *Practical Education,* co-authored with her progressive father, is not so unashamedly clear as West's. Here Edgeworth disclaims—though she does not outright dismiss—any progressive concern for the condition of women, illuminating their problems, but disavowing any intention to solve them: "Their happiness is of more consequence than their speculative rights." Accordingly, she recommends that female children should be taught restraint, sweetness, and submission, because these, like it or not, are to be expected from them throughout their lives as adults. Women, she continues, "*must* trust to the experience of others; they cannot always have recourse to what *ought to be*, they must adapt themselves to what is. . . . Timidity, a certain tardiness of decision, and reluctance to act in public situations, are not considered as defects in a woman's character." Edgeworth's statement, of course, is already a stunning piece of intertextuality, imbedded as it is with a number of conservative truisms: it is wiser to trust to the accumulated experience of others than to advance and pursue one's own ideals, to submit to what "is" rather than quixotically striving for what "ought to be," and to habituate male, but especially female, children to what Edgeworth a little later terms dutiful "forebearance" rather than self-willed "precipitation."[6]

Wentworth's contempt for what he perceives as Anne's failure to be decided, forward, and strong thus implicates and dissents from an already firmly established and widely available tradition of debate about women's manners. To Wentworth, a woman is guilty of "weakness and timidity" when she evinces a readiness "to oblige others" (P 61), and when, deferring to the judgment of family or friends, she credits fearful rather than hopeful predictions about her betrothed. A strong man himself, Wentworth knows, or at least thinks he knows, that he wants the same qualities in a woman. He "seriously described the woman he should wish to meet with. 'A strong mind, with sweetness of manner,' made the first and the last of the description" (P 62). Wentworth's description appears straightforward enough. But as his subsequent remarks attest, he is in fact caught within highly charged tensions about women's manners, and his description of the ideal woman is oxymoronic, because however much he may desire "strength" in women, he considers it essentially inconsistent with the sweetness he also exacts. The narrator's remarks on the "large fat sighings" of Mrs. Musgrove "over the destiny of a son, whom alive nobody had cared for" (P 68) are relevant here. They will appear less like the gratuitous and tasteless cruelties which the subversive school has so relished when we consider them in light of Wentworth's contradictory assumptions about women. The narrator in fact brings up the grotesqueness of Mrs. Musgrove's grief only to ponder the irrationality of our response to it: "Personal size and mental sorrow have certainly no necessary proportions. A large bulky figure has as good a *right* to be in deep affliction, as the most graceful set of limbs in the world. But, fair or not fair, there are unbecoming conjunctions, which reason will patronize in vain,—which taste cannot tolerate,—which ridicule will seize" (P 68, emphasis added).

The tendency of *Persuasion* as a whole is to consider conjunctions which perhaps have even less basis in reason, but which are so much more pervasive that their arbitrariness is not even noticed. This discredited association of physical size with emotional delicacy prefaces a debate between Wentworth and Mrs. Croft about female manners, in which Wentworth takes a position very different from what Lady Russell would expect. If a large, bulky figure has a "right" to affliction, then conversely perhaps a "graceful set of limbs" has a "right" to venturesomeness as well. To Wentworth, however, the very idea seems as ludicrously incongruous, if not indeed as repellent, as fat grief may be to us, and this despite his declared wish to find "a strong mind, with sweetness of manner" in a woman. With the haughtiness typical of him, Captain Wentworth announces his principled opposition to carrying women on board ships precisely on account of their delicacy. His objections, he explains, arise not from mean-spirited misogyny, but rather from high-minded chivalry: "There can be no want of gallantry, admiral, in rating the claims of women to every personal comfort *high*—and this is what I do. I hate to hear of women on board, or to see them on board; and no ship, under my command, shall ever convey a family of ladies any where, if I can help it" (P 69). Having spent the best years of her life on a man-of-war, Mrs. Croft regards her brother's opinions as "idle refinement!" (P 69). But Mrs. Croft's claim that "any reasonable woman" can be "perfectly comfortable" (P 70) on board actually loses points with her brother. To a man fixed in his ideas about female delicacy, women so "reasonable" are simply not ladies. He is willing to transport women on his ships insofar as they are a dear friend's property—"I would bring any thing of Harville's from the world's end, if he wanted it" (P 69)—but the possibility that women themselves may not consider such journeys a violation of their lovely and amiable natures is obnoxious to him: "I might not like them the better for that, perhaps. Such a number of women and children have no *right* to be comfortable on board" (P 69, emphasis Wentworth's).

The objections not only to female sturdiness, but also to a female "*right*" to it, that Wentworth expresses here explain why it was and still is impossible for him to recognize "strength of mind" and "sweetness of manner" in Anne Elliot, until Anne's sturdiness and her forwardness to take control after the the catastrophe at Lyme oblige him to surrender his notions about delicacy. Like female modesty, which is suspected to the same degree as it is commanded, female strength is disapproved to the same degree as it is desired. Although the introduction of the tearful Benwick and the domestic Harville upsets conventional conjunctions of ideas about gender, for Wentworth delicacy and strength are sex-typed oppositions reinforced by class, and where he finds them conjoined in women of his own class—officer's wives—he is by his own admission displeased. Mrs. Croft's extraordinary rebuttal seizes on what she regards as absurd in her brother's ideas about manners and class: "I hate to hear you talking so, like a fine gentleman, and as if women were all fine ladies, instead of rational creatures" (P 70). As we recall, Mr. Knightley can convincingly oppose the modish primitivism of Mrs. Elton's projected "gipsy party" to the "nature and simplicity of gentlemen and ladies, with their servants and furniture" (E 355), because *Emma* as a whole is predicated upon the worthiness of the gentry ideal and the gentlemen and ladies who comprise it. But in *Persuasion*, gentlemen and ladies are excluded from the category of "rational creatures." Not that rational creatures of either sex here abandon the amenities of life, like Mrs. Elton's impossibly idealized gypsies. Indeed, the conditions Wentworth imagines to be too grueling for a lady to bear turn out to be quite accommodating after all. It is Wentworth himself who ridicules land-loving civilians for supposing that sailors rough it, "living on board without any thing to eat, or any cook to dress it if there were, or any servant to wait, or any knife or fork to use" (P 64).

But though Mrs. Croft may not repudiate some of the comforts of gentility, she does repudiate the system of sexually differentiated manners ladies and gentlemen depend upon. Her views on the subject are actually quite remarkable, given the renewed importance ascribed to female manners during the period in question. Conservatives and radicals alike agreed that amiable weakness and loveliness in women guarantee the continuance of patriarchy itself. "The age of chivalry is gone," as Burke famously wailed in a passage of the *Reflections* which Lady Russell seems to remember, and along with the chivalric sensibility, he predicts, will die the conditions which make the old regime possible: the gallant disposition in men to feel fondly disposed to the amiable softness of women restrains the otherwise indecent and uncivilized rapacity of their appetites, and the retiring docility and dutiful chastity of women insures the identity and survival of the blood lines of good families. Of course not all of Burke's allies believed that the civilized world was held together by chivalrous opinion. Jane West, for one, opined that Burke's notions of chivalry bordered on idolatry, and granted women far more than they intrinsically deserved, filling their weak heads with silly ideas about their own importance, when it is they instead who should study to please, and to be sensible helpmates and useful companions rather than lovely and ever-distressed females.[7]

While conservative and progressive discourse sometimes intersects on the phrase "rational creatures," the insistence that men and women's shared status as rational creatures takes precedence over sexual difference in questions relating to their manners and their morals was generally perceived to be the progressive position. Wollstonecraft's critique of the cultivation of speciously differentiating delicacy in women was often treated as though it were a wholesale recommendation of grossly viraginous strength. Thus Robert Bisset, for example, scoffs that Wollstonecraft included among the *"rights of women"* the right to serve as "soldiers, sailors, senators, politicians, scholars, philosophers, and rakes. . . . She trusted the time would soon arrive when the sex would require high renown in boxing matches, sword and pistol."[8] Seen in this light, Mrs. Croft is a tour de force of characterization. Though her comportment has not the slightest hint of mannish impropriety about it—Lady Russell, for one, finds her a pleasing and sensible neighbor—her manners are conspicuous by their lack of features usually construed as feminine, such as bashfulness, roundness, sweetness, and daintiness. She "had a squareness, uprightness, and vigour of form, which gave importance to her person" and "a weatherbeaten complexion, the consequence of her having been almost as much at sea as her husband" (P 48). She omits that self-doubt and reluctance that Edgeworth, for one, exacted from women, particularly in public situations. She looks "as intelligent and keen as any of the officers around her" (P 168), and her manners are "open, easy, and decided, like one who had no distrust of herself, and no doubts of what to do; without any approach to coarseness, however, or any want of good humour" (P 48). And finally, without ever really appearing to be the eccentric she is, Mrs. Croft prefers warships to the most comfortable manors in the kingdom, throwing overboard as needless weight the excellencies of the proper lady, and she "shares with him [Admiral Croft] in everything" (P 168).

Mrs. Croft appears never to consider robustness and self-confidence an oxymoronic violation of her feminine nature, and she could bid farewell to the age of chivalry without worrying much about the future of the civilized world. To her chivalry and the way of life it guarantees are superfluous: Wentworth's solicitude for women's comfort is a "superfine, extraordinary sort of gallantry" (P 69), which appears even more unnecessary in his case, since he in particular, as his sister implies, has the good fortune not to be a "fine gentleman" to begin with. Sir Walter, for his part, does not regard Wentworth as a "gentleman" at all, and his usage, however unpleasant, is far from idiosyncratic. Wielding a fortune in war prizes of mythically immense proportions, Wentworth is nouveau riche with a vengeance. Sir Walter restricts the term "*gentle-men*" to "some man of property," and thus does not recognize the claim even of Wentworth's clerical brother to the title: "Mr. Wentworth was nobody, I remember; quite unconnected; nothing to do with the Strafford family" (P 23). He objects besides to the tendency of Wentworth's profession itself to contend with and confound the established networks of social prestige, for the military is "the means of bringing persons of obscure birth into undue distinction, and raising men to honours which their fathers and grandfathers never dreamt of" (P 19). In all fairness, the contempt is entirely mutual. To a man who prides himself on "the gratification of believing myself to earn every blessing that I enjoyed" (P 247) the famous "Elliot pride" (P 88) in membership within their own family—as well as the precedence-, title-, and pedigree-mongering that goes along with it—is offensive. Mary Musgrove's eagerness to assure him that she regards the Hayters as unworthy connections only arouses in him "a contemptuous glance, as he turned away, which Anne perfectly knew the meaning of" (P 86). Furthermore, the record of filial piety which makes up an important part of Darcy's characterization, for example, has no place in Wentworth's history, and his impatience with Anne's hesitation at nineteen to defy paternal displeasure surely suggests how little store he sets by paternal authority in general. Since Wentworth has no place in, and indeed is actually hostile to, the patriarchal world of family and neighborhood which Sir Walter represents, though none too well, his "superfine" gallantry has no rationale and operates at political cross-purposes with his own designs and energies.

Wentworth's argument with Admiral and Mrs. Croft does not settle any issues, for no sooner does the subject reach an impasse than Wentworth breaks off and withdraws altogether. To their assurance that he will change his mind when he marries, he rather angrily returns: " 'I can only say, "No, I shall not;" and then they say again, "Yes, you will," and there is an end of it.' He got up and moved away" (P 70). Wentworth's words here both recapitulate his quarrel with Anne Elliot eight years ago and prefigure the same dilemma he will face in a matter of days when Louisa wants to jump down from the stiles at the new Cobb: "He [Wentworth] advised her against it, thought the jar too great; but no, he reasoned and talked in vain; she smiled and said, 'I am determined I will' " (P 109). Recurring to the imagery of hardness and to such related concepts as complaisance and determination, elasticity and fixation, impressionability and obstinacy, *Persuasion* continues to explore the antinomies of autonomy and authority that figure promi-nently in Austen's other novels as well. The subject of one of Elizabeth's

and Darcy's first debates, after all, is the worth of ductility and reso-
luteness: "To yield readily—easily—to the *persuasion* of a friend," Elizabeth taunts, "is no merit with you" (PP 50, emphasis Elizabeth's). But
while both novels attempt to delimit the legitimate boundaries of authoritative interference, the later novel deals with conflicts which, as
with the conceit of fat sighings, "reason will patronize in vain" (P 68),
and where persuasion accordingly is more problematic.

In *Persuasion* neither giving in on the one hand, nor holding out to
get one's way on the other, are very attractive options. Conservative
apologists, of course, cut the Gordian knot by submitting such conflicts
to the arbitration of persons wisely vested by tradition with the authority
to decide. But if *Persuasion* does not specifically indict this method, it
also stops far short of adopting it, since the "authorities" so vested are
inadequate. In Anne's case, an older woman friend, and no venerable
father, carried the day. Lady Russell stands not in place of a mother, but
rather "in the place of a parent" (P 246), and the very need to replace
a living but morally dysfunctional father itself points to a problem with
the conservative model. Moreover, although Anne is steadfast in refusing
to apologize for having once been persuaded by a woman who takes the
place of a parent, she soon eschews Lady Russell's prudential reasonings
on the grounds that they "insult exertion and distrust Providence" (P
30), and she never allows herself to be persuaded again. When Anne
receives a proposal from Charles Musgrove, she solicits neither her
father's opinions nor Lady Russell's, but "left nothing for advice to do"
(P 29). Anne's gentle imperviousness to interference is fortunate, for
Lady Russell's approval of Charles Musgrove's suit and her championship of William Elliot's do not testify to her powers of discrimination.
Like *Northanger Abbey*, *Persuasion* reflects on its own refusal to ratify
received notions: the narrator validates the perseverance of young people
in carrying their points even though doing so is, as she says, "bad
morality to conclude with" (P 248). In erased notes of the cancelled
chapter covering the same material, Austen dwells at greater length on
her departures from conventional wisdom in fashioning a story where
the older and unassailably "proper" woman is wrong, not once, but
twice: "Bad Morality again. A young Woman proved to have . . . more
discrimination of Character than her elder—to have seen in two Instances
more clearly what a Man was . . . But on the point of Morality, I confess
myself almost in despair . . . and shall leave it . . . to the mercy of
Mothers & Chaperons & Middle-aged Ladies in general" (P 282, n. 23).
Even though Anne finally avers in defense of her own infelicitous, but
not culpable, deference to Lady Russell, "if I mistake not, a strong sense

of duty is no bad part of a woman's portion" (P 246), the efficacy of "submission" is, if not utterly undone, then at least called into question by authorially emphasized criticism of the principles which underpin and valorize such duty.

The unyielding firmness and independence Wentworth advocates is likewise tested and found wanting. After persuading Henrietta to visit Charles Hayter despite the interference of Mary Musgrove, Louisa proclaims:

> "And so I made her go. . . . What!—would I be turned back from doing a thing that I had determined to do, and that I knew to be right, by the airs and interference of such a person?—or, of any person I may say. No,—I have no idea of being so easily persuaded. When I have made up my mind, I have made it." (P 87)

This speech, and Wentworth's enthusiastic response to it, are not the simple assertions of principled self-determination they appear to be. Louisa, after all, did not disinterestedly supplement her sister's faltering powers of mind with the strength of her own. Instead, she took advantage of her sister's persuadability in order to clear the field for Wentworth and herself.[9] Further, Louisa recommends independence even as she congratulates herself for her own interference: "I made her go" (P 87). Finally, Wentworth disdains the feeble malleability of "too yielding and indecisive a character" (P 88) when it defies him as Anne's did, but he does not seem to mind or even to notice the same qualities when they malleably conform to his own influence. Louisa has really done no more than give Wentworth what he wants to hear, and unaware that Louisa's strength of mind is really only persuadability to him in disguise, he rewards her with his praise: "Happy for her [Henrietta], to have such a mind as yours at hand" (P 287).

Clearly, Wentworth's preference for singlemindedness is as indiscriminating and self-serving in its own way as Lady Russell's prejudice in favor of wealth and family is in its. If "complaisance" can be, as Louisa terms it, "nonsensical" (P 87), inflexibility can be so as well. Wentworth takes little notice of this possibility. "[L]et those who would be happy be firm," he intones, anticipating the moral of his parable about the hazelnut: ".To exemplify,—a beautiful glossy nut, which, blessed with original strength, has outlived all the storms of autumn. Not a puncture, not a weak spot anywhere.—This nut . . . while so many of its brethren have fallen and been trodden under foot, is still in possession of all the happiness that a hazel-nut can be supposed capable of" (P 88).[10] The most salient feature of the glossy hazel-nut, however, is not that it holds impressions well, but that it is not susceptible to them at all. The efficacy of determination is undermined when Louisa, "armed with the idea of merit in maintaining her own way" (P 94), withholds herself from advice and falls headlong onto the pavement at the Cobb. Even Wentworth eventually surrenders resolution so fixed and intransigent. After the accident, he turns desperately to Anne for help, to be ordered and told what to do. And throughout the novel, his immovable resentment of her loosens under the influence of other peoples' admiration of her. He arrives at Uppercross swearing that Anne has aged beyond recognition, but he changes his tune when he observes William Elliot to be struck by her, and later when connoisseurs of beauty sing Anne's praises in his hearing (P 177–78).

Wentworth's determination is generally considered to mark him as a "new man," temperamentally as well as ideologically opposed to the way of life Sir Walter represents. But like his gallantry towards women, his steadfastness to the point of inflexibility actually aligns him with Sir Walter, and he must mitigate his self-will before reconciliation is possible. When Anne defies him by suspending their engagement, she encounters "all the additional pain of opinions, on his side, totally unconvinced and unbending, and of his feeling himself ill-used by so forced a relinquishment" (P 28). Wentworth's tenacity in holding "unbending" opinions, his tendency to remain "unconvinced" by and inaccessible to opposition, and most alarmingly of all, his readiness to feel "ill-used" place him in the unflattering fellowship of none other than the Elliots themselves. Like spoiled children, Elizabeth and Sir Walter bitterly blame the world for the necessities their own debts place them under. They feel "ill-used and unfortunate" (P 10), and steadfast in their foolishness, they refuse to forego expensive "decencies"—'Journeys, London, servants, horses, table" (P 13)—that alone make life supportable even to "private" ladies and gentlemen. Having inherited "a considerable share of the Elliot self-importance" (P 37) without commanding any comparable hauteur, Mary Musgrove manifests their tyrannical self-pity in a particularly degraded form. She always fancies herself "neglected or ill-used" (P 37), always thinks with bullheaded obstinacy "a great deal of her own complaints" (P 33), and feels everything as a wound. Wentworth has his own version of the "Elliot self-importance" which prompts him in like fashion to be headstrong and absolute. True, he may not have behaved like "an ill-used man" (P 172) when Louisa falls for Benwick, but this is not, as the Admiral thinks, because he has "too much spirit" to kick against the goad, but rather because he came to regret their flirtation to begin with. As the Admiral could not have known, eight years ago, when it counted, Wentworth did feel like "an ill-used man," and he does "murmur" and "whine and complain" (P 172)—not with Mary's sorts of whimpers, but rather with icy vindictiveness nursed over a period of eight years.

In the Elliots' case, of course, self-importance is a birthright, a benefit conferred upon them by their social position. Sir Walter believes he is somebody to the "nobody" of virtually everyone else. But though Sir Walter is convinced that, as a public figure, he carries his importance around with him irrespective of place, people only three miles away at Uppercross are contentedly oblivious to "the affairs which at Kellynch-hall were treated as of such general publicity and pervading interest" (P42) by Sir Walter himself. Anne's mortification to discover that Sir Walter and Elizabeth "see nothing to regret" in relinquishing "the duties and dignity of the resident land-holder" (P 138) bespeaks her lingering sympathy with the life of the manor, but landholders less distinguished than her father are not spared either. As presented in *Persuasion*, at least, landed existence itself fosters an immobility that fixes delusions of self-consequence which cause so much conflict. Anne is an adept in "the art of knowing our own nothingness beyond our own circle" (P 42), and this is what makes her wise. But the otherwise unobjectionable Musgroves, whose views are bounded by the narrowness of their neighborhood, cannot share such wisdom. Except in *Pride and Prejudice*, where a countrified Mrs. Bennet takes umbrage at Darcy's cosmopolitan pretentions, only in *Persuasion* does Austen portray the provinciality of her characters as a disadvantage. Taken by himself, Charles Hayter, for example, could appear as an earnest and respectable gentleman. But placed alongside Frederick Wentworth and ineffectually pleading with a troublesome child, he fades into nonentity. And just as the Admiral's tendency to confuse Henrietta and Louisa suggests their indistinguishability, so the redundancy of Hayter's Christian name, doubling with that of Charles Musgrove, calls attention to what is undistinctive about eldest sons in general. And in no other novel is a gentry matron exposed to such painful comparisons with a woman with wider horizons. When Mrs. Croft summarizes her travels, adding "We do not call Bermuda or Bahama, you know, the West Indies," poor Mrs. Musgrove finds herself baffled: "Mrs. Musgrove had not a word to say in dissent; she could not accuse herself of having ever called them any thing in the whole course of her life" (P 70).

Landed life is not taken to task simply because it promotes mediocrity or ignorance, but rather because its insularity is psychologically damaging, especially for women. Conservatives laud membership within a neighborhood precisely on account of the strong and stabilizing attachments, the changeless pace, and the unceasing familiarity that it carries with it. But for women it also carries with it a particularly narrow and unwholesome confinement, and discussion of this problem in *Persuasion* is specific, prolonged, and dramatically charged. Whatever baronetcy does for Sir Walter, it has not helped a daughter who has reached the age of twenty-nine without marrying. For Elizabeth the *Baronetage* cannot be the never-ending fund of solace unalloyed it is for her father. Every reading mercilessly reiterates an ever-receding birthdate and an unchanging status as spinster. Mr Bennet's sarcasm—"a girl likes to be crossed in love a little now and then. . . . It is something to think of" (PP 137–38)—has a disturbing relevance to *Persuasion*, where such crosses are all that women have to think of. Being the mistress of Kellynch-hall—"doing the honours, and laying down the domestic law at home" (P 6–7)—is not as engaging, as satisfying, and as adequate to Elizabeth's imagination as running Hartfield and its environs is to Emma's. Elizabeth is haunted by her disappointment in love, and the cares and duties of "her scene of life" are not enough to keep her from revisiting and fixing her pain. Bitterness, mortification, regret, and worry are all she has "to give interest to a long, uneventful residence in one country circle, to fill the vacancies which there were no habits of utility abroad, no talents or accomplishments for home, to occupy" (P 9). Nor is Elizabeth's condition unique. Anne has more "resources," as they are termed in *Emma*, than her sister Elizabeth, yet she understands that her regret over Wentworth lingers because "no aid had been given in change of place . . . or in any novelty or enlargement of society" (P 28) that could dislodge and eventually efface her painful impressions.

   Whether it is because we typically exclude Austen in general from access to, capability for, or interest in arcana of any sort, or whether it is because we have a habit of regarding *Persuasion* in particular as a tender love story that is not conducive to such considerations, rather scant attention has been accorded to Austen's affiliation with the eighteenth-century tradition of liberal psychology.[11] But readers of Johnson's essays, who recall his fears about the corrosiveness of hopes and disappointments, his recommendation of "change of place" (*Rambler* 5, 47), and his anxieties about the "vacuities of recluse and domestick leisure" (*Rambler* 85), will recognize the provenance of her concerns and the character of her diction, and will appreciate how, by linking women's confinement within their changeless neighborhoods to the strength and longevity of their feelings, she develops this tradition with particular emphasis on women's problems. Anne herself tells Harville that women do "not forget you [men], so soon as you forget us" (P 232). But far from presenting the constancy of woman's love in the light of a virtue, for example, loyalty, she presents it as a burden—"our fate rather than our merit" (P 232). Men will love faithfully "so long as [they] have an object," but woman's love can subsist indefinitely as fantasy alone: "All the privilege I claim for my own sex . . . is that of loving longest, when existence or when hope is gone" (P 235). A dubious privilege indeed, this liability to hopeless fixation. Anne's rather technical explanation for the stubborn durability of women's love combines social criticism with psychological acuity:

> "We live at home, quiet, confined, and our feelings prey upon us. You are forced on exertion. You have always a profession, pursuits, business of some sort or other, to take you back into the world immediately, and continual occupation and change soon weaken impressions." (P 232)

To Maria Edgeworth, whose access to moral psychology, unlike Austen's, is undisputed, Anne's analysis held special interest. The marginalia in her personal copy of *Persuasion* are very sparse until this episode, which prompts a flurry of scratches, underlinings, and comments. She, for example, reiterates Anne's socio-psychological argument here with "our mind is continually fixt on one object"; to the claims that occupation and change weaken impressions, she writes a heartily concurring "That it does"; and she brushes aside Harville's analogy between the strength of men's "bodily frames" and the constancy of their feelings (P 233) with an emphatic "No".[12] But whereas Edgeworth in conservative fashion upholds the traditional social arrangements that expose women to the problems she herself laments, on the grounds that defying such arrangements will not promote their happiness, *Persuasion* asks us to consider whether women's happiness may not be better served by cutting loose from those arrangements. Mrs. Croft disapproves of long and uncertain engagements because they expose women to perilous anxieties and fantasies— and her brother, eavesdropping, appears to acknowledge that the application to his own case with Anne has a compelling legitimacy which he had never before considered. Mrs. Croft's example as a wife suggests that life on the high seas, for all its dangers, is to be preferred to the "safety" of helpless immobility she experienced when she lived conventionally, as most wives such as Mrs. Musgrove do: "The only time I ever really suffered in body or mind, the only time I ever fancied myself unwell, or had any ideas of danger, was the winter that I passed by myself at Deal, when the Admiral (*Captain* Croft then) was in the North Seas. I lived in perpetual fright at that time, and had all manner of imaginary complaints from not knowing what to do with myself" (P 71).

The phenomena of change and relativity in *Persuasion* have long been considered symptoms of the dizzying modernity to come, a modernity usually described as either brave or degenerate, according to the axis of the critic. But to those characters who take notice at all, the deracination and relativity presented in *Persuasion* are not felt to be disturbing or disorienting. Except when she has pangs in tender remembrance of her dear mother, Anne cannot regret the Croft's tenancy at Kellynch-hall. She cannot say of her family seat what she knows social orthodoxy would have her say: "These rooms ought to belong only to us. . . . How unworthily unoccupied! An ancient family to be so driven away!" (P 126). Rather than feel that their removal to the diminished accommodations at Camden-place constitutes a fall, Sir Walter and Elizabeth themselves find more than enough "extent to be proud of between two walls, perhaps thirty feet asunder" (P 138). Anne is not bewildered to learn that our some-thingness is tenuous and relative, or sad to confront her nothingness be-yond her family circle—she, after all, is rather less than something *in* her family circle as well. Only from within a mentality which organizes peo-ple hierarchically from somebodies down to nobodies, and often according to whether or not they yield or are yielded to, does that status of noth-ingness feel so degrading. Anne does not possess such a mentality, and detached from a single neighborhood and a fixed world of traditional in-stitutions that make that mentality possible, she allows the alienation she experiences upon first coming to Uppercross to be a benefit. Anne finds it "very fitting, that every little social commonwealth should dictate its own matters of discourse" (P 43), and by learning different social dis-courses she is able to be a citizen of many commonwealths. Accordingly, she considers it "highly incumbent on her to clothe her imagination, her memory, and all her ideas" (P 43) in Uppercross. Though first undertaken as a duty, this reinvestiture is later experienced as a boon. After leaving, Anne discovers that subjects which she had felt obliged to "smother among the Musgroves" assume only "secondary interest" (P 124). She is "sen-sible of some mental change": her sorrow about Kellynch and even her tenacious loyalty to Wentworth loosens, and she now entertains thoughts of Benwick, and even of Walter Elliot.

If processes of inuring can be therapeutic—Anne, for example, "was become hardened to such affronts" (P 34) as she receives at home—some kinds of malleability can bring relief as well, even if it makes possible a certain erasure. Anne finally refuses to take sides in the debate about hardness and softness, and determination and submission, setting her sights instead on "elasticity of mind, that disposition to be comforted, that power of turning readily from evil to good, and of finding employment" (P 154). When Wentworth wittily explains how in marrying Anne he is not getting what he deserves, he elaborates on this quality: " 'Like other great men under reverses,' he added with a smile, 'I must endeavour to subdue my mind to my fortune.' " (P 247). The ironic mode of his state-ment is oddly fitting, for the "reverse" in question of course is the hap-piness of reconciliation, possible only after relinquishing the obduracy of his resentment and becoming susceptible to opposition. But the people in *Persuasion* who are preeminent for elasticity of mind are significantly far more remote than Wentworth, who after all by the end of the novel is acceptable even to Sir Walter. By the standards set in Austen's fiction, in fact, they are unusual, and by those set in conservative fiction, far too marginal to be the models they are here. They are mostly without the kinds of affiliations, idealized in such writing, that exact a high cost— confinement, unventuresomeness, fixity, boredom—for the stability they guarantee. Some Sir Walter regards as scarcely human: "A Mrs. Smith. A widow Mrs. Smith. . . . And what is her attraction? That she is old and sickly.—Upon my word, Miss Anne Elliot, you have the most extraordinary taste! Every thing that revolts other people, low company, paltry rooms, foul air, disgusting associations are inviting to you" (P 157). Yet Mrs. Smith above all others typifies the "elasticity of mind" Anne values, and this is not only despite the reverses that have marginalized her, but also in some ways because she has undergone them.

Insofar as salvos like these would console the unfortunate by contending that it is better to suffer after all, they condone the processes and conditions which cause such suffering to begin with, and so may be considered implicitly conservative. *Persuasion* is sometimes deeply tinged with such quietism. And yet Anne's preference of "low company, paltry rooms, foul air" to the companionship of her father and those he would choose for her is nevertheless a pretty piece of social criticism. Fortune, Providence, luck, chance—these are extremely prominent entities in the novel, and are emblemized here by the sea itself. And the person with "elasticity of mind"—the "choicest gift of Heaven" (P 154)—takes and resigns what they give with equal cheer, and makes her- or himself malleable to their impressions, much as the Crofts have let the sea air write itself onto their complexions without bothering with applications of Gowland's Lotion. On Mrs. Smith, who lives beyond the margins of "good" society, their marks have been the deepest: "She had been very fond of her husband,— she had buried him. She had been used to affluence,—it was gone. She had no child to connect her with life and happiness again, no relations to assist in the arrangement of perplexed affairs, no health to make all the rest supportable" (P 154). But though she is the least sheltered from fortune's blows—and as Mrs. Croft says, "We none of us expect to be in smooth water all our days" (P 70)—she is also the most resilient for having "weathered it" (P 154), the least inclined to feel "ill-used." Her bodily immobility—roughly similar in kind, if not in degree, to the confinement undergone by proper ladies in their provincial homes—serves only to highlight her resources more brilliantly. In a similar way Harville lives just beyond society, bordering out onto the sea itself, which has not served him a fraction so generously as it has Wentworth. If his case is not so dire as Mrs. Smith's—he is less crippled, less cramped, less destitute, and with a loving family, less disattached—by Sir Walter's standards he still ranks as a "disgusting association." But though even Anne herself suffers a "moment's astonishment" at the meanness of his lodgings, she later regards them as the seat of "great happiness" (P 99).

While the people Anne casts her lot with are well-traveled citizens of many different commonwealths, to recall Anne's metaphor, they are proprietors of none. Always ready to determine orders of precedence and to feel "ill- used" if opposed or neglected, Mary Musgrove decides after only a little consideration that even though Anne's accession to marriage restores her "to the rights of seniority," her own situation is still superior: "Anne had no Uppercross-hall before her, no landed estate, no headship of a family; and if they could but keep Captain Wentworth from being made a baronet, she would not change situations with Anne" (P 250). To Anne, however, these lacks are a virtue. Religious intimations are more frequent in *Persuasion* than in any of Austen's other novels and more enmeshed into its outlook. But whereas in other novels the world of wealthy gentry in which Mary takes such pride is either genuinely or at the very least nominally in the service of such intimations, in *Persuasion* it is not. Characters here who are most like the glossy but impermeable and therefore irredeemable hazelnut in Wentworth's parable are not Wentworth himself, who finally yields after all, but members of the privileged class, such as Sir Walter, who is devoted to avoiding crow's-feet, and the "polished" William Elliot, who is suspect precisely because he "endured too well" (P 161) and gives no evidence of friction or wear.

From the very beginning of the novel, Anne has valued "cheerful confidence in futurity" and scorned to "distrust Providence!" (P 30). Peopled more with friends than family, and accepting the "dread of war" that sometimes dims the "sunshine" (P 252) of domestic felicity, the society Anne finally selects—the "best" company (P 150)—removes itself from the institutions of the country manor to front more directly and hospitably onto Providence. But while the break Anne accomplishes with those institutions is more complete than what we find in any other novel, and while her efforts at accommodation are the most perfunctory, she and the alternative society she joins are also the least prone to overt indictment, and this constitutes a departure from Austen's early fiction especially. Whereas *Sense and Sensibility* and *Northanger Abbey* derive much of their dramatic tension from the defiance of tyrannical parents, *Persuasion* eludes, even frowns upon, overt rebellion. Social forms may be neglected—Anne dislikes "give-and-take invitations, and dinners of formality and display" (P 98)—but not outright opposed. Accordingly, Anne herself is capable of betraying some shame about her association with Lady Dalrymple and Miss Carteret, but she politely keeps it under wraps: " 'Yes,' sighed Anne, 'we shall, indeed, be known to be related to them!'—then recollecting herself . . . not wishing to be answered" (P 150–51). But William Elliot's history of expressed disrespect for rank itself is not acceptable. The narrator makes no bones about averring that "Sir Walter was not very wise" (P 24), but Anne shudders "with shock and mortification" to learn that his heir applies words as irreverent as "fool" (P 204) to him. But before we conclude that Austen's willingness to cover for Sir Walter betrays deplorable bad faith, or perhaps less damningly, loyalties too deep and residual to permit penetrating social criticism, we would do well to ponder the typically confounding twist in her characterization of William Elliot. Surely to identify the person who mouths social disrespect with the person who then panders to the very people of "credit and dignity" (P 151) whom he admits are "nothing in themselves" (P 150) is to underscore the particularly sterile conventionality of the entire system of "blood and connexion" (P 206) and the cynicism on which it subsists.

Of none of Austen's works, but of *Persuasion* perhaps least of all, can it be said, as Trilling has, "Nothing in the novels questions the ideal of the archaic 'noble' life which is appropriate to the great beautiful houses with the ever-remembered names—Northanger Abbey, Donwell Abbey, Pemberly, Hartfield, Kellynch Hall, Norland Park, Mansfield Park. In them 'existence is sweet and dear,' at least if one is rightly disposed. . . . With what the great houses represent the heroines of the novels are, or become, completely in accord."[13] Northanger Abbey is far from a haven to Catherine Morland, and this is not because *she* fails to be "rightly disposed"; Norland Park provides no values with which the Dashwood sisters can accord; and Kellynch Hall, not even "ever-remembered" by its own proprietors, is bidden a rather wistful good riddance by a daughter far superior to what it now "represents." Works of fiction written on the conservative model tirelessly exhort us to accept infelicity as the condition of life and urge us instead to seek our modest satisfactions in the consciousness of prescribed attachments well honored, and duties well done. But Austen's novels are pervasively concerned, not with according ourselves to an existence "sweet and dear," but with achieving a more active, expansive, and personally fulfilling happiness, and they persistently suggest that this is well worth the striving. Sometimes, as in *Pride and Prejudice*, Austen contrives to locate such happiness within conservative institutions themselves, but as we have seen, it takes some work before Pemberly will accommodate Elizabeth. And once Pemberly does make a place for her, one suspects that it is the "great beautiful house" itself, rather than Elizabeth, that will be essentially improved for her presence there, because whatever its previous dignity, it never seemed a place of pleasure. The word "happy" rings as frequently across the pages of *Persuasion* as it does those of *Pride and Prejudice*, and it should tell us something that in *Persuasion* it is the nefarious Walter Elliot who wishes to dissuade Anne from pursuing the highest happiness she can conceive of. When he discovers that she prefers the "best" company to merely "good" company, he warns, "You have a better right to be fastidious than almost any other woman I know; but will it answer? Will it make you happy? Will it not be wiser to accept the society of these good ladies in Laura-place, and enjoy all the advantages of the connexion as far as possible?" (P 150). Fortunately, Anne's fastidiousness, like Elizabeth's, finally does "answer." But unlike Elizabeth's, it is achieved not at a great beautiful house with an ever-remembered name, but rather in a disposition only discernible in people who do not belong to such houses, people such as the Crofts, who walk "along in happy independence," (P 168) or like Harville, whose weather-beaten lodgings are a "picture of repose and domestic happiness" (P 98).

The interests of happiness, piety, and well-being demand removal from Kellynch Hall, its proprieties and priorities. But whether moving beyond Kellynch or any equivalent bespeaks a victory of autonomy from what a great house represents, or a despair of its ever improving enough to be desirable, is hard to say. Not surprisingly, since they belong exclusively to the years which assured the reaction, Austen's last three novels reflect a strong sense of the increasing immovability of established authority. While *Sense and Sensibility* concludes with an opposition and a withdrawal that are angry, permanent, and committed, in *Northanger Abbey* General Tilney finally does yield, if minimally, and in *Pride and Prejudice* Darcy is improved by confrontation, and eventually even Lady Catherine comes around. But even though Sir Thomas's judgment in *Mansfield Park* is thoroughly impeached, his authority is fixed. In *Emma*, when his kind of authority is transformed and feminized, and joined with Knightley's, it assumes a benign aspect. But in *Persuasion*, stately houses and their proprietors are no longer formidable, and their intransigence is matched only by their vapidity. Good characters depart from them without a breach, differ from them without defiance. Thus the overarching structure of *Persuasion* as a whole reproduces and asks us to accept the same sorts of unresolved tensions found in so many of its shorter, characteristically oxymoronic formulations—such as "fat sighings," or "she was deep in the happiness of such misery, or the misery of such happiness" (P 229). *Persuasion* settles little: it resumes a debate interrupted eight years in the past without reaching an agreement, and without requiring one. Wentworth does not concede that Lady Russell had been right, Anne refuses to concede that yielding was wrong: "cheerful confidence in futurity" precludes such regret, and Providence has been equally served by delay.

The "elasticity of mind" celebrated in *Persuasion* accepts and surpasses both of these, as well as the broader social conflicts the book details. It is tempting to see in this effort to define and endorse extensive difference from established institutions, without effecting an overt or impassible breach from them, as the perfection of the strategies and the positions that have marked Austen's fiction from the start. Austen, no less than Blake, wrote for an audience with what one critic has called "war-man-acled minds," and her works, no less than Blake's, attempt—inevitably with only limited success—to shed those manacles which she perforce wore too.[14] Among the least doctrinaire of all her contemporaries, Austen from the outset took on the materials which political controversy endowed with such importance, without inviting or aggravating partisan impulses. During a time when all social criticism, particularly that which aimed at the institution of the family in general and the place of women in particular, came to be associated with the radical cause, Austen defended and enlarged a progressive middle ground that had been eaten away by the polarizing polemics born of the 1790s. If she very early opted definitely not to ratify the anarchism of the radical opposition, despite an allegiance to the liberal tradition which underlay much of it, she also avoided its irritability, its confusion, and its very early defeat. Conservative fiction was Austen's medium because it very quickly became the only fiction there was, other voices being quelled, and Austen persistently subjected its most cherished mythologies to interrogations from which it could not recover. The highly parodic style developed in the juvenilia, when applied to the stuff of conservative fiction, constituted a kind of piracy which commandeered conservative novelistic discourse and forced it to hoist flags of different colors, so to speak, to say things it was not fashioned to say—as when Catherine Morland, for example, assures herself with perfect trust that the good General Tilney "could not propose any thing improper for her" (NA 156); or when Marianne's "sensibility" and Elinor's "sense" turn out not to be antithetically opposed; or most optimistically, when Darcy himself absorbs the values of his antagonist in order to make her as well as himself happy. In none of the novels can conservative ideology be entirely overcome, but in all, as most forcibly in *Mansfield Park*, its basic imperatives—benevolence, gratitude, family attachment, female modesty, paternal authority—are wrested from their privileged claims and made, like Edmund Bertram, to relinquish their "moral elevation" (MP 158).

NOTES

INTRODUCTION

1. Scott's remark, recorded in a journal entry of 1826, is reprinted in *Jane Austen: The Critical Heritage*, ed. B. C. Southam (London: Routledge and Kegan Paul, 1968), p. 106.

2. Southam, *Critical Heritage*, p. 131.

3. J. W. Croker, *Quarterly Review*, xi (April 1814), 123–24 (Article IX); see also Croker's even lengthier and more vituperative attack on Burney's *Memoirs of Dr. Burney* in *Quarterly Review* 49 (April 1833): 97–125.

4. From his review of *Northanger Abbey* and *Persuasion* in *Quarterly Review* (January 1821), reprinted in Southam, *Critical Heritage*, p. 95.

5. From his review of the *Memoir of Jane Austen* in the *North British Review* (April 1870), reprinted in Southam, *Critical Heritage*, pp. 257, 250.

6. From "The Novels of Jane Austen," *Blackwood's Edinburgh Magazine* (July 1859), reprinted in Southam, *Critical Heritage*, p. 163. Donald Greene coined the phrase "myth of limitation" and takes the whole phenomenon to task in "Jane Austen and the Myth of Limitation," in *Jane Austen Today*, ed. Joel Weinsheimer (Athens: University of Georgia Press, 1975), pp. 142–75.

7. Southam, *Critical Heritage*, p. 166. Also see the "'historical' view" from *St. Paul's Magazine* (March 1870) which repeatedly praises Austen for knowing better than to step out of her sphere. Reprinted in Southam, pp. 226–40.

8. *Jane Austen: A Critical Bibliography*, ed. R. W. Chapman (Oxford: Clarendon Press, 1953), p. 53.

9. The same nostalgia haunts much of Trilling's writing on Austen, particularly his posthumously printed essay in *The Times Literary Supplement* 5 (March 1976): 250–52; reprinted in *The Last Decade: Essays and Reviews, 1965–75*, ed. Diana Trilling (New York: Harcourt, 1979), pp. 204–25.

10. For example, see, respectively, Gilbert Ryle, "Jane Austen and the Moralists" *Oxford Review* 1 (February 1966): 5–18; Lionel Trilling, *Sincerity and Authenticity* (Cambridge: Harvard University Press, 1972), pp. 70–80; Alistair Duckworth, *The Improvement of the Estate* (Baltimore: Johns Hopkins University Press, 1971). Viewing Austen in essentially the same way as Janeites do, only without a fraction of their pleasure, some recent Marxist critics have been extremely severe with Austen as a result of their equally unquestioned assumption of her incapacity to be conscious of ideology. Generous allowances are made for Blake's inability completely to stand outside ideology, but for Austen ideology is never more than a "hindrance" and a "screen" which prevents her

from questioning the "market values" she is "utterly committed to" and which "systematically closes up her imagination against critical alternatives." See David Aers, "Community and Morality: Towards Reading Jane Austen," in *Romanticism and Ideology: Studies in English Writing 1765–1830*, ed. David Aers, Jonathan Cook, and David Punter (London: Routledge and Kegan Paul, 1981), pp. 118–36. For a political reading which holds, by contrast, that Austen radically criticizes market values, particularly as these oppress women, see Mary Evans, *Jane Austen and the State* (London and New York: Tavistock Publications, 1987).

11. Marilyn Butler, *Romantics, Rebels and Reactionaries* (New York: Oxford University Press, 1982), p. 102.

12. Marilyn Butler, *Jane Austen and the War of Ideas* (Oxford: Clarendon Press, 1975), p. 298. Although I obviously disagree with Butler quite strenuously on the subject of Austen's politics, I am also, like all Austenians, deeply indebted to her for having been the first to demonstrate Austen's involvement with the war of political ideas. Butler somewhat softens her position on Austen's conservatism in "History, Politics, and Religion," in *The Jane Austen Companion*, ed. J. David Grey, A. Walton Litz, and Brian Southam (New York: Macmillan, 1986), pp. 190–208.

13. Southam, *Critical Heritage*, pp. 64, 116.

14. See Lord David Cecil, *A Portrait of Jane Austen* (New York: Hill and Wang, 1979). I am particularly indebted to David Spring's essay, which situates Austen in the rentier class of "pseudo-gentry." See "Interpreters of Jane Austen's Social World: Literary Critics and Historians," in *Jane Austen: New Perspectives*, Women and Literature, New Series, Vol. 3, ed. Janet Todd (New York: Holmes and Meier), pp. 53–72.

15. David Halperin, *The Life of Jane Austen* (Baltimore: Johns Hopkins University Press, 1984), pp. 108–10. Many of Halperin's views were put forward earlier by Marvin Mudrick, whose *Jane Austen: Irony as Defense and Discovery* (Princeton: Princeton University Press, 1952) still sets the terms of much Austenian criticism.

16. "Jane Austen and the Conflict of Interpretations," in Todd, *Jane Austen: New Perspectives*, pp. 45–46.

17. Among the works of feminist criticism and scholarship to which I have been particularly indebted are Patricia M. Spacks, *Imagining A Self* (Cambridge: Harvard University Press, 1976); Elaine Showalter, *A Literature of their Own: British Women Novelists from Brontë to Lessing* (Princeton: Princeton University Press, 1977), which, though focusing exclusively on Victorian fiction, establishes a female novelistic tradition; Sandra M. Gilbert and Susan Gubar, *The Madwoman in the Attic: The Woman Writer and the Nineteenth-Century Literary Imagination* (New Haven: Yale University Press, 1979), which examines the problems women writers encounter writing in a culture that severely limits the female voice; and above all Mary Poovey, *The Proper Lady and the Woman Writer: Ideology as Style in the Works of Mary Wollstonecraft, Mary Shelley, and Jane Austen* (Chicago: University of Chicago Press, 1984), which unfolds the ideological contradictions in conduct literature requiring female modesty and subordination. Although they do not bear so directly on my enterprise here, I

have been much informed by Judith Fetterley, *The Resisting Reader: A Feminist Approach to American Fiction* (Bloomington: Indiana University Press, 1978), and Margaret Homans, *Bearing the Word: Language and Female Experience in Nineteenth-Century Women's Writing* (Chicago: The University of Chicago Press, 1986). General works on historical method which I have found helpful include, Jerome J. McGann, *The Beauty of Inflections: Literary Investigations in Historical Method and Theory* (Oxford: Clarendon Press, 1985); Jerome J. McGann, ed., *Historical Studies and Literary Criticism* (Madison: University of Wisconsin Press, 1985); Hans Robert Jauss, *Toward an Aesthetic of Reception* (Minneapolis: University of Minnesota Press, 1982); Fredric Jameson, *The Political Unconscious: Narrative as a Socially Symbolic Act* (Ithaca: Cornell University Press, 1981); Terry Eagleton, *Criticism and Ideology* (London: Verso Editions, 1976).

18. For the best recent essay on this subject, see Margaret Anne Doody, "Jane Austen's Reading," in *The Jane Austen Companion*, pp. 347–63. See also Ellen Moers, *Literary Women: The Great Writers* (Garden City, N.Y.: Doubleday, 1976), which restores the intellectual dignity of Austen's predecessors. J. M. S. Tompkins's *The Popular Novel in England, 1770–1800* (London: Constable, 1932; reprint, Lincoln: University of Nebraska Press, 1961) is still valuable. Other discussions of Austen's relation to her predecessors include Frank W. Bradbrook, *Jane Austen and Her Predecessors* (Cambridge: Cambridge University Press, 1966); Kenneth Moler, *Jane Austen's Art of Allusion* (Lincoln: University of Nebraska Press, 1968); and Henrietta Ten Harmsel, *Jane Austen: A Study in Fictional Conventions* (The Hague: Mouton, 1964).

19. Gary Kelly illuminates the difficulties posed by the terms "anti-Jacobin" and "Jacobin"—terms which, by relegating social criticism to the realm of treason, serve reactionary ends. See *The English Jacobin Novel, 1780–1805* (Oxford: Clarendon Press, 1976). Also see Raymond Williams's review article "The Fiction of Reform," in *Times Literary Supplement*, 25 March 1977, reprinted in *Writing in Society* (London: Verso Editions, n.d.), pp. 142–49.

20. Needless to say, although it was not exclusively Lockean, the rhetoric of liberty could be associated with Locke, just as, although it was not exclusively the heritage of the gentry, it was associated with and adoptable by the gentry. The volatility of such rhetoric was readily apparent well before the French Revolution. John Brewer has demonstrated how as early as the 1760s many warring political interests were adopting the discourse of liberty; see his *Party Ideology and Popular Politics at the Accession of George III* (Cambridge: Cambridge University Press, 1976). For other studies of political language in its historical contexts I am particularly indebted to J. E. A. Pocock, *Politics, Language and Time: Essays on Political Thought and History* (New York: Atheneum, 1971), and *Virtue, Commerce, and History* (Cambridge: Cambridge University Press, 1985); and Quentin Skinner, *Foundations of Modern Political Thought* (New York and Cambridge: Cambridge University Press, 1978). Also see James T. Boulton, *The Language of Politics* (London: Routledge and Kegan Paul, 1963).

21. Lionel Trilling, "Introduction" to *Emma* (Boston: Houghton Mifflin, 1957), p. x.

CHAPTER ONE

1. Jane West, *Tale of the Times* (London, 1799), 3 vols., vol. 2, pp. 274–75.

2. Charlotte Smith, *Desmond*, 3 vols. (London, 1792), p. iii.

3. Jane West, *The Infidel Father*, 3 vols., (London, 1802), p. ii.

4. *Reflections on the Revolution in France*, in *The Works of the Right Honourable Edmund Burke*, 16 vols. (London, 1826), vol. 5, pp. 141–42.

5. I have been pervasively influenced by Ronald Paulson's *Representations of Revolution (1789–1820)* (New Haven: Yale University Press, 1983), especially pp. 57–73; Thomas Weiskel, *The Romantic Sublime: Studies in the Structure and Psychology of Transcendence* (Baltimore: Johns Hopkins University Press, 1976); Neil Hertz, "Medusa's Head: Male Hysteria Under Political Pressure," *Representations* 4 (Fall, 1983): 27–54. For a helpful and necessary corrective to these largely Freudian approaches see J. G. A. Pocock's discussion of political economy in the *Reflections* in *Virtue, Commerce, and History*, pp. 193–212.

6. See, for example, Robert Kiely, *The Romantic Novel in England* (Cambridge: Harvard University Press, 1972); and Mary Poovey, "Ideology and 'The Mysteries of Udolpho,' " *Criticism* 21 (1971): 307–30.

7. "Letter to a Member of the National Assembly," in Burke, *Works*, vol. 6, pp. 38–41.

8. *Reflections*, in Burke, *Works*, vol. 5, p. 100.

9. West, *Tale of the Times*, vol. 1, p. 4.

10. Elizabeth Hamilton, *Memoirs of Modern Philosophers*, 3 vols. (Bath, 1800), vol. 2, p. 280. Italics are Hamilton's, denoting direct quotations from Godwin's *Political Justice*.

11. West, *Tale of the Times*, vol. 1, pp. 66, 72, 147.

12. For a discussion of the political novel as it evolved throughout the eighteenth century, particularly as it can be illuminated by Hobbes, Hume, and Burke, see Carol Kay, *Political Constructions of Eighteenth-Century English Fiction*, forthcoming, Cornell University Press. For discussions of social criticism in the fiction of the later-eighteenth- and early-nineteenth-century novels, see Mona Scheuramann, *The Novel of Social Protest in England* (Columbus: Ohio State University Press, 1985); and Judith Lowder Newton, *Women, Power, and Subversion: Social Strategies in British Fiction, 1778–1860* (Athens: University of Georgia Press, 1981).

13. West, *Tale of the Times*, vol. 1, p. 57.

14. Hamilton, *Memoirs of Modern Philosophers*, vol 1, p. 202.

15. Hamilton, *Cottagers of Glenburnie* (Edinburgh, 1808), p. 120.

16. Hamilton, *Modern Philosophers*, vol. 3, p. 51.

17. Hamilton, *Modern Philosophers*, vol. 2, p. 397.

18. Jane West, *Letters Addressed to a Young Man*, 3 vols. (London, 1801), Letter 14, vol. 3, pp. 153, 158, 160. West conveys her theory about the conspiracy of the intellectuals on the authority of Abbé Barruel's counterrevolutionary *Mémoires pour servir à l'histoire du Jacobinisme* (London, 1797–98).

19. For compelling discussion of the similarly politicized lexicon of Wordsworth's poetry see James K. Chandler, *Wordsworth's Second Nature: A Study*

of the Poetry and Politics (Chicago: University of Chicago Press, 1984). I am also much indebted to Edward Duffy, Rousseau in England: The Context for Shelley's Critique of the Enlightenment (Berkeley and Los Angeles: University of California Press, 1979).

20. Elizabeth Hamilton, Translation of the Letters of a Hindoo Rajah, 2 vols. (London, 1796), vol. 2, pp. 202–3.

21. Hamilton, Modern Philosophers, vol. 2, pp. 220–21.

22. Issac Disraeli, Vaurien, 2 vols. (London, 1797), vol. 1, p. 53.

23. Amelia Opie, Adeline Mowbray; Or, The Mother and Daughter, 3 vols. (London, 1805), vol. 1, p. 104.

24. Opie, Adeline Mowbray, vol. 2, p. 16.

25. Opie, Adeline Mowbray, vol. 1, p. 28.

26. Smith, Desmond, vol. 2, pp. 62–65. The following studies of Locke have been particularly helpful to me: John Dunn, The Political Thought of John Locke (Cambridge: Cambridge University Press, 1969); John Yolton, John Locke and the Way of Ideas (London: Oxford University Press, 1956); John Locke: Problems and Perspectives (Cambridge: Cambridge University Press, l969); John Locke and Education (New York, Random House, 1976); Jeffrey Barnouw, "The Pursuit of Happiness in Jefferson and its Background in Bacon and Hobbes," Journal of Political Philosophy 11 (May 1983): 225–48; John Richetti, Philosophical Writing: Locke, Berkeley, Hume (Cambridge: Harvard University Press, 1983).

27. Hamilton, Modern Philosophers, vol. 2, p. 397.

28. Mary Robinson, The False Friend: A Domestic Story, 4 vols. (London, 1799), vol. 4, pp. 98–99.

29. Gilbert Imlay, The Immigrants, 2 vols. (London, 1793), vol. 1, pp. 203–4; emphasis Lord B's.

30. For a survey of responses to Wollstonecraft's Vindication as they evolved throughout the 1790s, see Regina M. Janes, "On the Reception of Mary Wollstonecraft's A Vindication of the Rights of Woman," Journal of the History of Ideas 39 (1978): 293–302, which demonstrates that Wollstonecraft's Vindication was well received until the pressures of war and reaction and, later, disclosures about Wollstonecraft's personal life made it seem radical and threatening. In an act that required considerable daring, the conservative Hamilton specifically defended Wollstonecraft's good sense long after her disgrace had been sealed; see Hamilton, Modern Philosophers, vol. 1, pp. 196–99. For a compelling discussion of Wollstonecraft's affiliations with earlier moral and political philosophy, see Carol Kay, "Canon, Ideology, and Gender," New Political Science 15 (Summer, 1986): 63–75.

31. Charles Lucas, The Infernal Quixote: A Tale of the Day, 4 vols. (London, 1801), vol. 1, pp. 135–36.

32. Robert Bisset, Modern Literature: A Novel, 3 vols. (London, 1804). See vol. 3, pp. 197–209. The entire fourth chapter of volume 3 (pp. 124–226) is devoted to a discussion of Burke, Paine, Godwin, and Wollstonecraft, among others.

33. See Richard Polwhele, The Unsex'd Females: A Poem (London, 1798) and [Benjamin Silliman], Letters of Shacoolen (Boston, 1802). For a discussion

of the lasting influence of Polwhele's misogynist representations of Wollstone-craft, see Janet Todd, "The Polwhelean Tradition and Richard Cobb," *Studies in Burke and His Time* 16 (1974–75): 271–77. For a more general discussion of the anxiety aroused by the specter of female sexuality, see Patricia Meyer Spacks, " 'Ev'ry Woman is at Heart a Rake,' " *Eighteenth-Century Studies* 8 (1974–75): 27–46.

34. Jane West, *Gossip's Story*, 2 vols. (London, 1796), vol. 2, p. 25.

35. West, *Tale of the Times*, vol. I, p. 147.

36. West, *The Infidel Father*, vol. 1, pp. 151–52; vol. 1, p. 191.

37. Hannah More, *Coelebs in Search of a Wife*, 2 vols. (London, 1808), vol. 1, p. 347: vol. 2, p. 141. For a discussion of the contemporary importance of *Coelebs*, see Samuel Pickering, Jr., *The Moral Tradition in English Fiction, 1785–1850* (Hanover, N.H.: University Press of New England, 1976), For a discussion of More's work as a political writer, see Mitzi Myers, "Hannah More's Tracts for the Times: Social Fiction and Female Ideology," in *Fetter'd or Free? British Women Novelists, 1670–1815*, ed. Mary Anne Schofield and Cecilia Macheski (Athens: Ohio University Press, 1986), pp. 264–284. Myers attempts to rescue More's reputation as a mindlessly repressive and therefore dismissable propagandist by stressing the positive aspects of her bourgeois progressivism and her uniquely female contributions to political commentary. For other studies which restore intellectual as well as political dignity to a largely dismissed body of conservative literature by women, see "The Early Foundation of Victorian Domestic Ideology," in *Fit Work for Women*, ed. Sandra Burman (London: Croom Helm, 1979), pp. 15–32; Jane Tompkins, "Sentimental Power: *Uncle Tom's Cabin* and the Politics of Literary History," in *The New Feminist Criticism: Essays on Women, Literature, Theory*, ed. Elaine Showalter (New York: Pantheon Books, 1985), pp. 81–104; Vineta Colby, *Yesterday's Woman: Domestic Realism in the English Novel* (Princeton: Princeton University Press, 1974).

38. More, *Coelebs*, vol. 1. p. 348.

39. More, *Coelebs*, vol. 1, p. 323.

40. More, *Coelebs*, vol. 1, p. 195.

41. This problem is painfully conspicuous in Laetitia Hawkins's *Letters on the Female Mind* (1793), conceived as a response to Helen Williams's widely read *Letters Written in France* (London, 1790, 1792–95). While strenuously insisting to her radical countrywoman that a woman has no country, no grounds for patriotism, and that the "study" of "*politics*" is in the very "climax of unfitness" for women, she herself proceeds to apologize for the institution of slavery, to differentiate the English Revolution of 1688 from the French Revolution, and to attack the perniciousness of the "philosophy" of d'Alembert and Voltaire, all in addition to elaborating the political dimension of marriage and the social and economic considerations which dictate women's conformity to established customs. Whatever she may have *intended* to say about the proper limitations of the female mind, her own practice made her admonitions seem less credible, much as anti-Jacobins such as Richard Polwhele attacked literary ladies who engaged in social criticism, but praised those who defended throne and altar.

42. Hamilton, *Modern Philosophers*, vol. 1, pp. 2–3.

43. Warren Roberts has observed this in his cogent *Jane Austen and the French Revolution* (New York: St. Martin's Press, 1976), p. 184.

44. Hamilton, *Modern Philosophers*, vol. 1, p. 200.

45. Hamilton, *Hindoo Rajah*, vol. 2, p. 103.

46. Mary Brunton, *Self-Control* (Edinburgh, 1811), vol. 1, pp. 220, 241. For a sensitive discussion of how Brunton's novels are "feminist and egalitarian," in "effect, if not by conscious intention," see "Sarah W. R. Smith, "Men, Women, and Money: The Case of Mary Brunton" in Schofield and Macheski, *Fetter'd or Free*, pp. 40–58.

47. The characterization is Butler's in *War of Ideas*, p. 121; essentially the same view is expressed by one of Wollstonecraft's recent biographers, Claire Tomalin, in *The Life and Death of Mary Wollstonecraft* (New York: Signet 1974, reprint, Meridian Books, 1983), pp. 229–30.

48. Opie, *Adeline Mowbray*, vol. 3, p. 207.

49. Opie, *Adeline Mowbray*, vol. 3, p. 49.

50. See Marilyn Butler, *Maria Edgeworth: A Literary Biography* (Oxford: Clarendon Press, 1972).

51. I have found the following articles on Fanny Burney especially helpful: Susan Staves, "*Evelina*; or Female Difficulties," *Modern Philology* 72 (1974): 368–81; Mary Poovey, "Fathers and Daughters: The Trauma of Growing up Female," in *Women and Literature*, n.s., 2 (1982); 368–81.

52. Hamilton, *Hindoo Rajah*, p. 212, Opie, *Adeline Mowbray*, vol. 1, p. 71.

53. In a recent essay squarely confronting the problems with considering Austen as either a Jacobin or an anti-Jacobin, Gary Kelly attempts to distinguish the radical novel from the reactionary novel on formal grounds, and contends that Austen's belong to the reactionary camp. While I, of course, concur that Austen belongs to neither camp, I cannot agree that the novels, especially those by women, are politically distinguishable on the particular formal grounds that he suggests. Many counterrevolutionary novels, for example, are pervasively and insistently sentimental; progressive writers are frequently ironic and comical; see "Jane Austen and the English Novel of the 1790's," in Schofield and Macheski, *Fetter'd or Free*, pp. 285–306.

CHAPTER TWO

1. Virginia Woolf, *The Common Reader*, First Series (New York: Harcourt, Brace, 1953), p. 139.

2. A recent biographer considers Austen's self- confidence here too intense to belong to an "unpublished novelist" and so argues that the passage is an insertion dating from 1816; see Jane Aiken Hodge, *Only a Novel: The Double Life of Jane Austen* (London: Hodder and Stoughton, 1972), p. 178.

3. Austen's irony will appear more volatile if we consider the controversy over the placement of the apostrophe in "daughter's." The first edition has "daughter" in the singular. But Chapman notes that the following sentence makes sense only if "daughter" is plural, and many editors of widely read

paperbound editions accordingly emend the word to "daughters' " (P 292). If Sir Walter "prides himself" in making sacrifices like "a good father" to all his daughters, the passage cries out against him even more. Among the few financial cutbacks he actually approves is the elimination of gifts for Anne, and later, readily forgetting Mary's existence altogether, he alludes to Anne as his "youngest daughter" (P 143).

4. See George Steiner, *After Babel: Aspects of Language and Translation* (New York: Oxford University Press, 1975), pp. 8–11.

5. The compositional history of *Northanger Abbey* is still widely debated. For a clear summary of hypotheses see A. W. Litz, *Jane Austen: A Study of Her Artistic Development* (New York: Oxford University Press, 1965), pp. 175–6, and B. C. Southam *Jane Austen's Literary Manuscripts* (London: Oxford University Press, 1964), pp. 60–62. While Cassandra Austen's Memorandum dates the novel at "about the years 98 & 99," C. S. Emden has argued that *Northanger Abbey* evolved as early as 1794, a conjecture which would anchor the novel even more firmly to political controversies; see "*Northanger Abbey* Re-Dated?," *Notes & Queries* 105 (September 1950): 407–10.

6. Paulson, *Representations of Revolution*, p. 221.

7. Smith, *Desmond*, vol. 2, p. 174. For a discussion of radical character of Smith's novel, see Diana Bowstead, "Charlotte Smith's *Desmond*: The Epistolary Novel as Ideological Argument," in Schofield and Macheski, *Fetter'd or Free*, pp. 237–63. For a general essay on the relation of Smith to Austen—which does not, however, make an issue of the former's radical sympathies—see William H. Magee, "The Happy Marriage: The Influence of Charlotte Smith on Jane Austen," *SNNTS*, 7 (1975), 120–32.

8. See Paulson, *Representations of Revolution*, pp. 225–27, and Poovey, "Ideology and *The Mysteries of Udolpho*," *Criticism* 21 (1971): 307–30.

9. Marc Girouard, *Life in the English Country House: A Social and Architectural History* (New Haven: Yale University Press, 1978), p. 242.

10. Critics who have argued that *Northanger Abbey* shows "ordinary" life to be safe and fundamentally "a-gothic" include Butler, *War of Ideas*, pp. 178–79; Moler, *Art of Allusion*, pp. 38–40; and most recently P. J. M. Scott, who contends that much of this neither "profound" nor "even fairly interesting" novel is devoted to exposing a gap between "the worlds of art and the life outside them" which is doomed to triviality because the heroine "is simply not intelligent enough" to make her adventures interesting; in *Jane Austen: A Reassessment* (New York: Barnes & Noble, 1982), pp. 37–39. Most other readers feel that while *Northanger Abbey* does discredit the gothic, it nevertheless prohibits us from trusting too unsuspiciously in "common life," as represented by General Tilney. Such critics include Lionel Trilling, *Opposing Self* (New York: Viking Press, 1955), p. 207; A. W. Litz, *Artistic Development*, p. 63; Barbara Hardy, *A Reading of Jane Austen* (New York: New York University Press, 1976), pp. 130–31.

11. Olivia Smith, *The Politics of Language 1791–1819* (Oxford: Clarendon Press, 1984), p. 19. I am much indebted to this important study.

12. Judith Wilt, *Ghosts of the Gothic* (Princeton: Princeton University Press, 1980), p. 138. My views on the gothic have also been greatly influenced by George Levine, "*Northanger Abbey*: from Parody to Novel and the Translated Monster" in *The Realistic Imagination: English Fiction from Frankenstein to Lady Chatterley* (Chicago: University of Chicago Press, 1981), pp. 61–80; and by William Patrick Day, *In the Circles of Fear and Desire: A Study of Gothic Fantasy* (University of Chicago Press, 1985), pp. 22–67.

13. Eaton Stannard Barrett, *The Heroine* (London, 1813), 3 vols., vol. 3, pp. 288–89. Austen reports that she was "very much amused" by this novel, and that it "diverted" her "exceedingly." See *Letters*, p. 376 (2 March 1814).

14. My discussion owes much to Robert Hopkins, "General Tilney and Affairs of State: The Political Gothic of *Northanger Abbey*," *Philological Quarterly* 57 (1978): 213–25, and B. C. Southam, "General Tilney's Hot-Houses," *Ariel* 2 (1971): 52–62.

15. Hamilton, *Modern Philosophers*, vol. 3, pp. 56, 105.

16. Disraeli, *Vaurien*, vol. 1, p. 82.

CHAPTER THREE

1. Margaret Oliphant, "Miss Austen and Miss Mitford," *Blackwood's Edinburgh Magazine* (March 1870), in Southam, *Critical Heritage*, p. 216; Reginald Farrer, "An Anniversary Comment," *Quarterly Review* 228 (July 1917): 1–30; reprinted in *Critics of Jane Austen* (Coral Gables, Florida: University of Miami Press, 1970), pp. 20–21.

2. It will be observed that, following the example of Mary Poovey in *The Proper Lady and the Woman Writer*, I use the term "ideology" not exclusively to mean a set of politicized concepts or doctrines—although, especially when discussing reactionary and revolutionary propaganda, I certainly do mean this— but also and even more importantly to mean a system of values and priorities as lived. See also Raymond Williams, *Marxism and Literature* (Oxford: Oxford University Press, 1977), pp. 55–71; and Terry Eagleton, *Marxism and Literary Criticism* (Berkeley: University of California Press, 1977), pp. 16–17.

3. Hamilton, *Translation of the Letters of a Hindoo Rajah*, vol. 2, pp. 211–12.

4. Unsigned notice in *British Critic* (May 1812), reprinted in Southam, *Critical Heritage*, p. 40.

5. Hamilton, *Modern Philosophers*, vol. 2, pp. 218–19.

6. Hamilton, *Modern Philosophers*, vol. 2, p. 219.

7. Hamilton, *Modern Philosophers*, vol. 2, pp. 399–400. Hamilton notes that the italicized portion comes from *Emma Courtney*.

8. For a more detailed discussion of the importance of assent, hope, fear, and probability in this novel, and the Lockean and Johnsonian epistemology that underpins it, see my "The 'Twilight of Probability': Uncertainty and Hope in *Sense and Sensibility*," *Philological Quarterly* 62 (1983): 171–86.

9. Claire Tomalin has noted the relationship of *Sense and Sensibility* to controversies about Wollstonecraft's suicidal sensibility, and has also articulated the network of acquaintance by which Austen could probably have become apprised of Mary's story; see Tomalin, *Life and Death*, p. 291. Without referring to the political background of the novel, Leroy W. Smith argues that "feeling" in *Sense and Sensibility* makes one vulnerable to the males who control the world; see *Jane Austen and the Drama of Woman* (New York: St. Martin's Press, 1983). For recent overviews of the subject of sensibility, see Janet Todd, *Sensibility: An Introduction* (New York: Methuen, 1986); Jane Spencer, *The Rise of the Woman Novelist: From Aphra Behn to Jane Austen* (Oxford: Basil Blackwell, 1986), pp. 107–212.

10. West, *Gossip's Story*, vol. 2, p. 51.

11. Deborah Kaplan has noted that Austen contrasts male and female authority in *Sense and Sensibility*, but regards female versions as "illegitimate" and both kinds as narcissistic and fallacious; see "Achieving Authority: Jane Austen's First Published Novel," *Nineteenth-Century Fiction* 37 (1983): 531–51.

CHAPTER FOUR

1. Poovey, *Proper Lady*, p. 205.

2. Poovey, *Proper Lady*, p. 207. For a discussion of *Pride and Prejudice* as a powerful female fantasy, see Tania Modleski, *Loving With a Vengeance* (Hamden, Conn.: Archon, 1982), pp. 36, 49–51.

3. Poovey, *Proper Lady,*, p. 201.

4. Fordyce, *Sermons Addressed to Young Ladies*, 8th ed., corrected and greatly enlarged (Dublin, 1796), *Sermon* 3 ("On Female Reserve"), pp. 39ff.; *Sermon* 7 ("On Getting Wisdom and Understanding"), p. 124.

5. Fordyce, *Sermon* 3, p. 46; *Sermon* 2 ("On Modesty of Apparel"), p 24; *Sermon* 1 ("On the Importance of the Female Sex . . ."), p. 3.

6. For a contrasting view of Austen's artistic methods and objectives, see Jan Fergus, *Jane Austen and the Didactic Novel: Northanger Abbey, Sense and Sensibility and Pride and Prejudice* (Totowa, N.J.: Barnes & Noble, 1983). The act of generalizing itself was perceived as fraught with political import during the period in question. A misguided penchant for generalization was precisely what Burkeans laid at the door of Jacobin reformers, whom they variously dubbed geometricians, rationalists, economists, and the like. In stymieing efforts at generalization here, Austen, it could be argued, is in fact engaging in a very Burkean fondness for particularity. But the issue is more complex than this, especially when we remember that Burke's own supporters were embarrassed by and nervous about the uncontrollable particularity of his own prose, which seemed to indulge in precisely the sort of wildness and eccentricity he deplored. As Olivia Smith has observed, at the same time that counterrevolutionary writers suspected the efforts of cold, autonomous reason, they wished to retain the moral and political authority generalizing could yield, the kind of authority Austen's practice confounds; see O. Smith, *Politics of Language*, pp. 1–34.

7. Hamilton, *Modern Philosophers*, vol. 2, p. 221.

8. Johnson is often mentioned in passing in Austenian criticism, but the following studies discuss Austen's relation to Johnson in some detail: Peter L. De Rose, *Jane Austen and Samuel Johnson* (Washington, D.C.: University Press of America, 1980); Robert Scholes, "Dr. Johnson and Jane Austen," *Philological Quarterly* 54 (1975): 380–90; and my " 'The Operations of Time and the Changes of the Human Mind': Jane Austen and Dr. Johnson Again," *Modern Language Quarterly* 44 (1983): 23–38.

9. West, *Tale of the Times*, vol. 2, p. 181.

10. West, *Tale of the Times*, vol. 3, p. 18.

11. When inveighing against the license to "strangeness of behavior" and the "privilege of disgusting" which men of genius assume, West humorously limits the number of men who can so qualify to a quota of "half a dozen," so as to spare the community at large the offensiveness of their manners. Perhaps it was the occasional grossness of Johnson's own habits which prompted her to set a quota so liberal. See West's *Letters Addressed to a Young Man* (London 1801), Letter 12, vol. 3, pp. 30ff.

12. West, *Tale of the Times*, vol. 2, p. 181.

13. Macaulay alludes to the paradox of Johnson's conservatism in *Letters on Education* (London, 1790), pp. 166–67; Wollstonecraft recurs to Johnson, though not to Boswell, with great respect in *Vindication of the Rights of Woman*, and Hays opens her *Appeal to the Men of Great Britain* approvingly with a quotation from him. Although her study focuses on the political dimension of language theory, Olivia Smith briefly discusses the social as well as stylistic inconsistencies and contradictions that needed to be glossed over before Johnson could be offered up as an exemplar of authoritarianism; see O. Smith, *Politics of Language*, 13–17.

14. *Yale Edition of the Works of Samuel Johnson*, vol. 14, *Sermons*, ed. Jean Hagstrum and James Gray (New Haven: Yale University Press, 1978), p. 149. All further references from Johnson are drawn from the *Yale Edition* and will be indicated parenthetically.

15. Many historicist discussions of Austen's conservatism have borne the traces of decidedly late twentieth-century preoccupations and associations. Among these is Butler's emphatic insistence that "psychology" is an intrinsically amoral enterprise and that Austen, as a Tory conservative, abhorred and eschewed all such vile and subjectivist stuff; see Butler, *War of Ideas*, pp. 295–96. Of course the assumption that the interests of psychology and morality were not complementary would have been unintelligible to many an eighteenth-century moralist, Johnson foremost among them.

16. See, for example, Butler, *War of Ideas*, p. 206.

17. *The Young Philosopher*, 4 vols. (London, 1798), vol. 1, pp. 321–35.

18. On this subject, Donald Greene's "Jane Austen and the Myth of Limitation" is still illuminating.

19. The controversial phrase "affective individualism" is of course from Lawrence Stone's *The Family, Sex and Marriage in England, 1500–1800* (New York: Harper and Row, 1977).

20. Scholars who have considered Austen's views on the subject of women's friendship patriarchal include many who have influenced me: Janet M. Todd,

Women's Friendship in Literature (New York: Columbia University Press, 1980); and Nina Auerbach, *Communities of Women* (Cambridge: Harvard University Press, 1978), pp. 38–55. See also Edna L. Steeves, "Pre-Feminism in Some Eighteenth-Century Novels," *Texas Quarterly* 16 (1973): 48–58.

21. Auerbach, *Communities of Women*, p. 55.

CHAPTER FIVE

1. For the classic formulation of this view see Kingsley Amis, "What Became of Jane Austen? *Mansfield Park*," *Spectator* 199 (1957): 339–40.

2. Nina Auerbach, "Jane Austen's Dangerous Charm: Feeling As One Ought about Fanny Price," in *Jane Austen: New Perspectives*, pp. 209; reprinted in *Romantic Imprisonment: Women and Other Glorified Outcasts* (New York: Columbia University Press, 1986), pp. 22–37. Strictly speaking, this remark is not entirely sound. Emma, for example, has been said to exemplify the modern condition of inauthenticity, while Marianne has been said to embody protoromantic impetuosity. Still, I find profoundly suggestive Auerbach's basic assertion that unattractive heroines, by being happily or unhappily outside the possibility of critical flirtation, are often granted an extrapersonal seriousness denied their prettier counterparts.

3. Trilling, *Sincerity and Authenticity*, p. 81. Although Rousseau of course attacked actors as well as actresses, his attack on women's public self-representation is more strenuous and serious; see *Letter to M. D'Alembert on the Theatre*, trans. Allan Bloom (Ithaca: Cornell University Press, 1968), pp. 81–92. For a very persuasive analysis of gender as a constitutive element of Rousseau's political thought, see Joan Landes's forthcoming *Gendering the Public Sphere*.

4. Trilling, *Opposing Self*, p. 218; and *Sincerity and Authenticity*, p. 75.

5. Trilling, *Opposing Self*, pp. 213, 212.

6. For readings stressing the pernicious novelty of the Crawfords, see Tony Tanner, "Introduction" to *Mansfield Park* (Harmondsworth: Penguin, 1966), pp. 7–36; Avrom Fleishman, *A Reading of Mansfield Park: An Essay in Critical Synthesis* (Minneapolis: University of Minnesota Press, 1967); and Alistair Duckworth, *The Improvement of the Estate* (Baltimore: Johns Hopkins University Press, 1971), pp. 35–80.

7. For a discussion of Sir Thomas's heterodoxy regarding multiple incumbencies, see Fleishman, *Mansfield Park*, pp. 20–24; for an excellent analysis of debates about slavery in early-nineteenth-century England, see Catherine Gallagher, *The Industrial Reformation of English Fiction: Social Discourse and Narrative Form 1832–1867* (Chicago: University of Chicago Press, 1985), pp. 3–35.

8. On the interrelation of Burke's aesthetic and political rhetoric, see Paulson, *Representations of Revolution*, pp. 57–72; Neal Wood, "The Aesthetic Dimension of Burke's Political Thought," *Journal of British Studies* 4 (1964): 41–64.

9. For a convincing discussion of Sir Thomas's inability to be an accessible and personable mentor, and thus his failure to suit then-prevalent Lockean

pedagogical paradigms, see David Devlin, *Jane Austen and Education* (London: Macmillan, 1975).

10. Mary Wollstonecraft, *Vindication of the Rights of Men* (London, 1790), pp. 112, 54.

11. Burke, *Reflections*, in *Works*, vol. 5, p. 151.

12. A critique of the sentimental strategies Burke uses to exclude women from the rigors of moral agency figures in Wollstonecraft's *Rights of Men*, pp. 113–14. See also *Vindication of the Rights of Woman* (New York: Norton, 1975), pp. 131–40. Rousseau, along with conservative moralists in England, is assailed at greater length in *Rights of Woman*, pp. 25–52, 77–92.

13. For a similar argument, see Robin Grove, "Jane Austen's Free Enquiry: *Mansfield Park*," *Critical Review* 25 (1983): 132–50.

14. Burke, *Reflections*, in *Works*, vol. 5, p. 151.

15. West, *Letters Addressed to a Young Man*, Letter 12 , vol. 3, p. 37.

16. Polwhele describes the sexual-political immodesty of women in the following way:

> Survey with me, what ne'er our fathers saw,
> A female band despising NATURE's law,
> As "proud defiance" flashes from their arms,
> And vengeance smothers all their softer charms.
> *I* shudder at the new unpictur'd scene
> Where unsex'd woman vaunts the imperious mien;
> Where girls, affecting to dismiss the heart,
> Invoke the Proteus of petrific art;
> With equal ease, in body or in mind,
> To Gallic freaks or Gallic faith resign'd,
>
> . . . .
>
> Loose the chaste cincture, where the graces shone,
> And languish'd all the Loves, the ambrosial zone.

Polwhele continues by affirming that divine justice has been served by Wollstonecraft's death in childbirth. See *The Unsex'd Females: A Poem*, pp. 6–7; cf. pp. 8, 29–30. Polwhele also execrates authors such as Barbauld, Robinson, Smith, Yearsely, Hays, Kauffman, and Crewe for joining Wollstonecraft in vindicating the rights of womankind. It deserves emphasizing that Polwhele does not exactly denounce the presumptuousness of female authorship per se. So long as female authors mirror or reaffirm the wisdom and felicity of masculine supremacy, he is extravagant in their praise, and accordingly contrasts the "unsexed" republican females with supposedly chaste British matrons such as More, Burney, Radcliffe, Chapone, and Seward, among others. For Laetitia Hawkins's similar linkage of republicanism and licentiousness, see *Letters on the Female Mind*, vol. 1, pp. 80–81; 105–6.

17. Poovey, *Proper Lady*, pp. 15–30. I am much indebted to Poovey's pathbreaking discussion of this subject.

18. For some exceptions, see Fleishman, *Mansfield Park*, pp. 36–40; Roberts, *French Revolution*, pp. 109–54; Margaret Kirkham, *Jane Austen, Feminism and Fiction* (Totowa, N.J.: Barnes & Noble, 1983), pp. 101–120.

19. For Johnson's famous pronouncements against slavery, see *Boswell's Life of Johnson*, ed. George Birkbeck Hill, rev. L. F. Powell, 6 vols. (Oxford: Clarendon Press, 1934–50), vol. 3, pp, 200–205, and vol. 2, pp. 476–77. See also Cowper's "The Negro's Complaint" and "Sweet Meat has Sour Sauce or the Slave-trader in the Dumps."

20. "Madame de Fleury" (1809), from *Tales of Fashionable Life*, in *The Longford Edition of the Tales and Novels of Maria Edgeworth* (New York: AMS Press, 1967), vol. 6, p. 293.

21. Robert Bisset evidently felt the licentiousness of German drama to be noticeable and dangerous enough to merit his satire in *Modern Literature: A Novel*. Thus Bisset has his risible Jacobin, Scribble, summarize a German play in which a nun eagerly admits to breaking her vows of chastity during the repeated nocturnal visits of her sweetheart: "it was agreeable to benevolence to make such a youth happy when she could make herself happy to boot; forms were mere inventions of priests, to subjugate the best and most delightful of feelings of nature to their controul. Was it a crime to add the numbers of mankind? Here you have the liberal and expanded morality of German drama" (vol. 2. p. 208). West also devotes a lot of space to attacking the immorality of German drama; see *Letters Addressed to a Young Man*, Letter 14, vol. 3, pp. 190–99.

22. Catherine Gallagher, "Response," in *Representations* 4 (1983): 56.

23. Paulson, *Representations of Revolution*, pp. 63–66. For a contrasting, more untroubled view of Austen's treatment of erotic love, see Juliet McMaster, *Jane Austen on Love*, ELS Monograph Series, 13 (Victoria, B.C.; English Literary Studies, University of Victoria, 1978).

24. For a feminist analysis of how women figure in anthropological and psychoanalytic theories, see Gayle Rubin, "The Traffic in Women: Notes on the 'Political Economy' of Sex," in *Towards an Anthropology of Women*, ed. Rayna R. Reiter (New York and London: Monthly Review Press, 1975), pp. 157–210. Ruth Bernard Yeazell also employs an anthropological approach in her illuminating study of pollution in *Mansfield Park*; see her "The Boundaries of *Mansfield Park*," *Representations* 7 (1984): 133–52.

25. D. A. Miller accounts for the difficult closures in Austen's fiction differently. The kinds of qualities that make a "traditional" novel narratable in the first place (ambiguity, ignorance, deviation) are lapses from all of Austen's most cherished moral values (order, propriety, sincerity, stasis). Accordingly, closure, as Miller sees it, then involves an ethically motivated "passage" on the part of the hero or heroine from a polyvalent to a univalent discourse. Austen's conclusions thus bid an abrupt good riddance to subversive impulses in order to embrace the authority of the Law. Although I find this poststructuralist analysis exceedingly suggestive, it is worth noting how much of it depends upon the historically questionable premise that Austen is a Tory conservative in the first place, that she adheres to "official values" with which her own artistic constructions are, until the end, at odds. Clearly, I am more struck by how her conclusions undermine and elude, rather than confirm, "official values"; see D. A. Miller, *Narrative and Its Discontents: Problems of Closure in the Traditional Novel* (Princeton: Princeton University Press, 1981), pp. 3–106.

CHAPTER SIX

1. In Southam, *Critical Heritage*, pp. 263, 265.

2. R. Brimley Johnson, *Jane Austen* (London: Sheed and Ward, 1927), pp. 74, 72−3; R. W. Chapman, *Facts and Problems* (Oxford: Clarendon Press, 1948), p. 134; *Emma*, ed. Lionel Trilling (Boston: Houghton Mifflin, 1957), pp. xxv–xxvi.

3. *Memoir of Jane Austen*, p. 157.

4. Bernard Paris, *Character and Conflict in Jane Austen's Novels: A Psychological Approach* (Detroit: Wayne State University Press, 1978), pp. 69, 73.

5. Duckworth, *Improvement of the Estate*. p. 148.

6. Marvin Mudrick, *Jane Austen: Irony as Defense and Discovery* (Princeton: Princeton University Press, 1952), pp. 181−206; Edmund Wilson, "A Long Talk About Jane Austen," *New Yorker* 20 (24 June 1944), p. 69.

7. Wayne C. Booth, *The Rhetoric of Fiction* (Chicago: University of Chicago Press, 1961), p. 260.

8. Trilling, "Introduction" to *Emma*, p. x; *The Opposing Self*, p. 116. Such attitudes cannot be dismissed as the crudeness of a bygone era, for a tacit belief that for women, at least, biology is destiny still underpins recent criticism about *Emma*. P. J. M. Scott, for example, insists that "Miss Woodhouse"—as she is repeatedly called—is "frightened of the wedded state"; see Scott, *Reassessment*, p. 64.

9. *Letters*, p. 504 (16 February 1813); F. B. Pinion, *A Jane Austen Companion* (New York: St. Martin's Press, 1973, rev. ed. 1976), p. 21.

10. Scott, *Reassessment*, pp. 67−68.

11. Stuart M. Tave, *Some Words of Jane Austen* (Chicago: University of Chicago Press, 1973), p. 246. I am much indebted to Tave's now classic study which so illuminates the distinctive features of Austen's language.

12. For a complementary discussion of the ethical importance of the community, see Julia Prewitt Brown, *Jane Austen's Novels: Social Change and Literary Form* (Cambridge: Harvard University Press, 1979).

13. Barrett, *The Heroine*, vol. 3, pp. 168−69; vol. 3, p. 171.

14. For a discussion of the gothic elements in the characterization of Jane Fairfax, see Judith Wilt, "The Powers of the Instrument, or Jane, Frank, and the Pianoforte," in *Persuasions, The Jane Austen Society of North America*, no. 15 (16 December 1983), pp. 41−47.

CHAPTER SEVEN

1. For some of the many formulations of this view, see Virginia Woolf, *The Common Reader*, First Series, pp. 147−48; Nina Auerbach, *Romantic Imprisonment*, pp. 38−54, the chapter devoted to *Persuasion* in David M. Monaghan, *Jane Austen: Structure and Social Vision* (Totowa: Barnes & Noble, 1980).

2. For a historian's sceptical outlook on the way literary scholars have misused historical arguments about social change as reflected in *Persuasion*, see David Spring, "Interpreters of Jane Austen's Social World," in Todd, *Jane Austen: New Perspectives*, p. 65.

3. See, for example, Butler, *War of Ideas*, pp. 274–86; and Poovey, *Proper Lady*, pp. 224–40.

4. See B. C. Southam, "*Sanditon*: the Seventh Novel," in *Jane Austen's Achievement*, ed. Juliet McMaster (London: Macmillan, 1976), pp. 1–26. See also Joel J. Gold, "The Return to Bath: Catherine Morland and Anne Elliot," *Genre* 9 (1976): 215–29.

5. West, *Letters Addressed to a Young Man*, Letter 17, vol. 3, p. 371.

6. Maria Edgeworth, *Practical Education*, 2 vols. (London, 1798), pp. 167–68; 703–4.

7. West, *Letters to a Young Man*, Letter 14, Vol. 3, pp. 142–46; Cf. Hannah More, *Strictures on the Modern System of Female Education* (London, 1799), chap. 2.

8. Robert Bisset, *Modern Literature: A Novel*, 3 vols. (London, 1804), vol. 3, pp. 199–200; cf. the disgust with the idea of female vigor expressed in Benjamin Silliman, *Letters of Shahcoolen* (Boston, 1802). In an important discussion relevant to Mrs. Croft, David Monaghan argues that Austen differs from most contemporaries not only in granting "sex equality," but also in being willing to redefine gender roles in nontraditional ways; see "Jane Austen and the Position of Women," in *Jane Austen in a Social Context* (Totowa: Barnes & Noble, 1981), pp. 105–21.

9. I am indebted to the fine analysis in Tave, *Some Words*, p. 265.

10. For compelling discussions of the import of religious imagery throughout *Persuasion*, see Duckworth, *Improvement of the Estate*, pp. 195; and Jane Nardin, "Christianity and the Structure of *Persuasion*," *Renascence* 30 (1978): 43–55.

11. For some notable and welcome exceptions, see Frederick Keener, *The Chain of Becoming—The Philosophical Tale, the Novel, and a Neglected Realism of the Enlightenment* (New York: Columbia University Press, 1983), pp. 241–307; Lloyd W. Brown, *Bits of Ivory: Narrative Techniques in Jane Austen's Fiction* (Baton Rouge: Louisiana State University Press, 1973).

12. Edgeworth's copy of *Persuasion* is located in the Edgeworth Collection in the Special Collections Division of the University Research Library at The University of California, Los Angeles.

13. Trilling, *Sincerity and Authenticity*, pp. 73–74.

14. This phrase derives from David Erdman, *Blake, Prophet Against Empire* (Princeton: Princeton University Press, 1954).

INDEX

Advice: and absolute power in *Mansfield Park*, 101–2, 104; contrasted with domination, 85, 146; and persuasion, 155–57

Anti-Jacobin Review, xii, 16

Austen, Jane: artistic self-consciousness of, 31–32, 121–22, 134–35; authorial independence in *Emma*, 122, 126; authorial self-confidence of, 28–32, 47–48; biographical criticism of, 144–45; compared to partisan writers, xxii–xxiii, 27; as conservative writer, xv–xvi; gender and place of in canon, xii–xiii, 122; intellectual stature in criticism of, xiv–xvi; and irony as personal weakness, xvii; as parodist, 29–30, 34–35, 47–48, 96, 99–100, 114–16, 166; and treatment of illicit sex, 43–44, 55–57, 108–11; use of feminine novelistic tradition, xviii–xix. *See also specific works*

Authority: alternatives to, 69–72; benign in *Emma*, 140–42; critique of in *Mansfield Park*, 96–99, 107–8; evaded in *Persuasion*, 146–47, 154–56, 163–66; female versions of in *Emma*, 122–32, 143; female versions of in *Pride and Prejudice*, 88–89; idealized in conservative fiction, xix, 7–11; idealized in *Pride and Prejudice*, 73–74; problematized in progressive fiction, 24–26. *See also* Family

Bage, Walter: *Hermsprong*, 15; *Man As He Is*, 124

Barrett, Eaton Stannard, *The Heroine* as conservative critique of female imagination by, 40, 133, 136

Bisset, Robert, 153; *Modern Literature: A Novel*, 15

Blair, Hugh, 39

Booth, Wayne, 123

Brontë, Charlotte, xiv

Brunton, Mary *(Self-Control)*, 21, 100

Burke, Edmund: and celebration of patriarchal ideal, 4–5, 8, 11, 13; and chivalry, 98, 100, 152; and "drapery of decency," 99–100; fictions of scrambled by reformist novelists, 23–26; legacy to conservative novelists, 4–17, 33–34; and neighborhood as political unit, 5–6; and political import of sublime and beautiful, 97–99. Works: *Letter to a Member of the National Assembly*, 4–5, 10; *A Philosophical Enquiry into the Origin of the Sublime and Beautiful*, 98; *Reflections on the Revolution in France*, 4, 10, 98, 100, 152

Burney, Fanny, xiii, xviii, xxi, 8, 21, 24, 91, 133–34. Works: *Camilla*, 25, 48, 141; *Cecilia*, 25, 48; *Evelina*, 25, 133; *The Wanderer, or Female Difficulties*, xiii, xviii, 25, 134

Butler, Marilyn, xv

Cecil, Lord David, xvi

Chapman, R. W., xiv–xv

Conduct books: in conservative fiction, 16; didactic methods of confounded, 23–24, 32, 76–77; and Mr. Collins, 74–75; morality of interrogated, 50, 83, 155–56; as source for Austen's ideas, xvi

Cowper, William, 107

Croker, J. W., xiii

de Stael, Madame, xvi

Diderot, Denis, 11

Disraeli, Issac *(Vaurien)*, 12, 42

Duckworth, Alistair, 122

Edgeworth, Maria, xxi, 91, 153, 160. Works: *Belinda*, xviii, 16, 20, 24, 48, 100; "The Grateful Negro," 107; "Madame de Fleury," 107; "The Modern Griselda," 20; *Practical Education*, 149